POSTCARD HISTORY SERIES

# Maynard

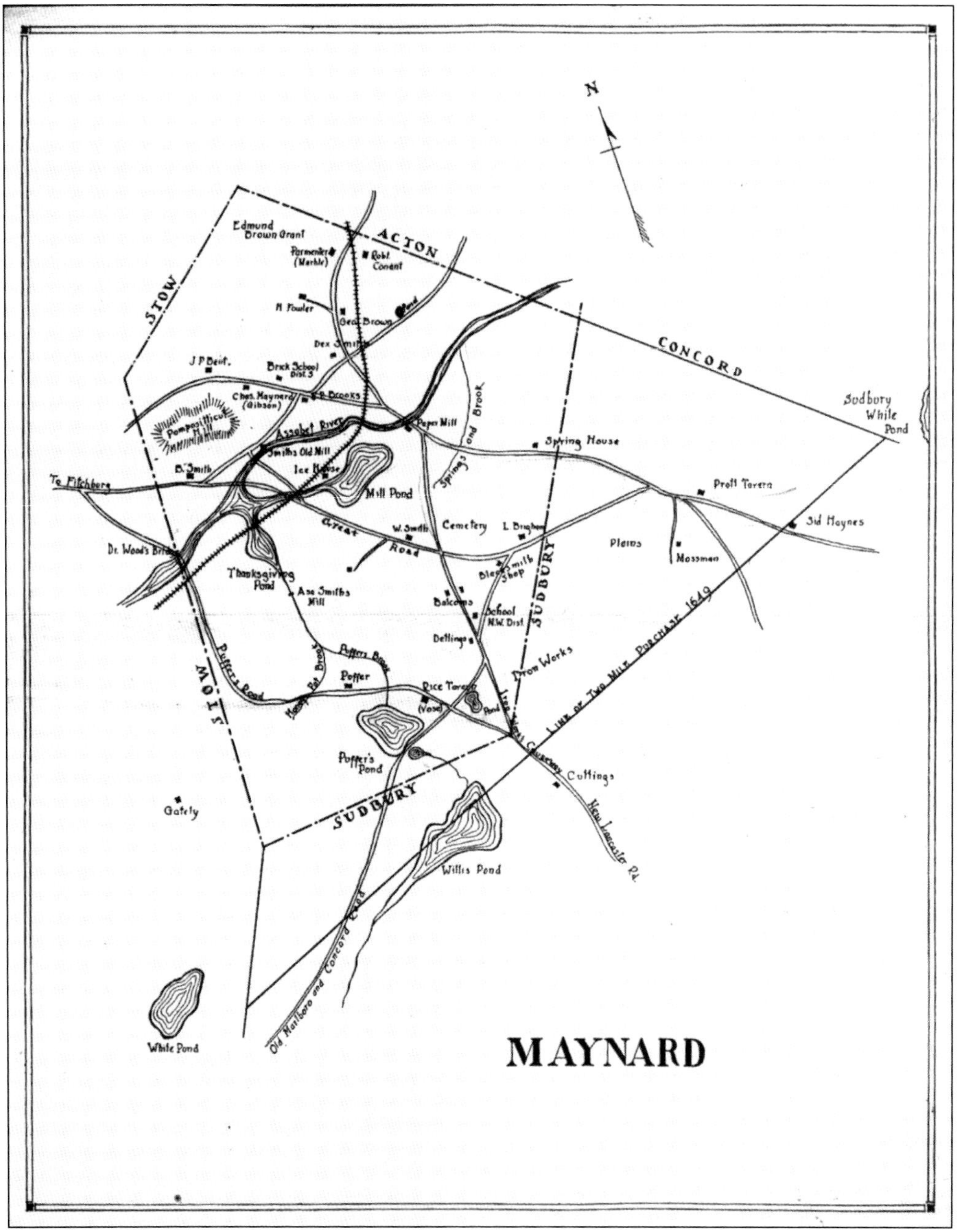


**MAP OF MAYNARD, 1921.** The town was incorporated on April 19, 1871, with 1,300 acres taken from the town of Stow and 1,900 acres taken from the town of Sudbury.

POSTCARD HISTORY SERIES

# Maynard

Paul Boothroyd and Lewis Halprin

ARCADIA PUBLISHING

ISBN 978-0-7385-3946-1

Published by Arcadia Publishing
Charleston, South Carolina

Printed in the United States of America

Library of Congress Catalog Card Number: 2005933681

For all general information contact Arcadia Publishing at:
Telephone 843-853-2070
Fax 843-853-0044
E-mail sales@arcadiapublishing.com
For customer service and orders:
Toll-Free 1-888-313-2665

Visit us on the Internet at www.arcadiapublishing.com

*On the front cover*: **TROLLEY STOP.** At the junction of Main and Nason Streets in the center of Maynard in 1906, people board a trolley on Main Street. This was one of the regular stops along the trolley line that ran from Acton through Maynard and Stow to Hudson.

*On the back cover*: **MAPLE AND BROOKS STREETS.** This postcard shows the peaceful corner of Maple and Brooks Streets. Brooks Street was named for Silas P. Brooks, who owned the land before it was cut into house lots. Maple Street was named for its five stands of maple trees.

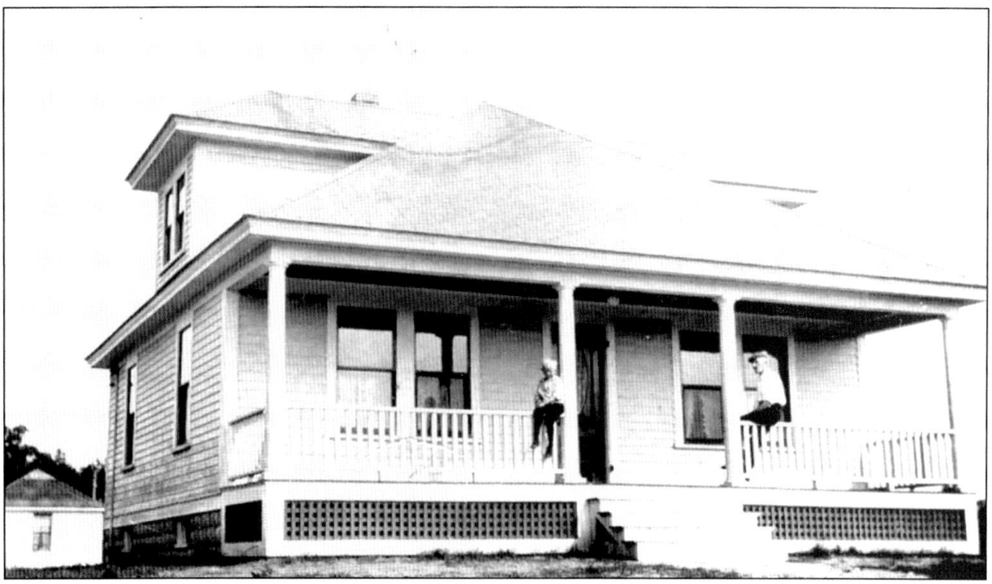

**TYPICAL MAYNARD BUNGALOW.** Located on Riverside Park along the Assabet River, William Salo, on the left, and an unidentified friend enjoy a warm summer day. (Courtesy of Judy Laasanen.)

# CONTENTS

# ACKNOWLEDGMENTS

I was born and raised in Maynard, went to school here, and worked all my life in my town of Maynard. I am now operating my own real-estate agency, have been appointed the chairman of the Maynard Historical Commission, and am an archivist of the Maynard Historical Society. During all these years, I have been collecting images of one sort or another of the town's history, both old and new. These images show the rich heritage that was created by the generations of mill workers who came to work at the town's big woolen mill but continued the customs and languages of their old country in the churches and societies they built in Maynard. I have been a deltiologist (serious postcard collector) of Maynard postcards for over 40 years. This collection of postcards represents the rich history of Maynard, and I am pleased to share that history with you through this book.

—Paul Boothroyd

This is the seventh Arcadia book I have written about my home on Lake Boon and my neighboring towns of Stow, Hudson, and Maynard. Although Maynard is the smallest of these towns if you go by area, it is almost the largest when you go by number of people and is definitely the largest when you go by the diversity of its people, coming from all over the world to work at the Assabet Mills in the center of town and to raise their family and pray to their god, each in their own way. This diversity is clearly shown in the collection of postcards Paul and I were able to gather, mostly from Paul's personal collection and many from the archives of the very active Maynard Historical Society. We are sure you will enjoy "flipping" through this stack of postcards, as Paul and I have done many times during the preparation of this book, never getting tired or bored with the images of this great compact town by the river.

—Lewis Halprin

Most of the postcards in this book are from the collection of Paul Boothroyd. Credit also goes to the Maynard Historical Society (MHS) archives for many additional postcards and much of the caption information used throughout the book. The author's son Todd Boothroyd provided helpful assistance in finding information for the introduction of this book. Postcards have also been provided for this book by Jack Malcolm, Brenda LeSage, Paul Polewacyk, and Judy Laasanen. Postcards not provided by the authors are identified at the end of such postcards' captions.

# INTRODUCTION

Discussing postcards in the town of Maynard, Massachusetts, seems an odd pairing. The tiniest of mail items seems connected to the town only in that Maynard is one of the smallest towns in the commonwealth. However, Maynard's early roots focused a ton of energy in a small area, and the postcard was the light that radiated out to the world.

At 5.7 square miles, Maynard is the third-smallest town in the state of Massachusetts. The territory was formed by 1,900 acres from the town of Sudbury and 1,300 acres from Stow, with the split between the two being the Assabet River. In fact, Maynard was known as Assabet Village due to this river, which fed the town with a new life.

Assabet Village was, initially, a quiet farming district until the Industrial Revolution finally reached full strength in America. Mills fueled this revolution, and rivers fueled the mills. So it was in Maynard where clothing and powder mills channeled the river.

These mills also created an economic boom, so much so that the town's namesake, Amory Maynard, and other influential people petitioned the Commonwealth of Massachusetts for a charter. The village had become its own entity, and on April 19, 1871, the charter was granted.

Soon the new town bustled. Houses were built. Streets created. Even a new cemetery was set aside, but why? Immigrants. From all over Europe, Maynard became known as a hotbed of America, where work was plentiful for the young man, and there was a great influx.

These men and their families gave up what they had known. They said good-bye to their loved ones, and they traveled half a world away. But they still kept in touch, and the main means was the tiny postcard.

Postcards were popular outside of the United States, and, technically and aesthetically, foreign postcards were ahead of the United States. The reason was, in part, that only the U.S. government was allowed to print or even use the term "postcard." Only the government could make use of the postcard's rear side for information. Privately created ones were "souvenir cards"—not the same caliber, and they required all messages to be on the front.

Still there have been private postcards issued as early as 1861, the recipient being a John P. Charlton, and plain postcards were in prior use. A true breakthrough in popularizing this mail item appeared at the Columbian Exposition in Chicago, May 1893. Pioneer postcards appeared in color.

By May 19, 1898, and by an act of Congress, private printers were granted permission to print and sell cards that bore the inscription "Private Mailing Card." Still writing was not permitted on the address side until 1907, when a new style of postcard emerged. On the flipside, the right was reserved for the address, while a message could be scribbled on the left. It was the postcard with the rear face divided, which is standard worldwide today.

At the beginning of the 20th century, postcards entered a golden age. Coincidentally, so did Maynard, becoming one of the most influential towns in Massachusetts. Furthermore, Germany's defeat in World War I ended that country's significant influence in the postcard business. Their factories had been destroyed. American companies found it easier to compete.

Locally in Maynard, artisans made use of new postcard techniques. The linen era from 1930 to 1960, also called the rag content, had cards with a textured feel. And the photo chrome era started in 1939 and persists to today. These postcards have the common photograph.

Arvid Blad, a local photographer, made many cards for family use as well as public sale. W. B. Case, a five-and-dime company, also captured many Maynard scenes. These individuals and companies provided a twofold historic flavor. Not only did they preserve images of Maynard so people can remember how it looked, the sent cards also captured the messages people were sending, giving insight into their lives, now nearly a century gone by.

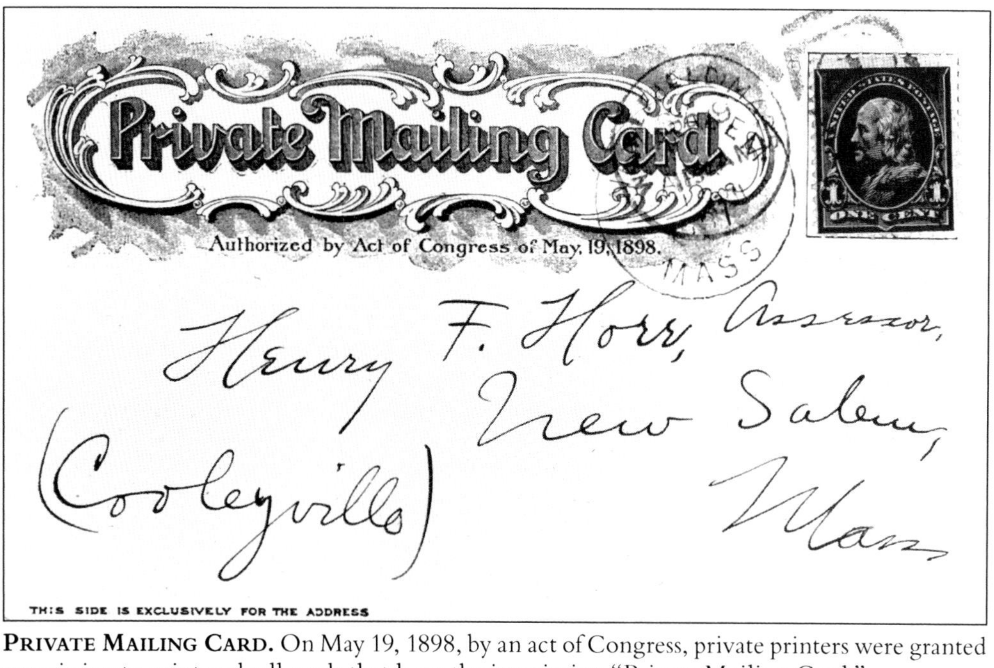


**PRIVATE MAILING CARD.** On May 19, 1898, by an act of Congress, private printers were granted permission to print and sell cards that bore the inscription "Private Mailing Card."

*One*

# BIRD'S-EYE VIEW OF MAYNARD

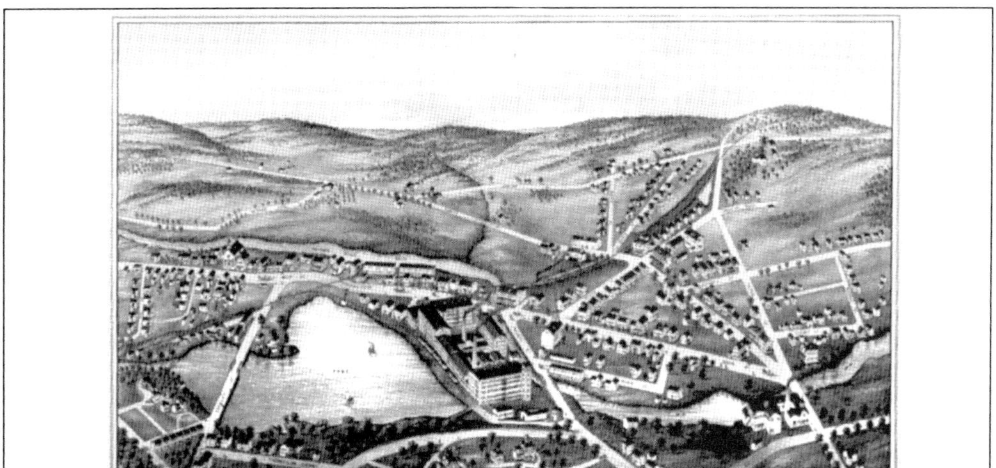


**ALL OF MAYNARD ON ONE POSTCARD.** The town of Maynard and the Assabet Mills in 1879 are seen here. In 1846, Amory Maynard built the village of Assabet, and in 1871, it became the town of Maynard.

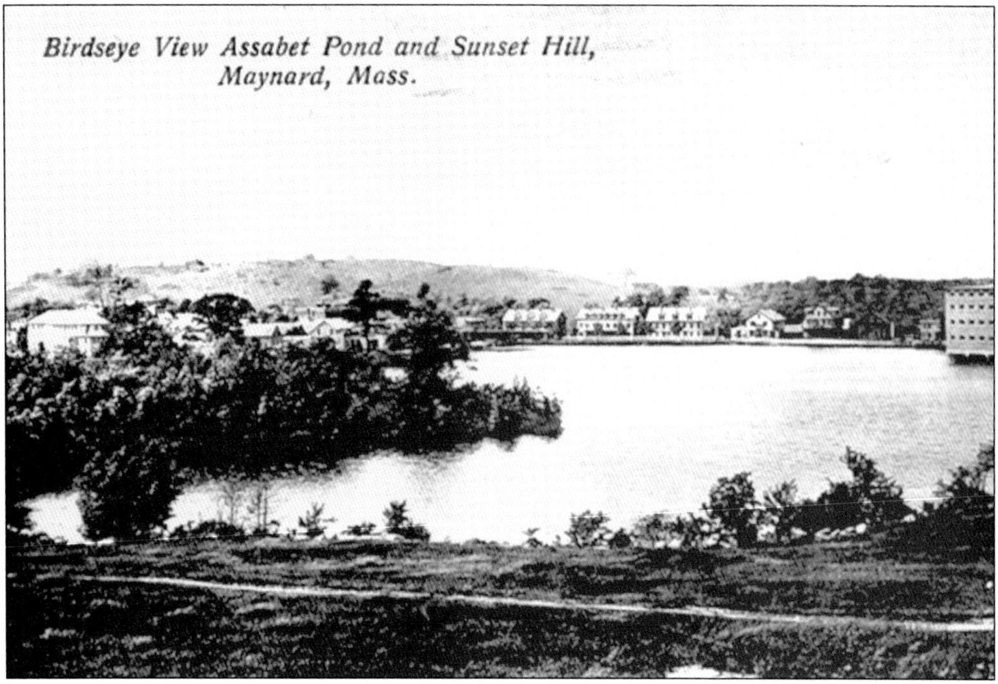


**POND VIEW.** Assabet Mills Pond is shown in the foreground with a view of Summer Hill in the left background. In 1676, during the King Phillip War, Native Americans would powwow on this hill. (Courtesy of Jack Malcolm.)

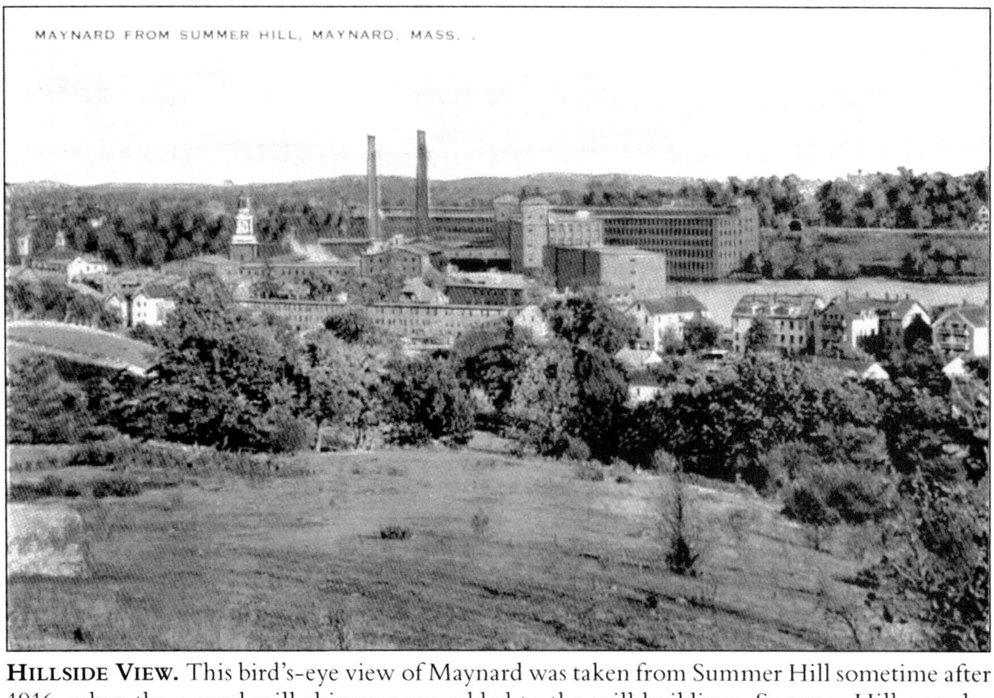


**HILLSIDE VIEW.** This bird's-eye view of Maynard was taken from Summer Hill sometime after 1916, when the second mill chimney was added to the mill buildings. Summer Hill was also called Pompociticut Hill.

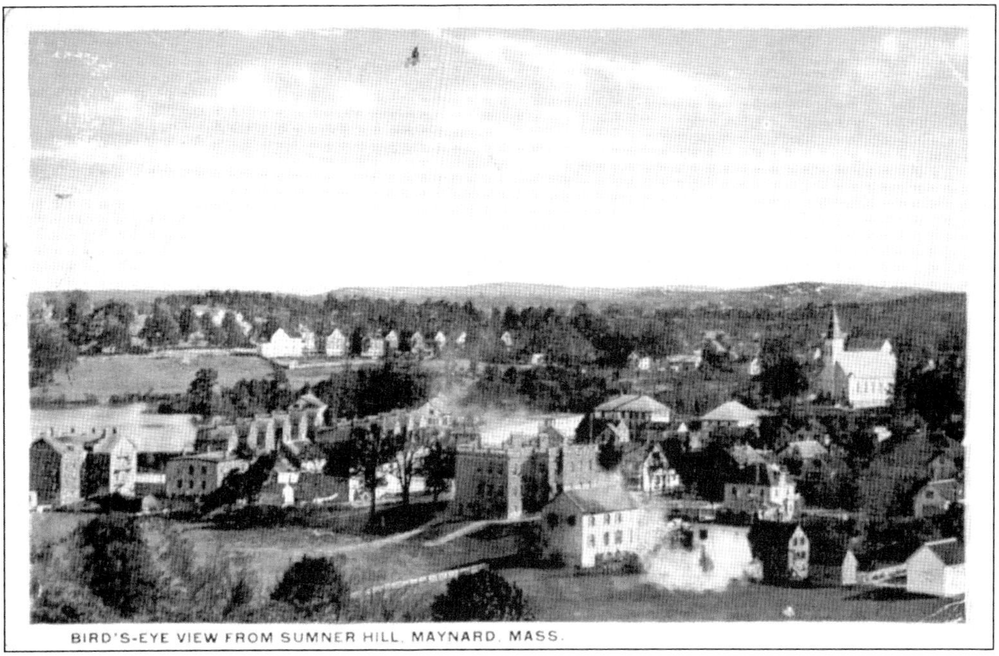


**Rear View of Main Street School.** Looking from Summer Hill, the Main Street School is seen in the center of the card and is the site of the Maynard Town Hall, with St. Bridget's Church seen in the right corner.

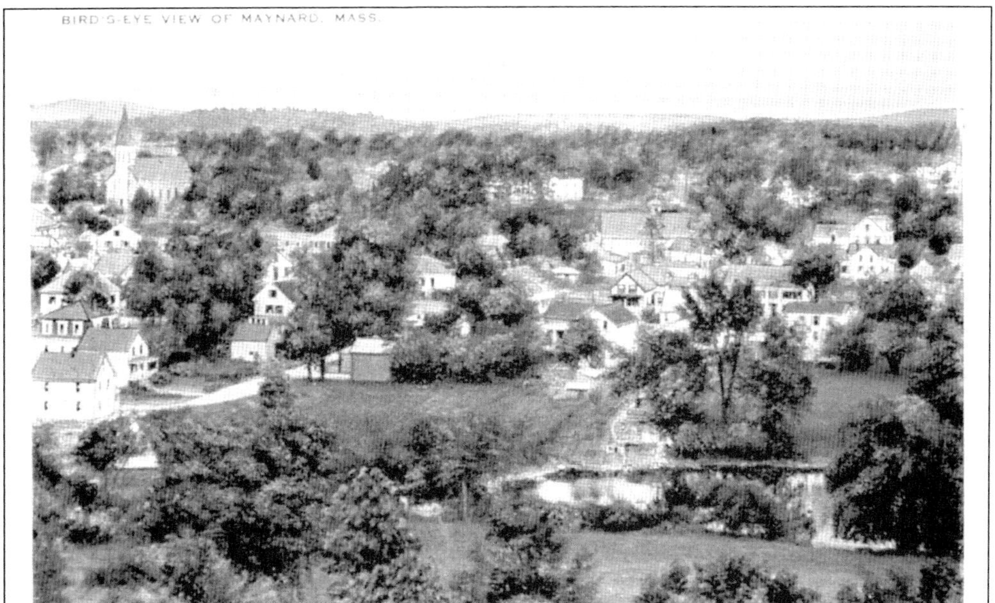


**West End View.** The homes in the west end of Maynard are seen along with the Assabet River as viewed from Summer Hill. St. Bridget's Church is seen in the upper-left corner of the picture.

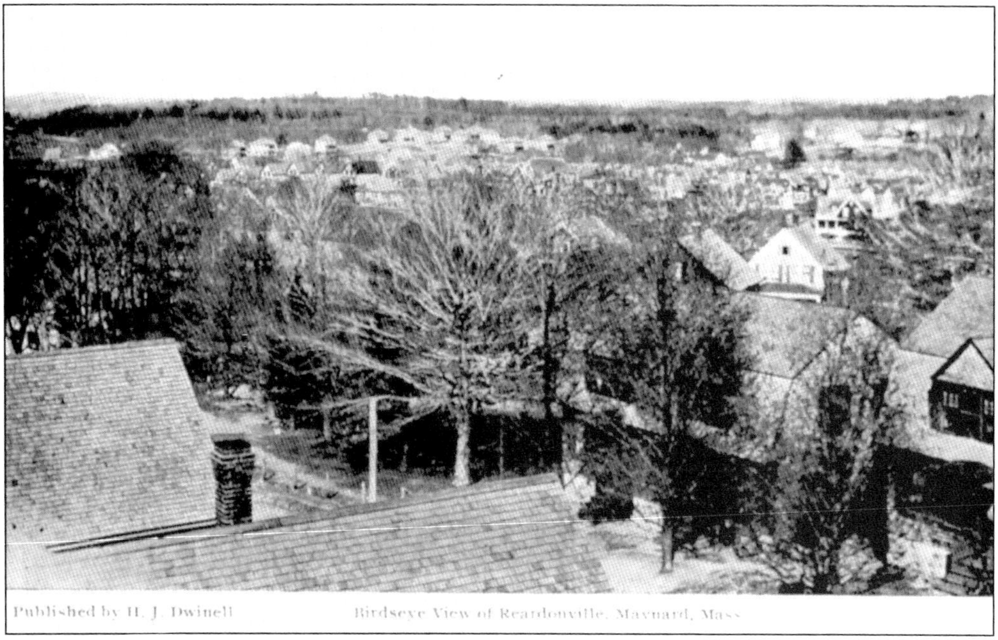


**Reardonville.** This part of Maynard is the housing development built by the American Woolen Company on the land of the Reardon farm between 1900 and 1918. They were all auctioned off in 1934, some to the people who lived in them.

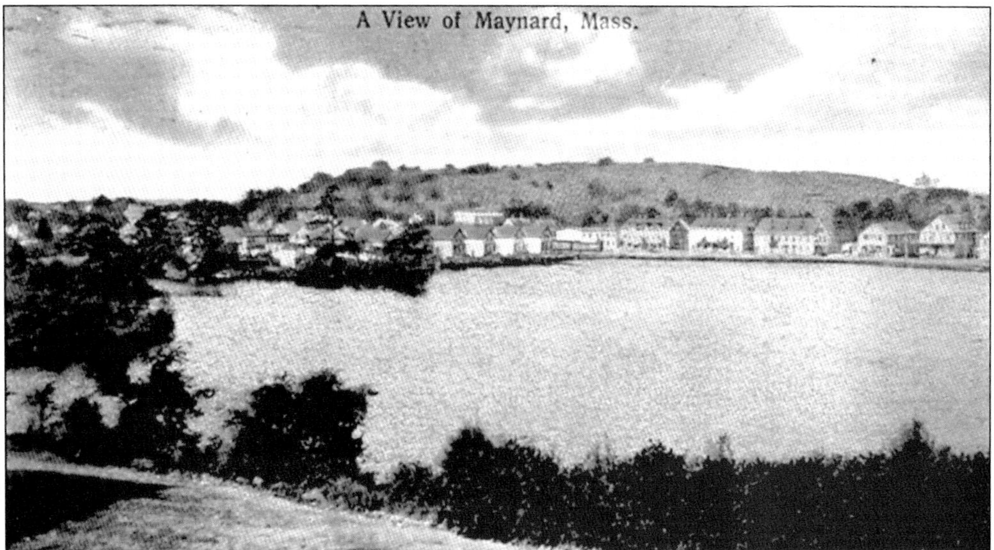


**View from the Hay Field.** This card features a view of Summer Hill, Main Street, and the millpond from a hay field by the millpond, as seen during World War II. Victory gardens were planted in the hay field.

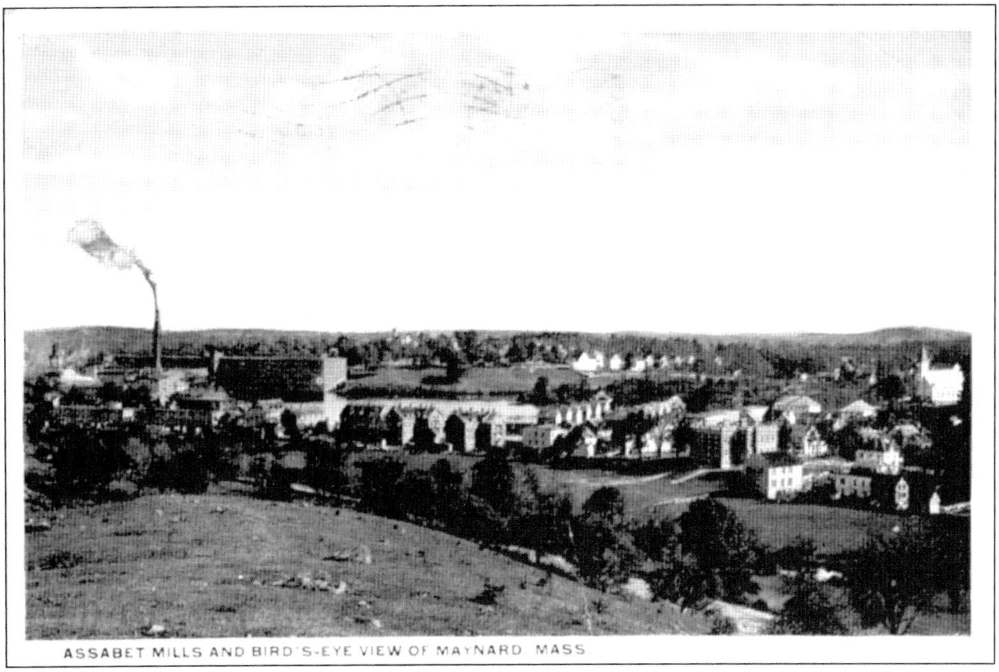


**ASSABET MILLS FROM SUMMER HILL.** Summer Hill Road is shown in the foreground and provides a good view of the mills as seen in these postcards sometime prior to 1916. Today Summer Hill and Summer Hill Road are built up with residential homes.

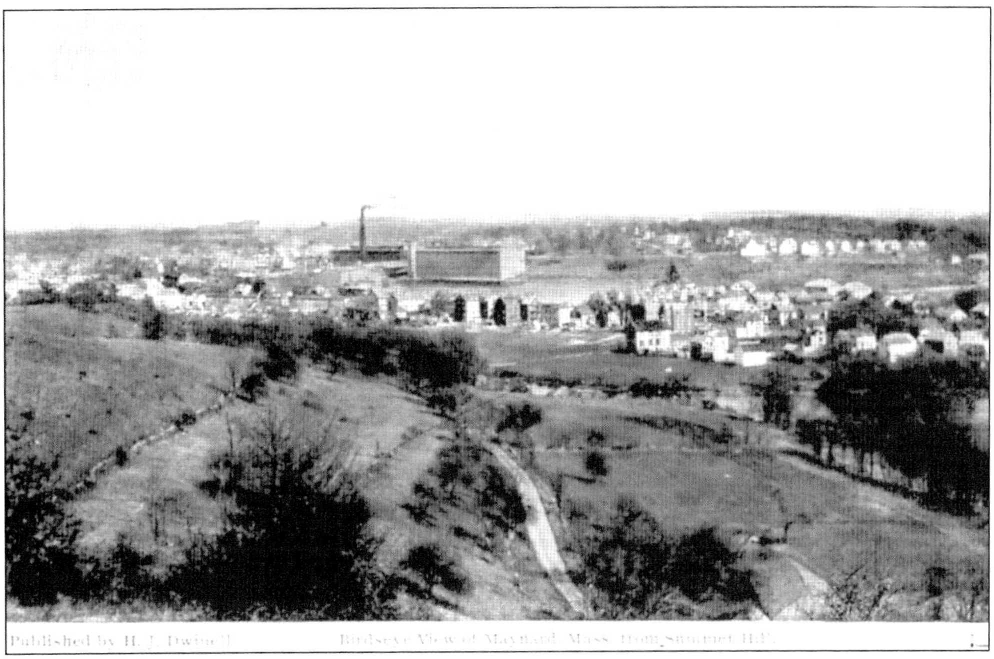

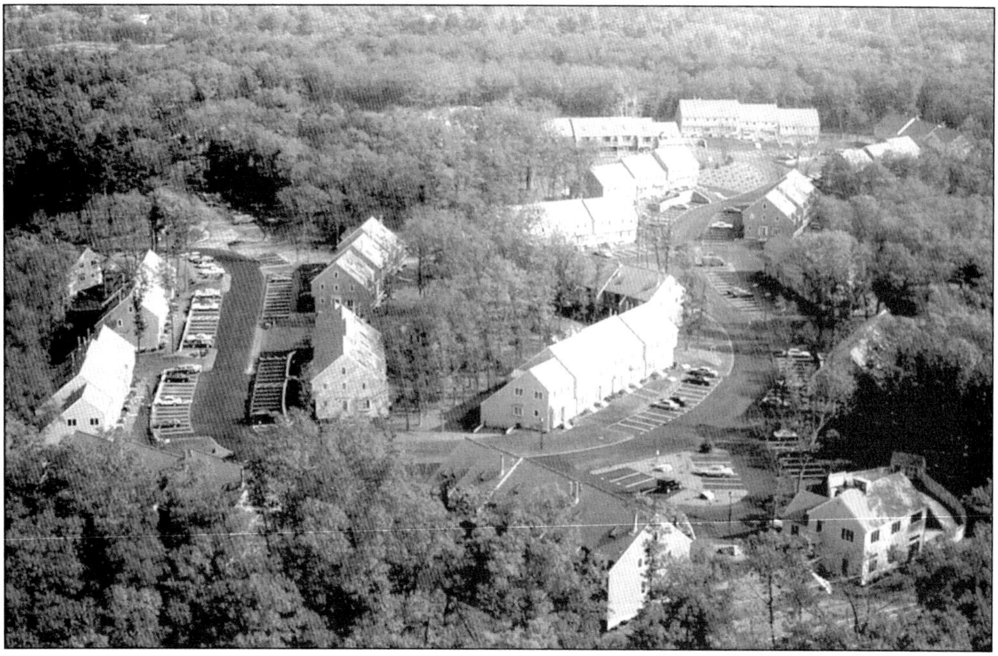

**DEER HEDGE RUN.** Nestled around a wooded hilltop, Deer Hedge Run is a housing development with 155 townhouse units on 37 acres.

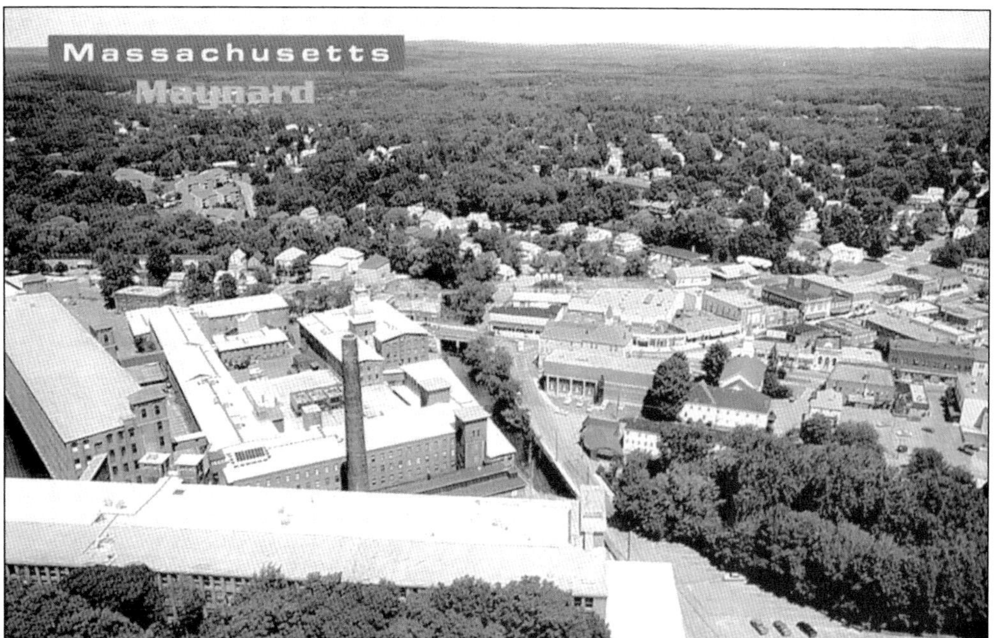


**THE MILL COMPLEX.** Once the world's largest woolen mill, this restored complex served as the Digital Equipment Corporation plant and headquarters between 1957 and 1990.

# *Two*

# The Assabet River and its Mills

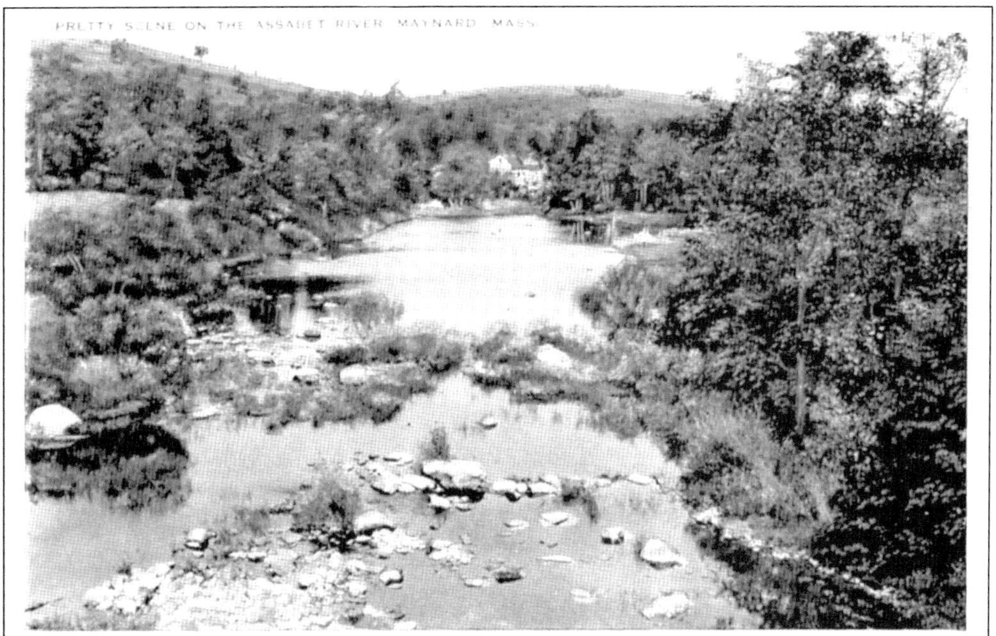


**Pretty Scene on the River.** Winding its way through the north-central part of Maynard, the Assabet River is a prominent feature of the natural beauty of the village. It enters Maynard at Russell's Bridge, formerly Dr. Wood's Bridge, at the Stow town line and flows to the Ben Smith Dam. The river continues on from the dam, through the center of the town, and exits at the Acton town line.

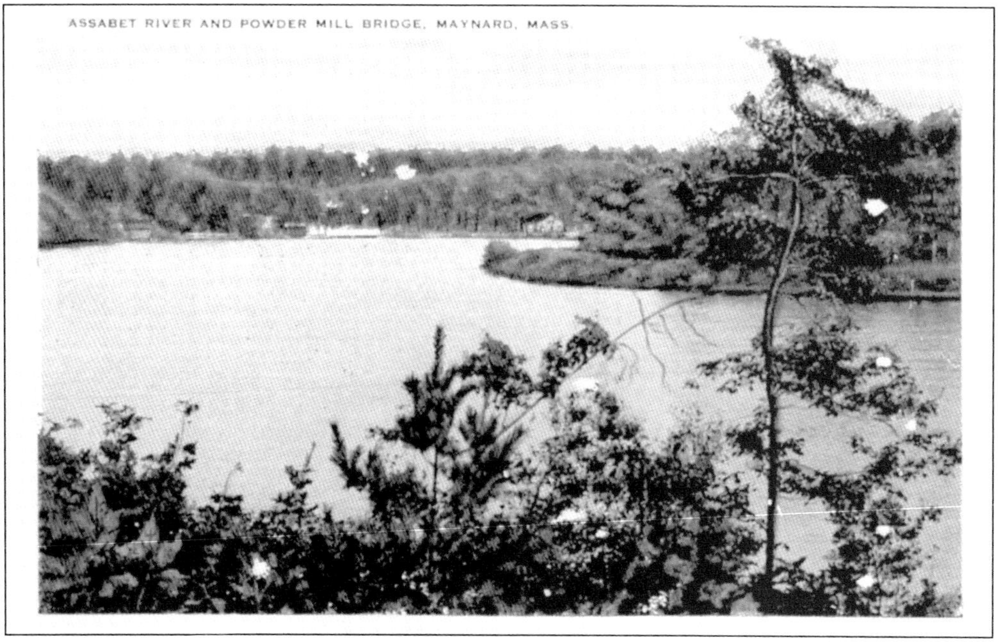


**POWDER MILL BRIDGE.** The Assabet River flows smoothly and quietly as it approaches the paper mill dam and bridge. (Courtesy of MHS.)

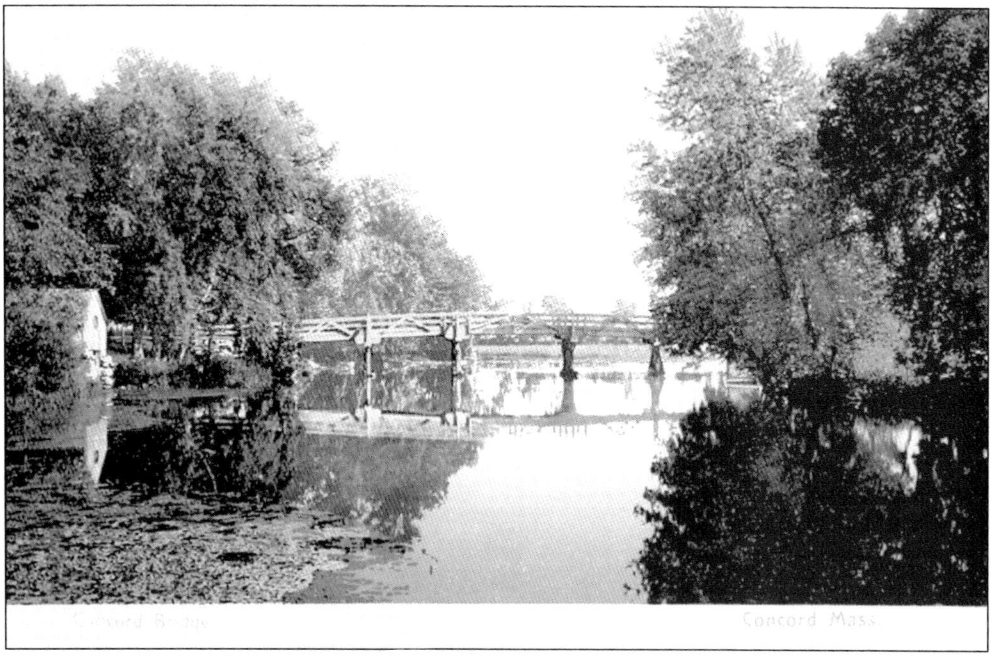


**OLD NORTH BRIDGE.** If one did not cross the Assabet River at the Dr. Wood's Bridge, or Russell's Bridge as it's called today, the next bridge was in Concord at the old North Bridge, or one would find a spot on the river where the water was shallow and ford across it.

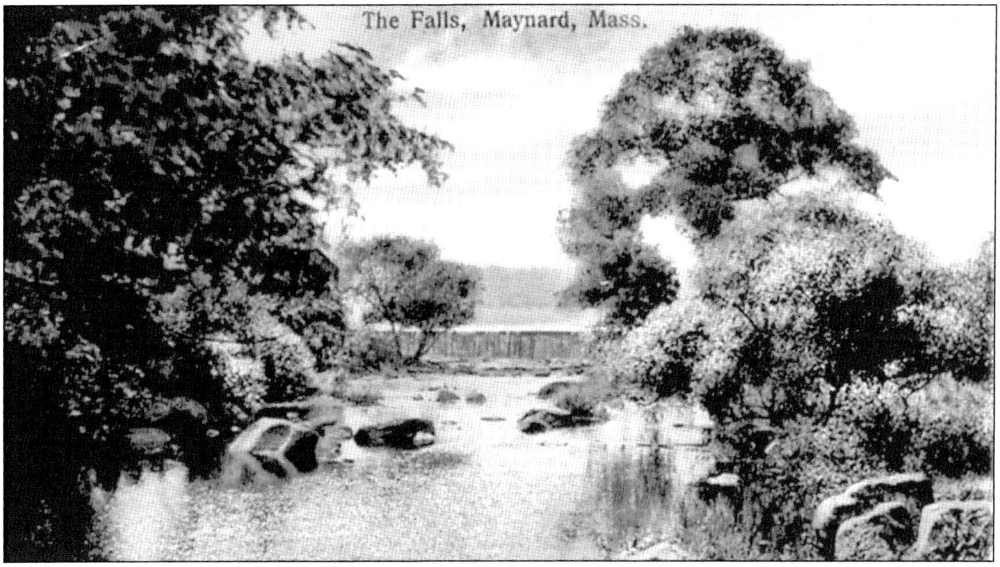


**BEN SMITH DAM.** Built in 1847 by Artemous Whitney for Amory Maynard, the Ben Smith Dam backs up the water of the Assabet River. The dam's high water entered a channel into the water storage basin next to the mills and was used to turn the mill's waterwheels.

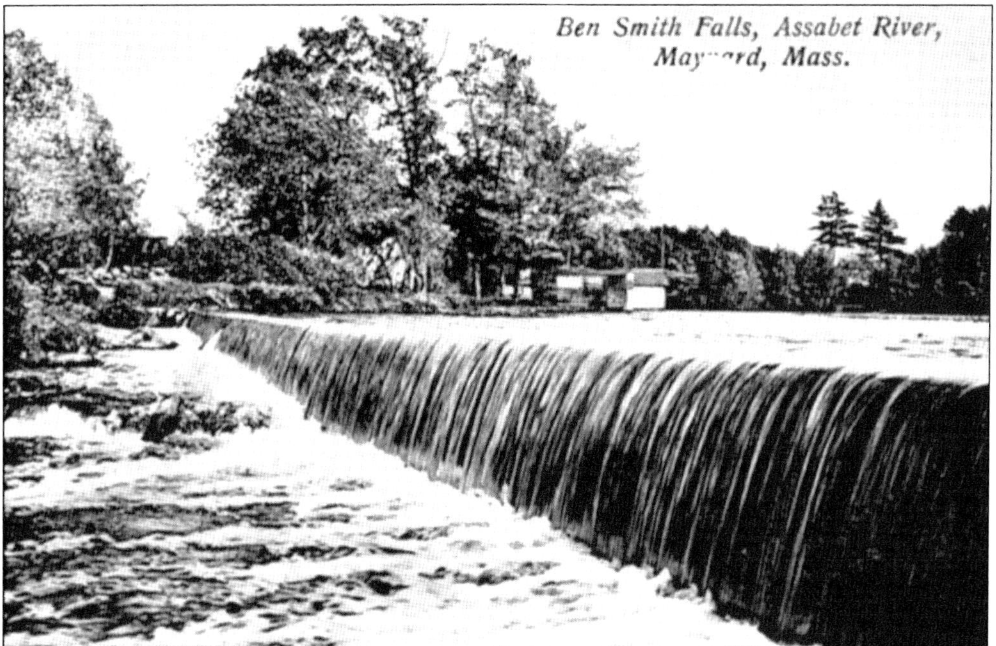


**THE QUEEN'S DOCK IN MAYNARD.** A boathouse and landing wharf (seen in the background) were built on the Assabet River near the Ben Smith Dam for use by the river launch *Queen*. The launch, run by Peter Wilcox and Fred Chandler of Maynard, transported parties between Maynard and Lake Boon up until 1914. (Courtesy of MHS.)

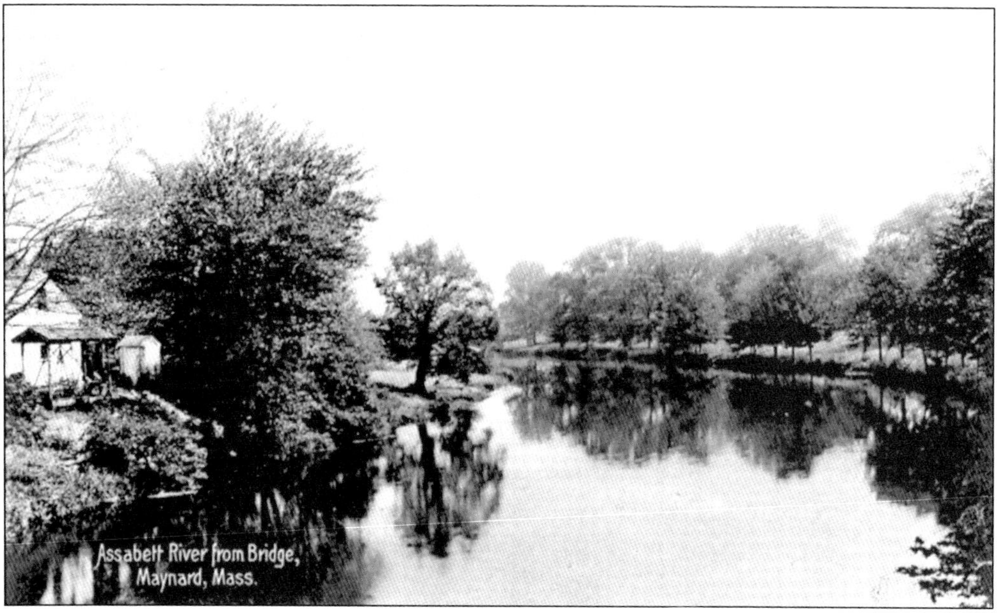


**THE ASSABET RIVER.** The name Assabet is from the Algonquin language and means "the place where materials for making fishnets grows." There has been considerable question concerning the correct spelling of the name. As early as 1650, it appears in the records and on maps variously as Asibath, Isabeth, Elsabeth, Elzibet, Elizabeth, Assabaeth, Assobet, and otherwise. It was standardized as Assabet in 1850.

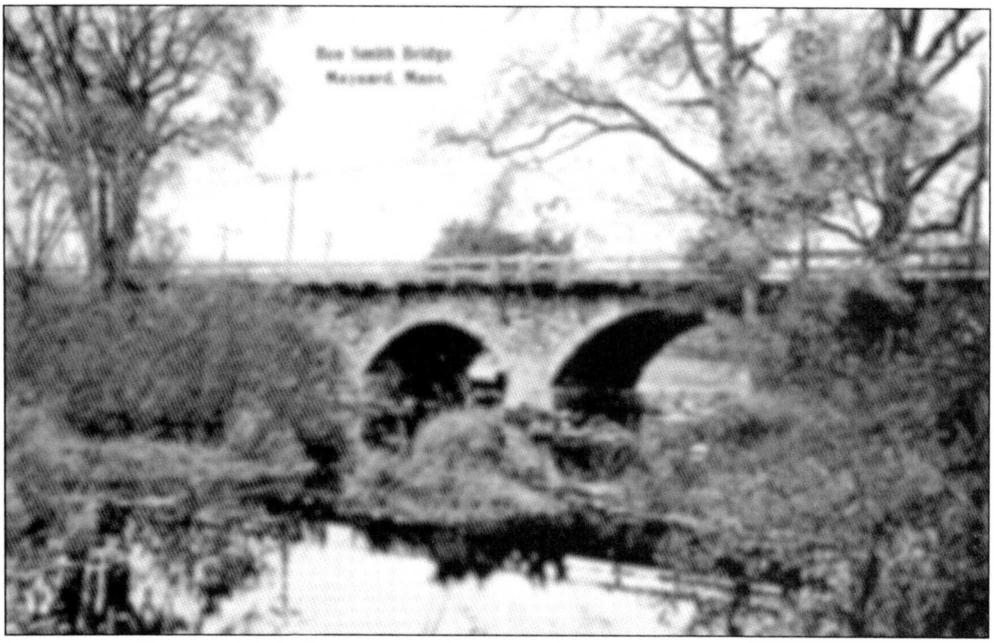

**BEN SMITH BRIDGE.** With the erection of Ben Smith Bridge in 1816, Great Road was opened to stagecoach travel. Levi Smith ran a tavern at what was later known as the Thompson or Eveleth farm.

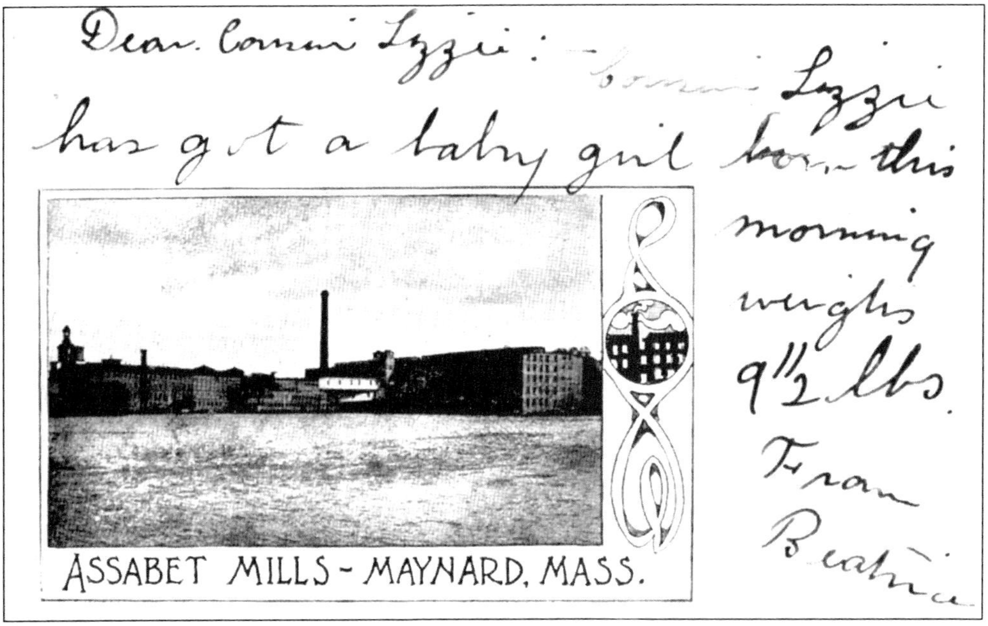


**My Job Was Here.** As seen from the millpond, this card features a view of the Assabet Mills, where many of the residents of Maynard worked and supported their families.

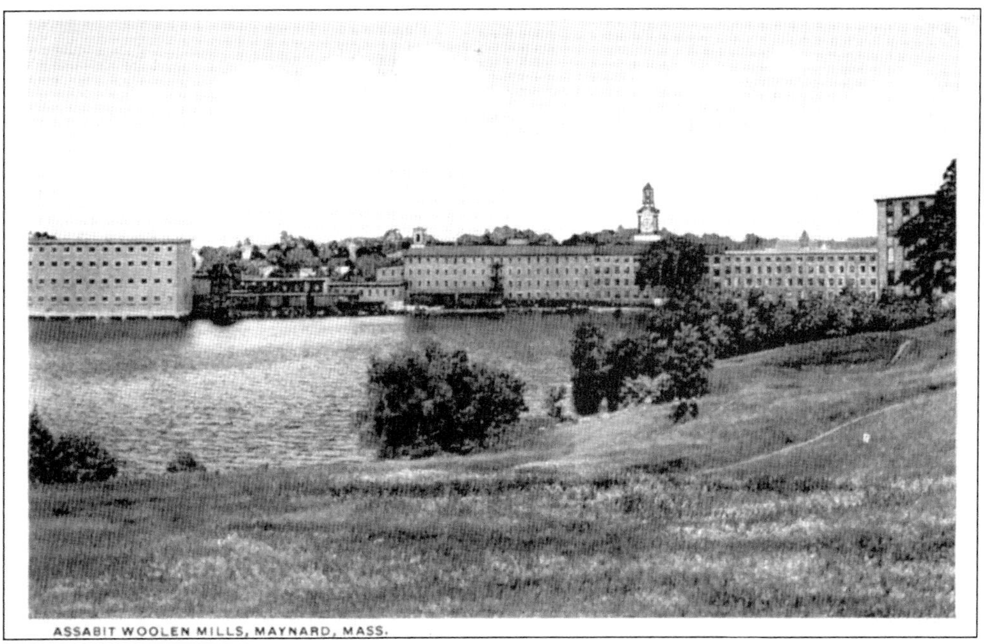


**Assabet Woolen Mills.** Located in the center of town, the millpond next to the woolen mills attracted lots of people to its parklike borders. In the winter, hundreds of ice-skaters were attracted to its smooth, flat surface.

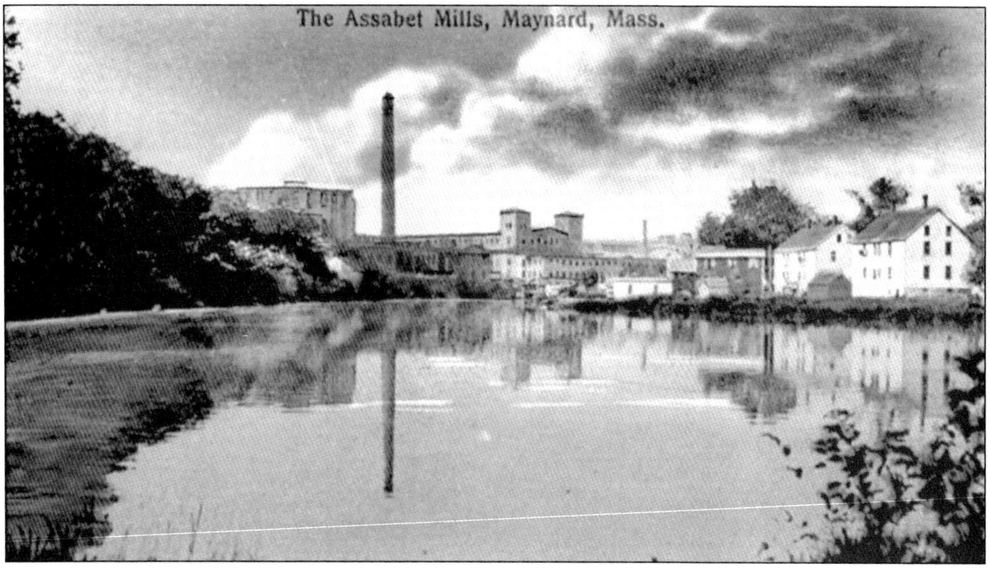


**WATER POWER.** The industrial developments of the territory were located near the river to make use of its waterpower. Communities such as Maynard developed as the hub for the supply of goods and services to the expanding area.

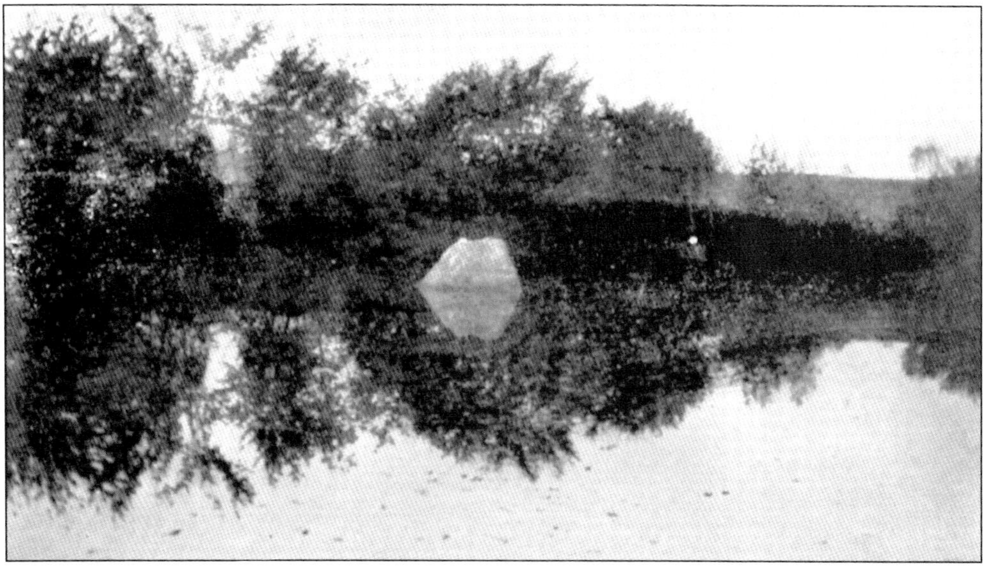

**NANNY GOAT ROCK.** On the Assabet River east of the present-day Elks, stands this unusual rock formation called Nanny Goat Rock. One can only surmise that a goat was stranded upon the rock at one time.

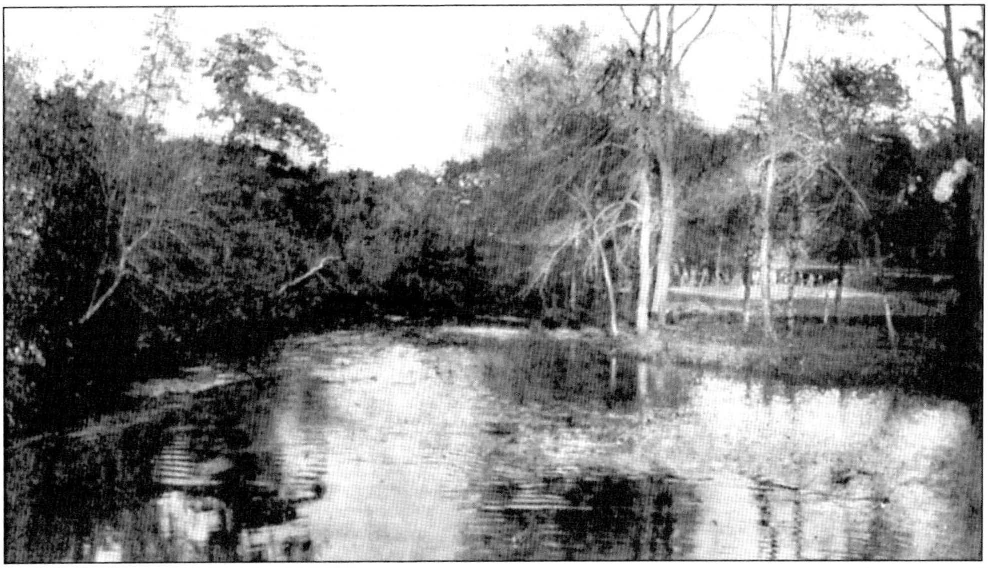

**THE RIVER FLOWS.** The 30-mile-long Assabet River originates in a swamp in the town of Westborough and flows through the towns of Northborough, Marlborough, Berlin, Hudson, Stow, Maynard, Acton, and into Concord, where it joins with the Sudbury River to form the Concord River.

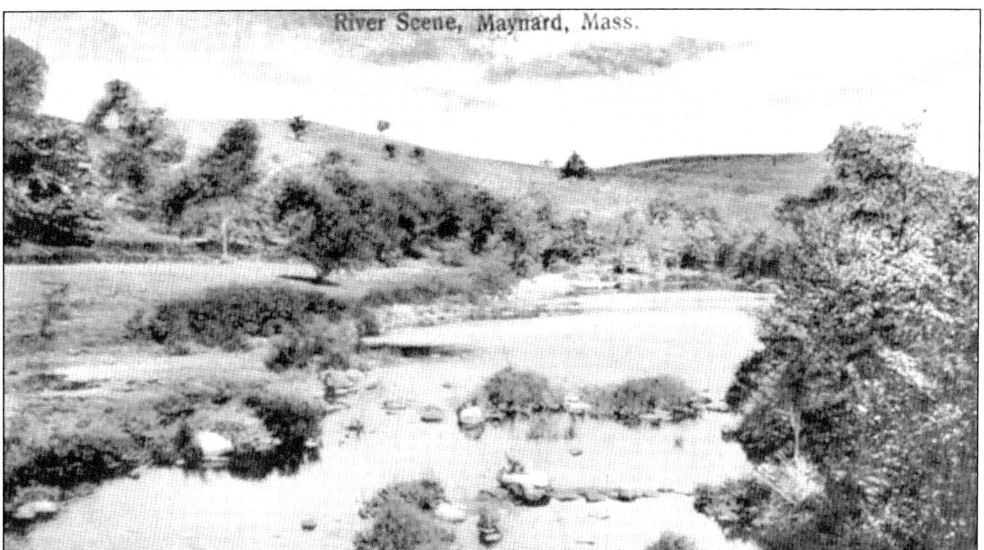


**EARLY RIVER SCENE.** For many years, there was no commercial center to the settlement of the Northwest District, but as the inhabitants took up residence close to the Assabet River, waterpower was used and a village took shape.

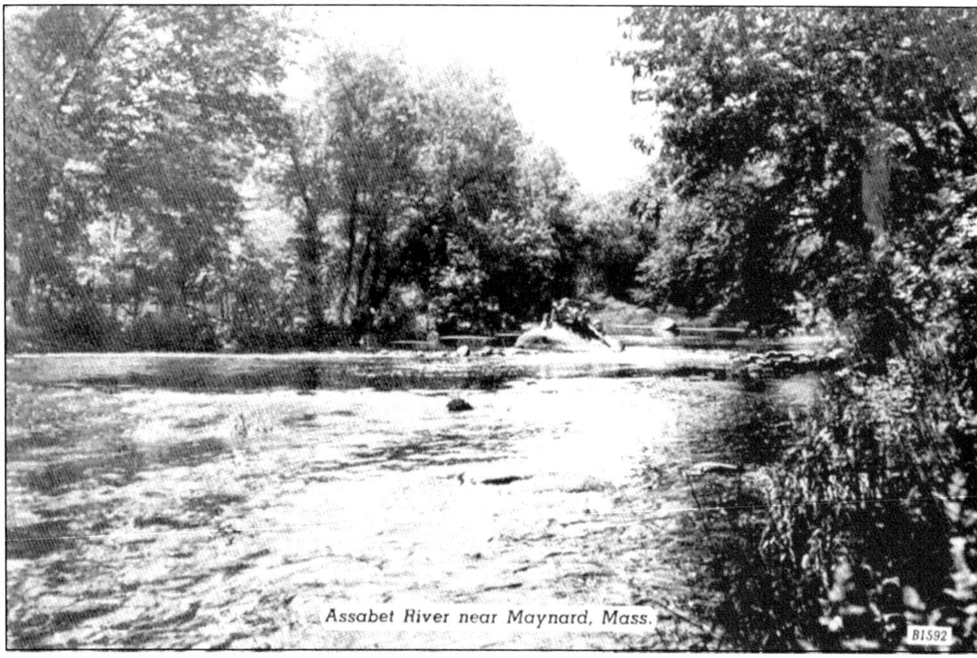


**RECREATION ON THE RIVER.** The building of the Ben Smith Dam created a large basin, which made it possible to use the river above the dam as a popular recreation area for boating, bathing, canoeing, skating, and fishing.

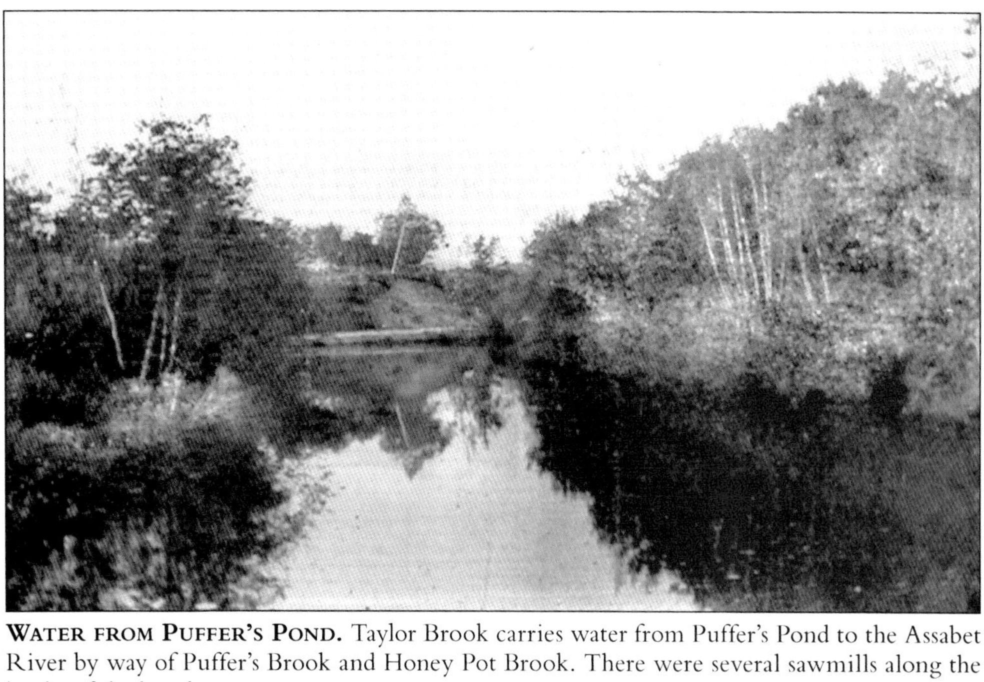

**WATER FROM PUFFER'S POND.** Taylor Brook carries water from Puffer's Pond to the Assabet River by way of Puffer's Brook and Honey Pot Brook. There were several sawmills along the banks of the brooks.

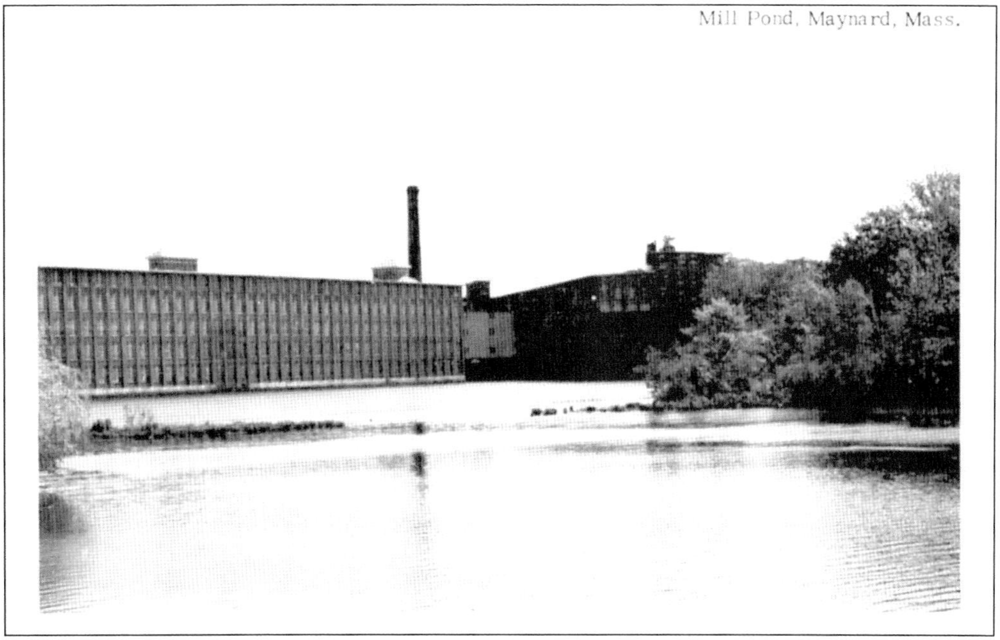


**THE THOMPSON STREET MILL.** This building was 640 feet long, 106 feet wide, and five stories high. It was known as a 100-set mill. Dynamos were installed, replacing the old gasameter that had supplied light to the mills and several of the nearby buildings.

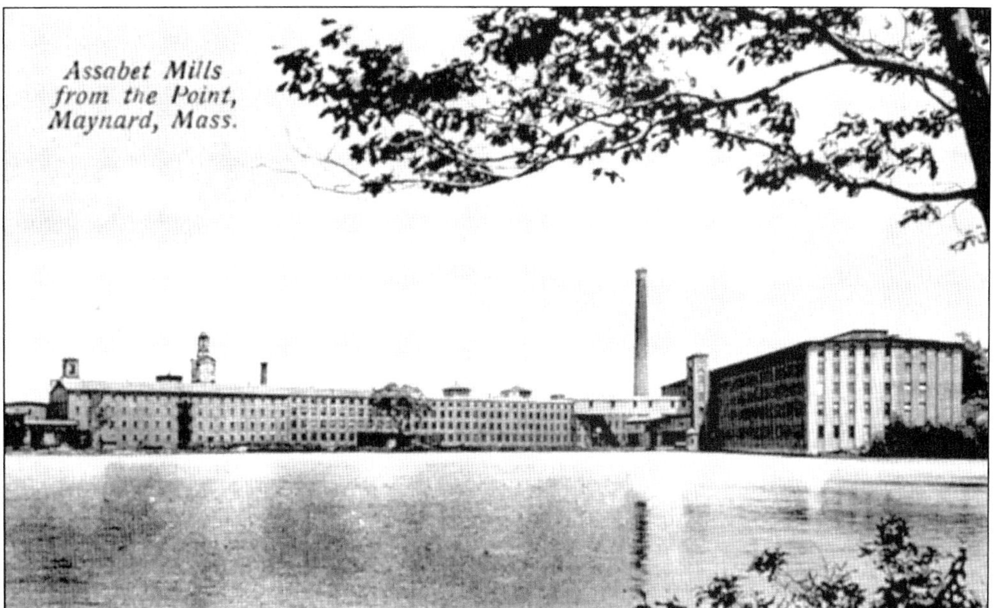


**AMERICAN WOOLEN MILLS IN MAYNARD.** The American Woolen Company was a large trust that operated 26 mills, one of them in Maynard. By 1923, it reached a total of 57 mills. Charles Rawlett was its presiding financial genius, and its president from 1905 through 1924 was William Madison Wood.

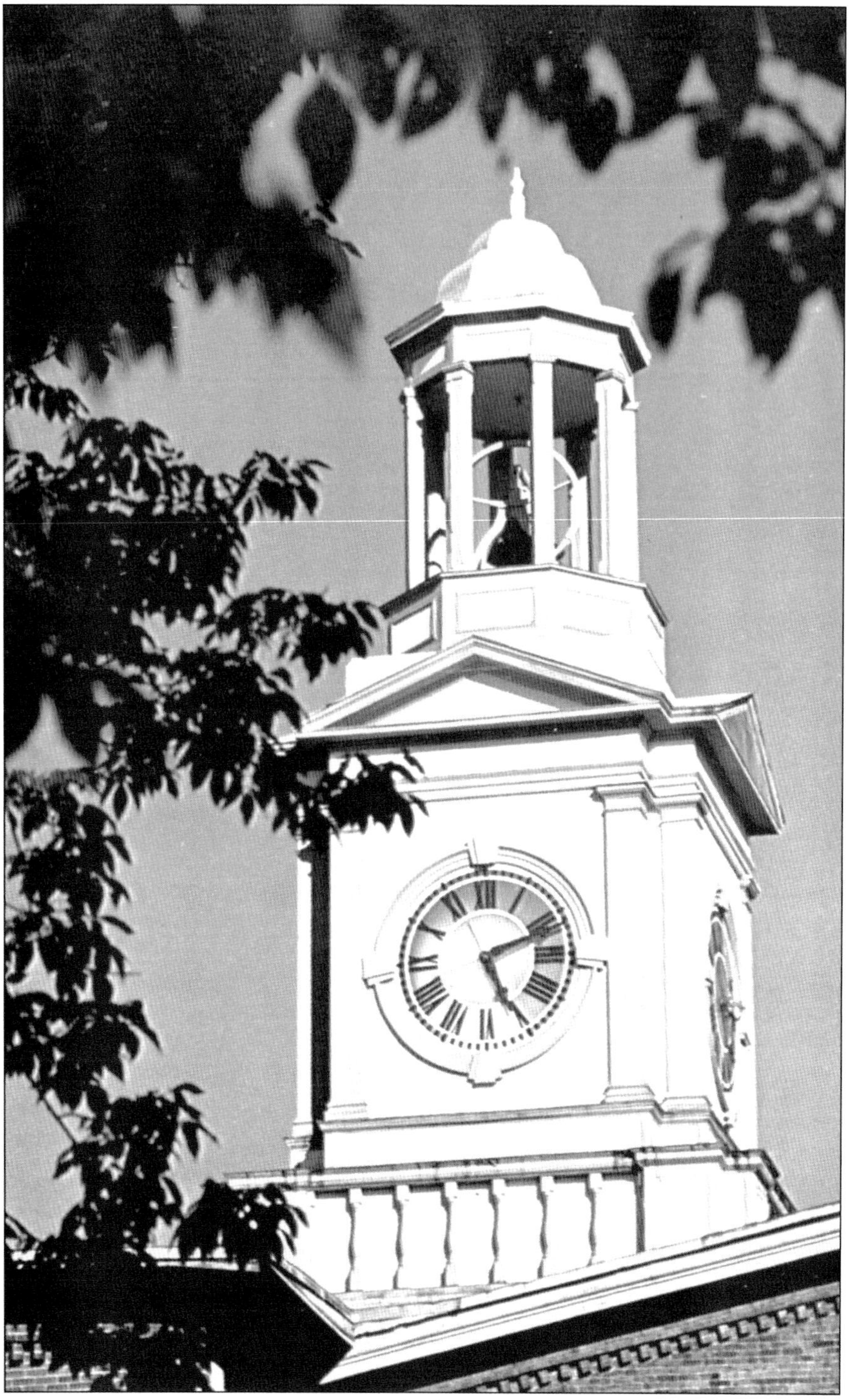

**MILL CLOCK AT ASSABET MILLS.** In 1892, the fine Mill Clock, often referred to as the Town Clock, was given by Lorenzo Maynard and placed in position in the fall of that year in the tower erected by the Assabet Manufacturing Company. It was adopted as the town seal for the town of Maynard.

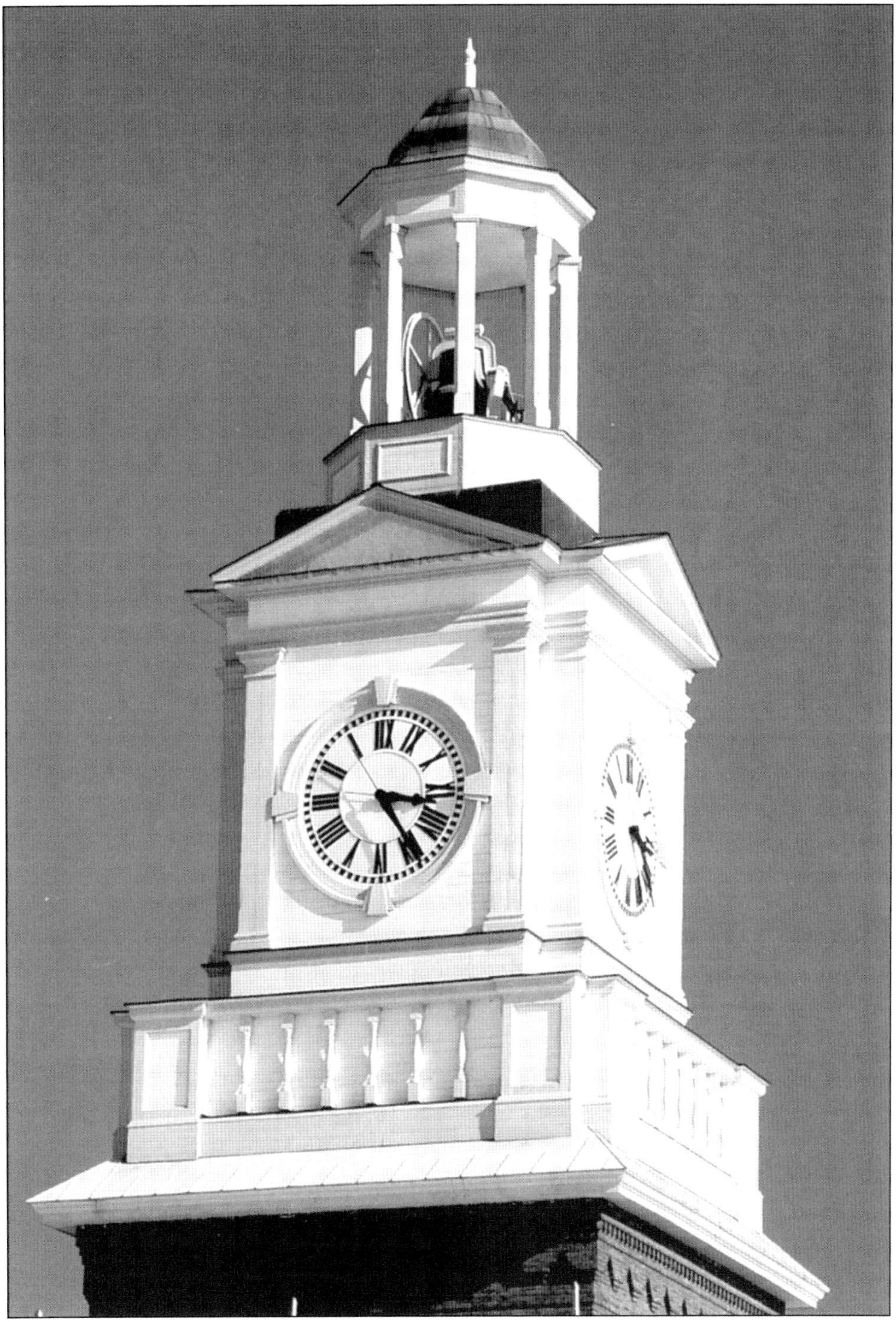

**BACKWARD MILL CLOCK.** The clock postcard shown above was printed with its negative reversed (note 1:00 p.m. is on the left where 11:00 p.m. should be). The card was already in circulation before it was noticed. It was quickly replaced with the correct view of the clock, which had become the symbol of Maynard.

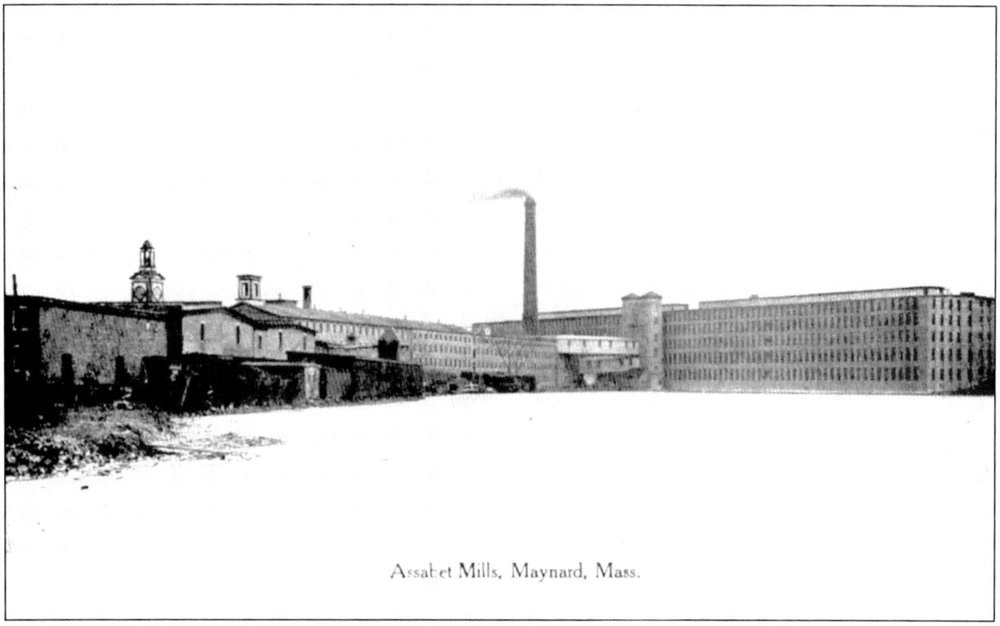


**A MILLPOND VIEW.** This view from the millpond shows building No. 5 (right), shortly after it had been completed. Buildings No. 1 and No. 21 had not yet been constructed. The trains ran along the edge of the millpond.

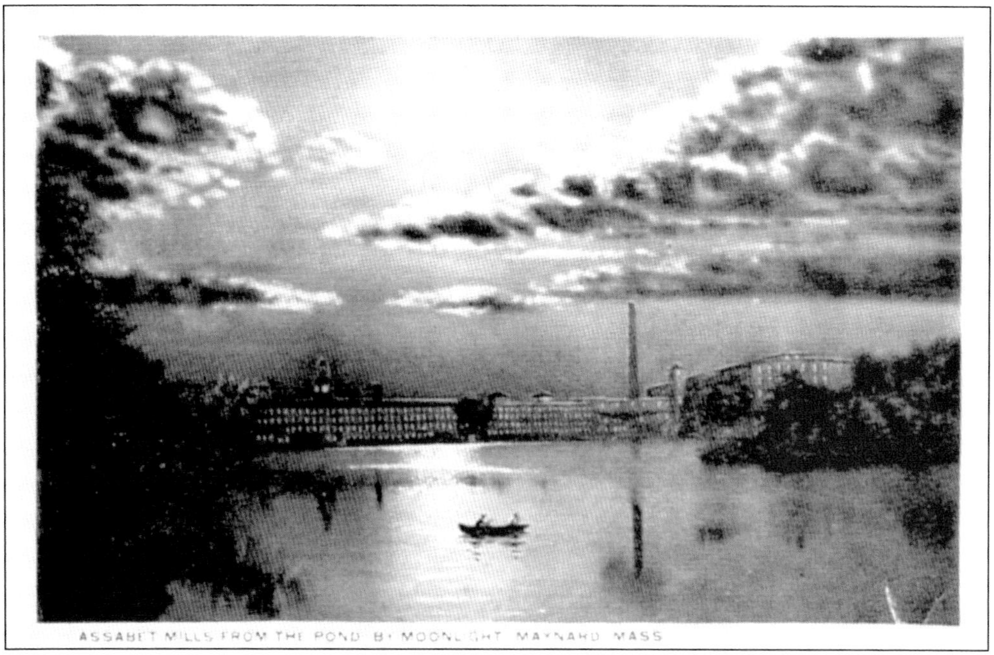


**MOONLIGHT OVER THE MILLPOND.** The millpond is very calm, and it provides a great place to take a canoe ride under a full moon. The pond also provides great fishing.

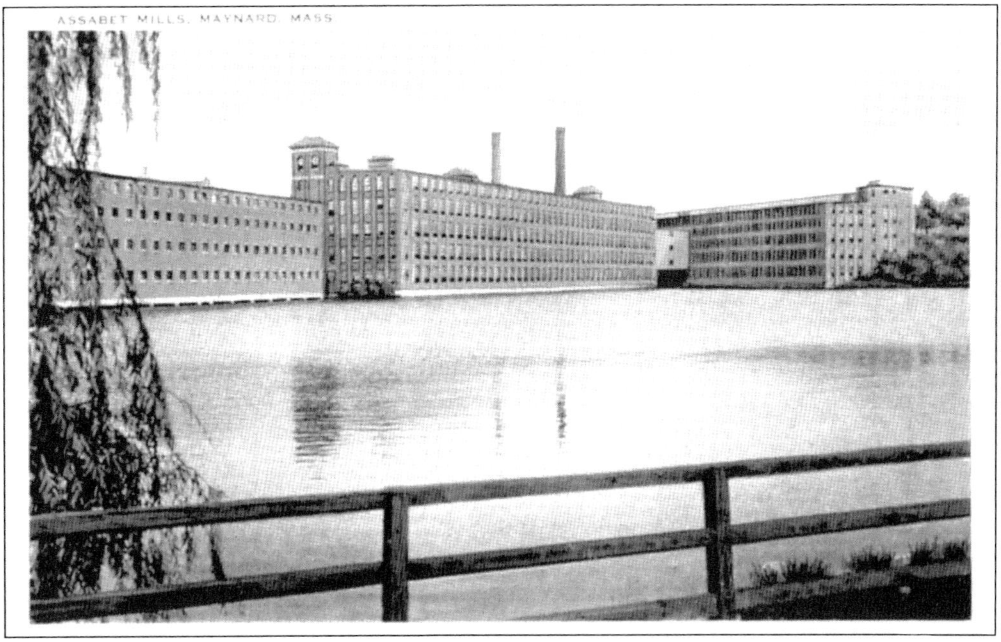


**FRONT STREET VIEW OF MILLS.** Most of the mills can be seen from Front Street with the millpond in the foreground. When the United States became involved in World War II, the mill was working seven days a week.

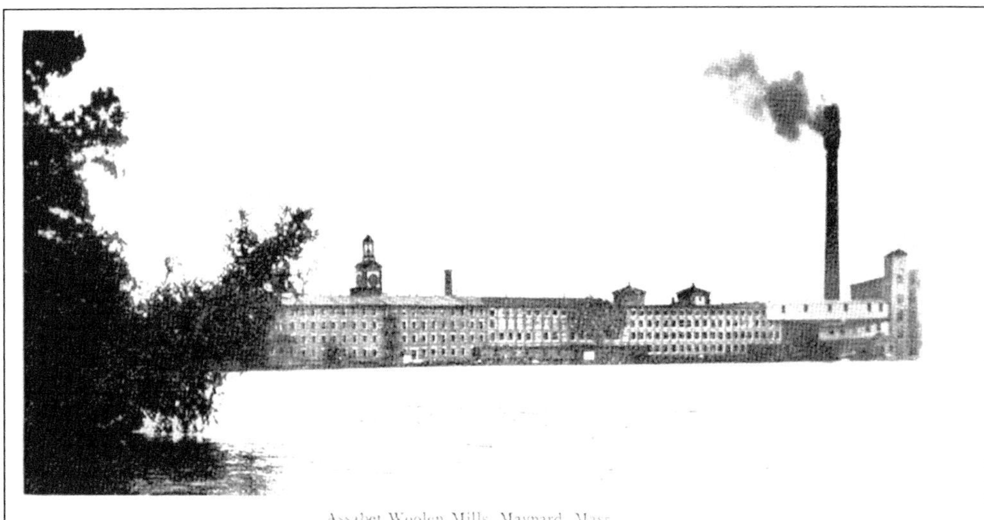


**ASSABET WOOLEN MILLS.** On May 19, 1846, Amory Maynard made his first land purchase from Eden S. Brooks to construct the first mill building. The land purchased was on both sides of the Assabet River.

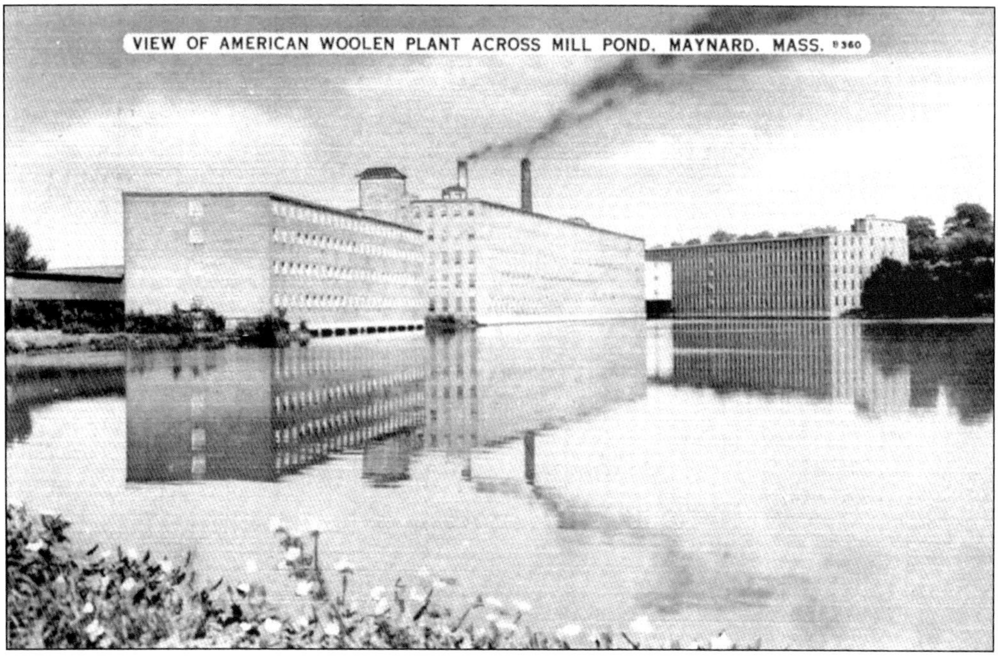


**NEW MILL ON THE POND.** The millpond is shown here during the heyday of the American Woolen Company. During the Digital Equipment Corporation era, since all its equipment was electric, there was no longer any need for waterpower, and half of the millpond was filled in for parking.

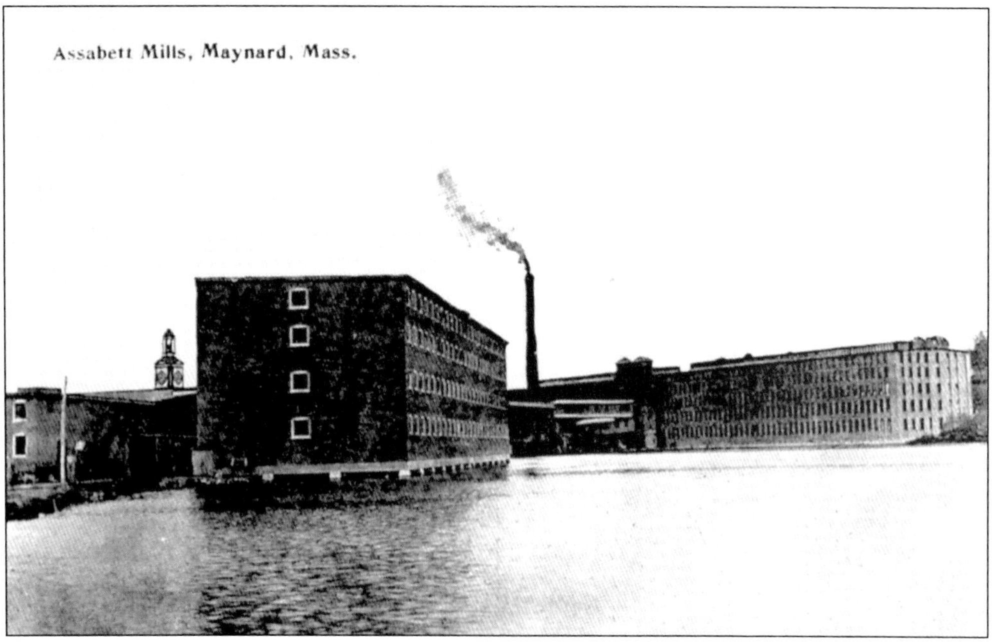

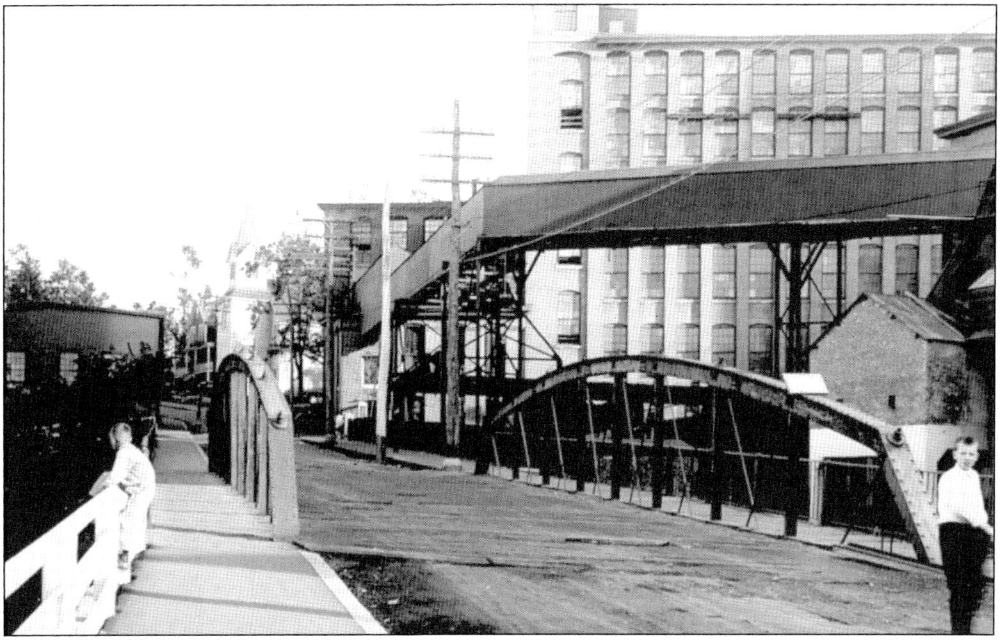

**IRON BRIDGE OVER THE ASSABET.** In 1872, an iron bridge was erected. Elevated steam pipes that went from building to building were covered, which made a warm shelter for pigeons. (Courtesy of MHS.)

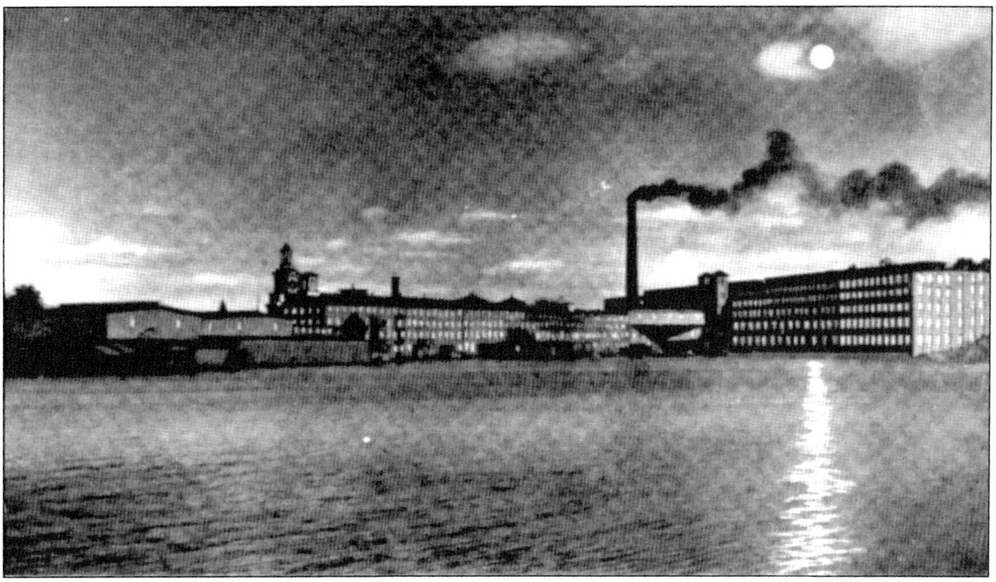

**MOONLIGHT OVER THE MILLS.** This view of the Assabet Mills was taken from the millpond at night, under a full moon and dramatic clouds. This image was taken prior to 1916, when the second chimney was added.

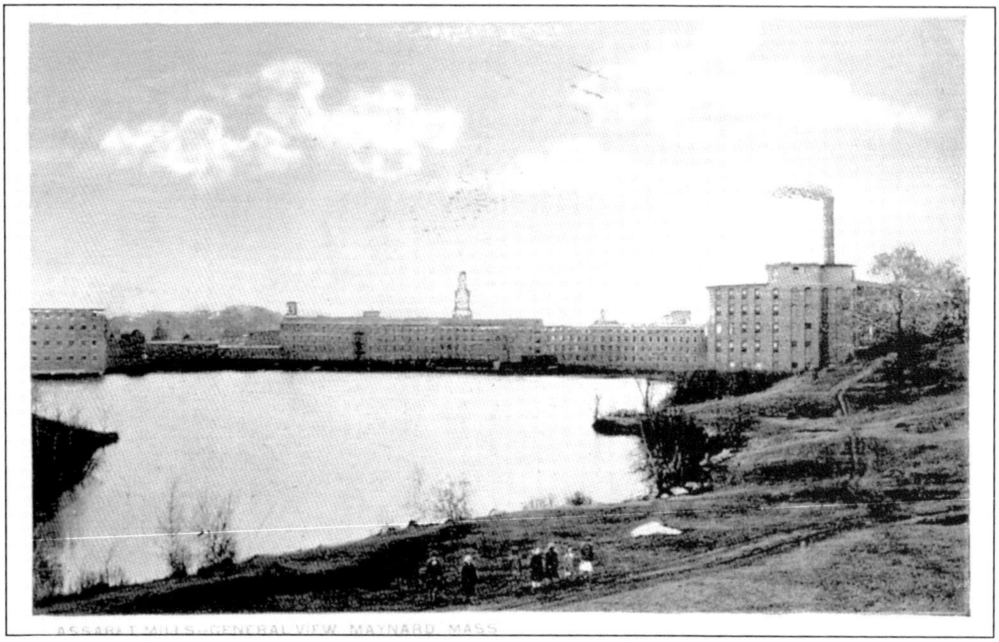


**OFF TO WORK.** Early morning workers are shown making their way along the millpond to their work areas in one of the brick plant buildings. No one took an automobile to work; they all walked, some up to a mile.

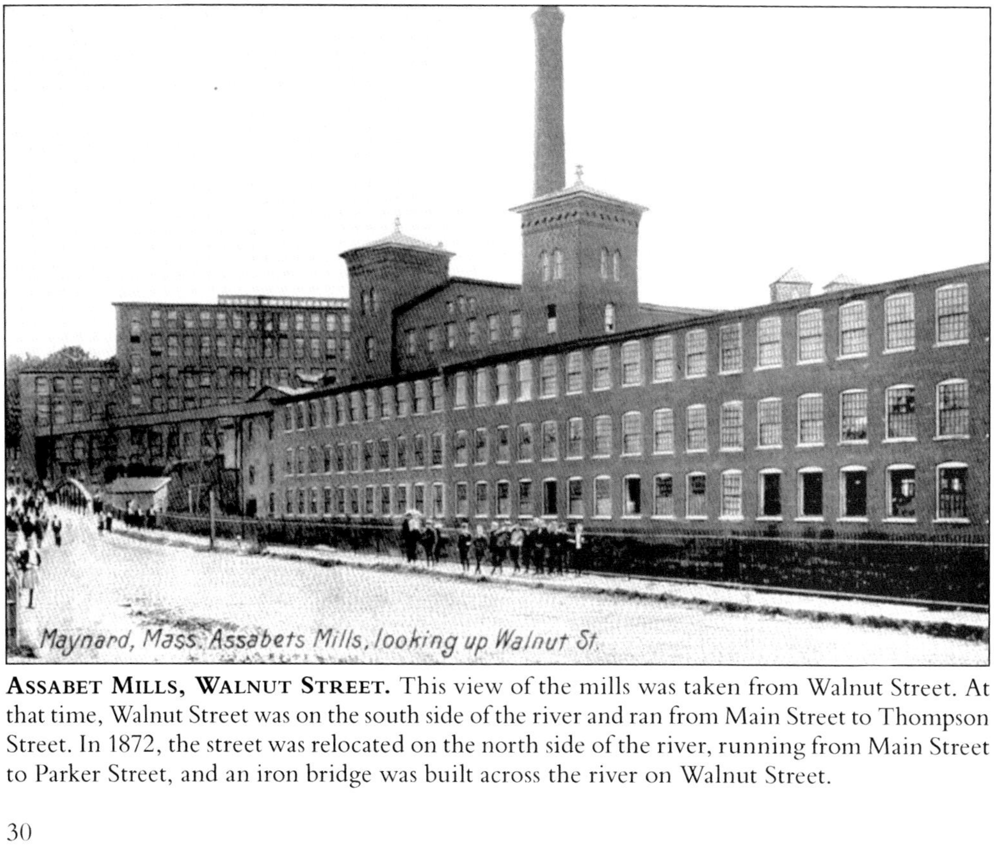


**ASSABET MILLS, WALNUT STREET.** This view of the mills was taken from Walnut Street. At that time, Walnut Street was on the south side of the river and ran from Main Street to Thompson Street. In 1872, the street was relocated on the north side of the river, running from Main Street to Parker Street, and an iron bridge was built across the river on Walnut Street.

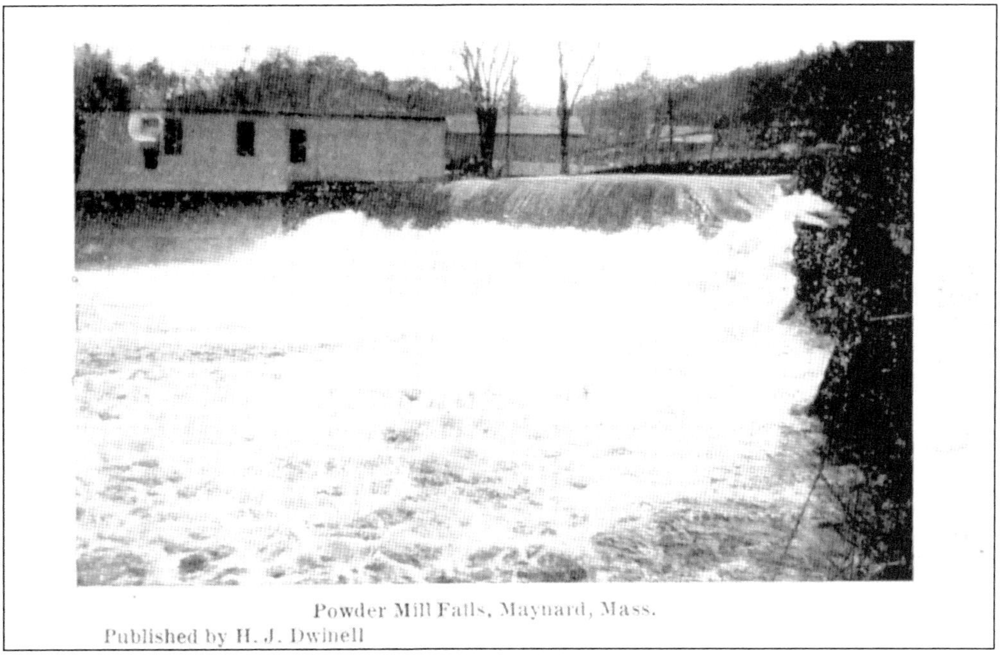


**POWDER MILL FALLS.** Nathan Pratt had the powder mill dam built, and he operated the powder mill that used the dam's waterpower until 1864. Waterpower for the creation of electricity is still possible at this site.

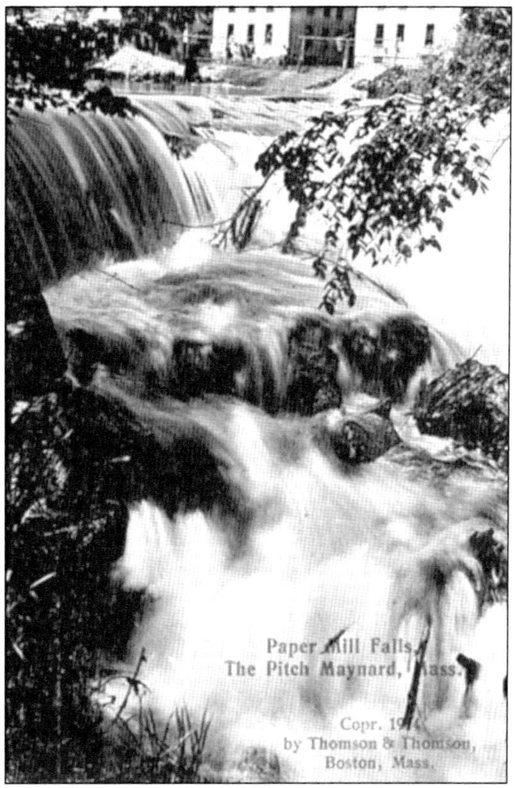


**THE FALLS AT THE PAPER MILL DAM.** Just below the center of the village were a paper mill and a powder mill. The powder mill manufactured powder for military and commercial purposes. The paper mill dam, shown here, was washed out in the spring flood of 1927. At the top of the picture are tenement blocks and the current site of McDonalds.

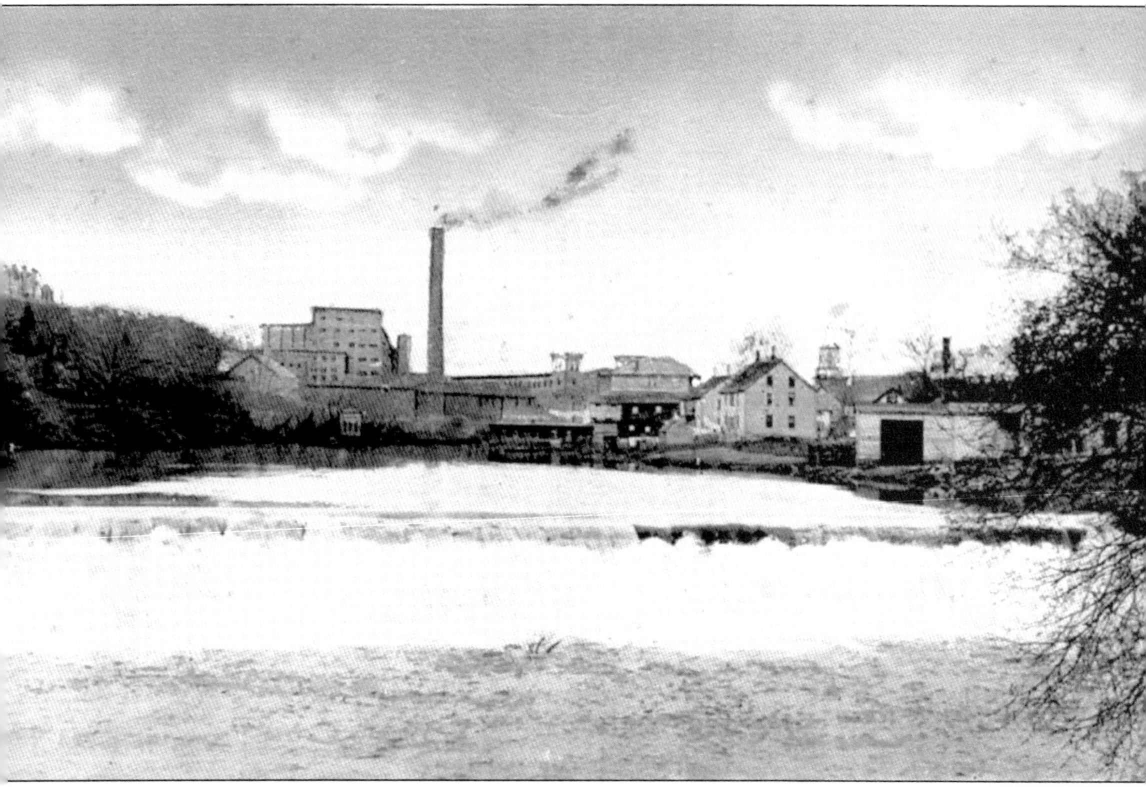

**PAPER MILL DAM.** In 1895, the mill bought the old paper mill dam and rebuilt its sluiceway. The 1927 flood destroyed the dam, and it was never rebuilt. The paper mill chimney was razed on August 14, 1914.

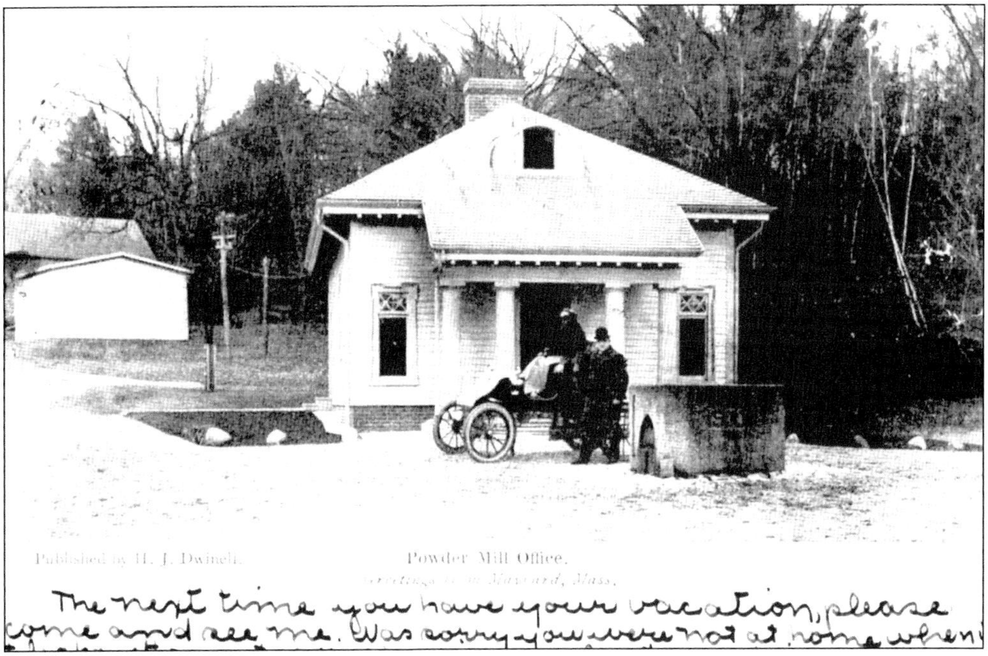


**Powder Mills in 1835.** The Powder Mills started along the Assabet River on the Maynard-Acton town line. In 1883, the company became the American Powder Company. There were many explosive accidents at the mill, which were heard up to 25 miles away.

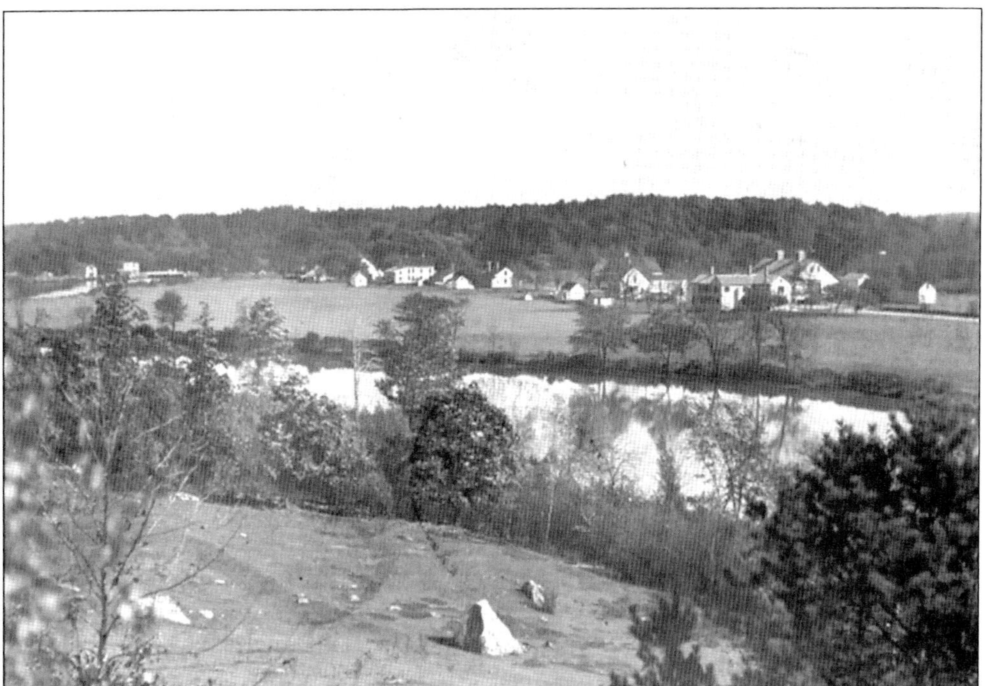

**Powder Mill Village.** This view from Pine Hill shows the Powder Mill Village. The dust from the milled powder was potentially explosive, and workmen and family lived under the constant potential of explosions. (Courtesy of MHS.)

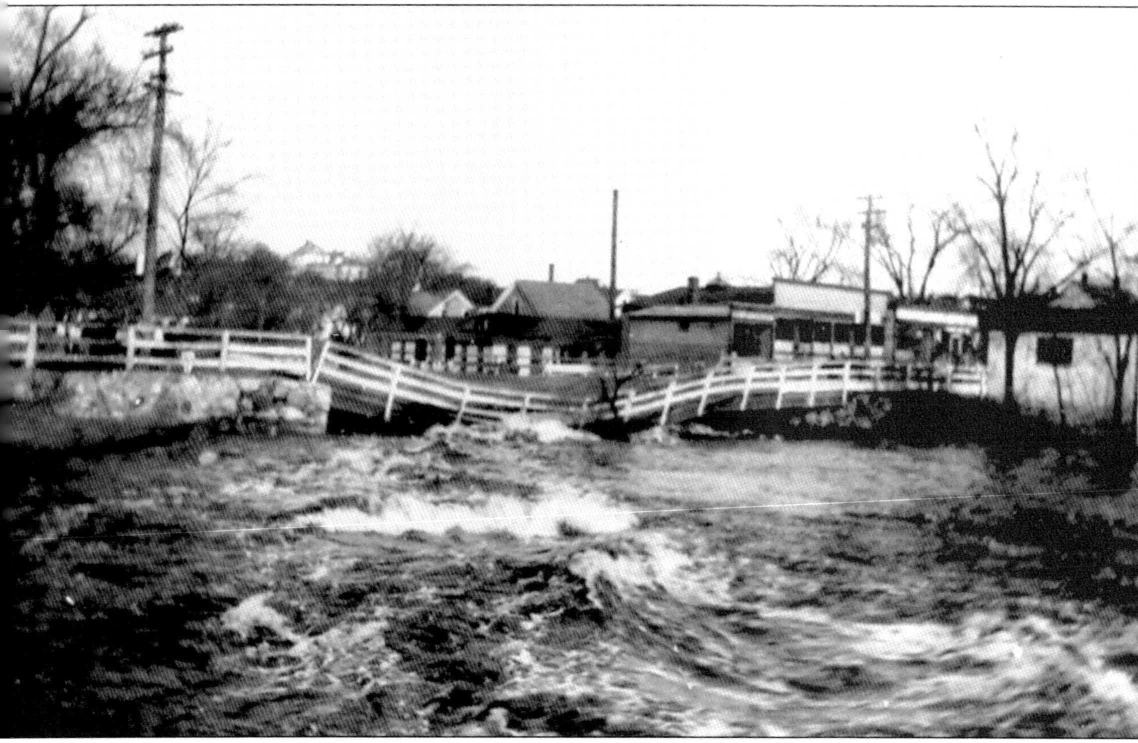

**THE FLOOD.** Until 1927, this dam was located south of where the Assabet River runs under the so-called paper mill bridge. Both the dam and the bridge were washed out in November 1927. Although the dam was not rebuilt, the bridge was replaced. (Courtesy of MHS.)

# *Three*

# STREET SCENES

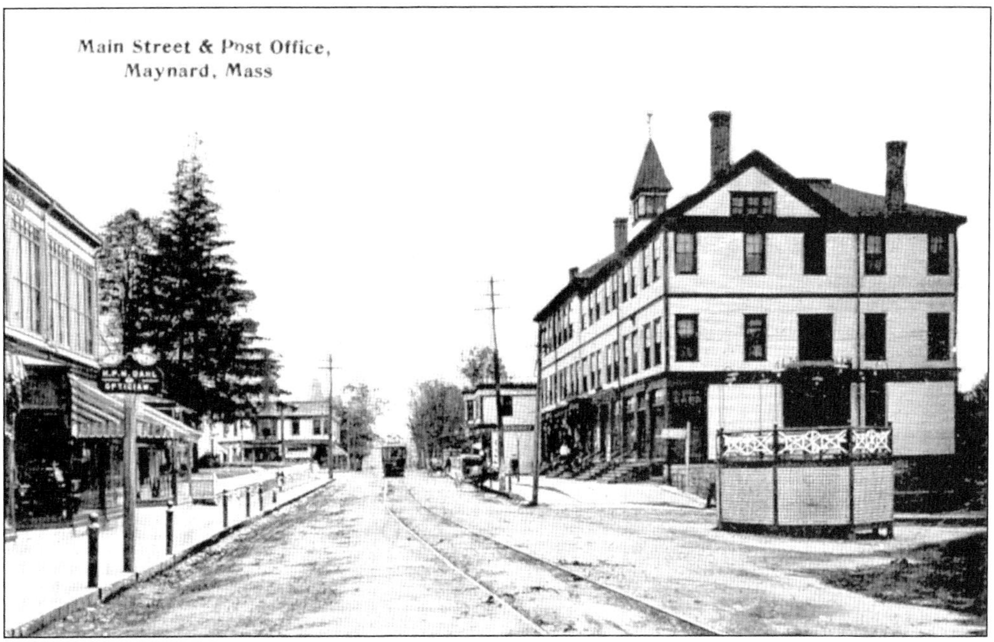


**MAIN STREET.** When Amory Maynard first came to Assabet Village, there was no Main Street. Rapid growth soon made it necessary to make a road through the valley, and in September 1848, Main Street was laid out, starting from Great Road.

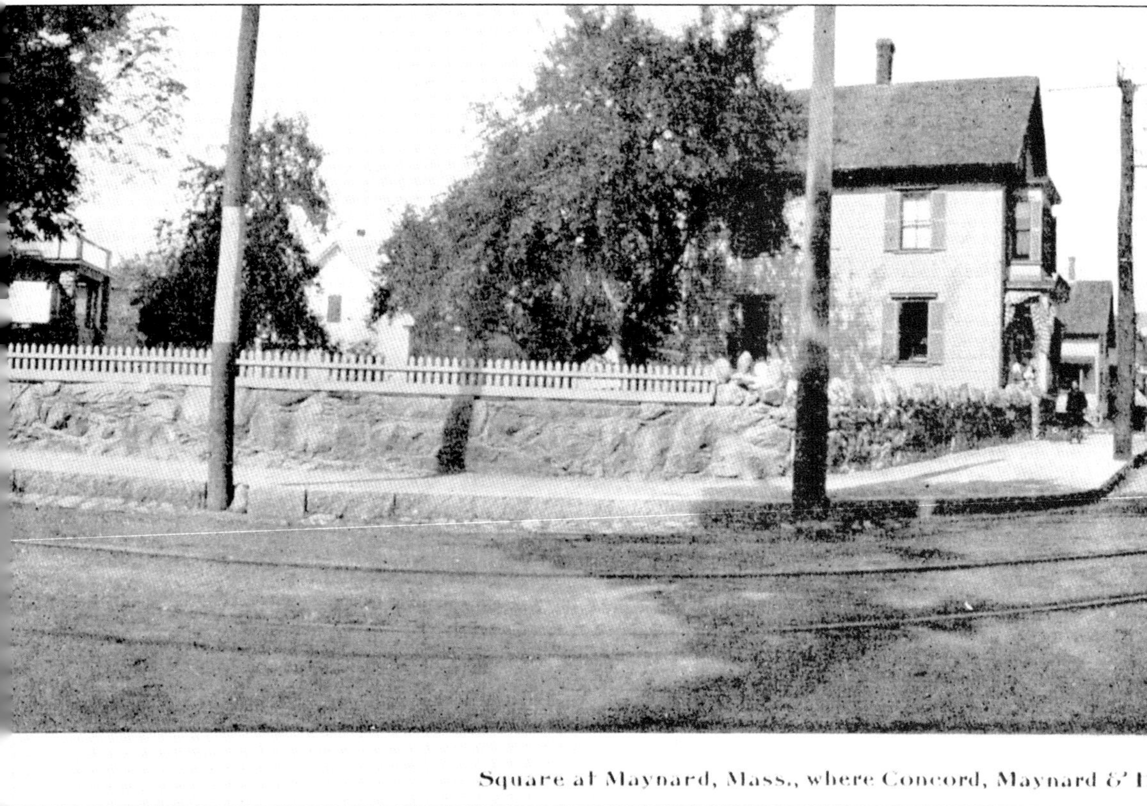

**PANORAMIC VIEW OF MAYNARD CENTER.** The home of Amory Maynard II (grandson of Amory, his son did not inherit his name) is on the left. A mall was built on the site of the home and has recently been demolished to make room for a new CVS store. The building on the far

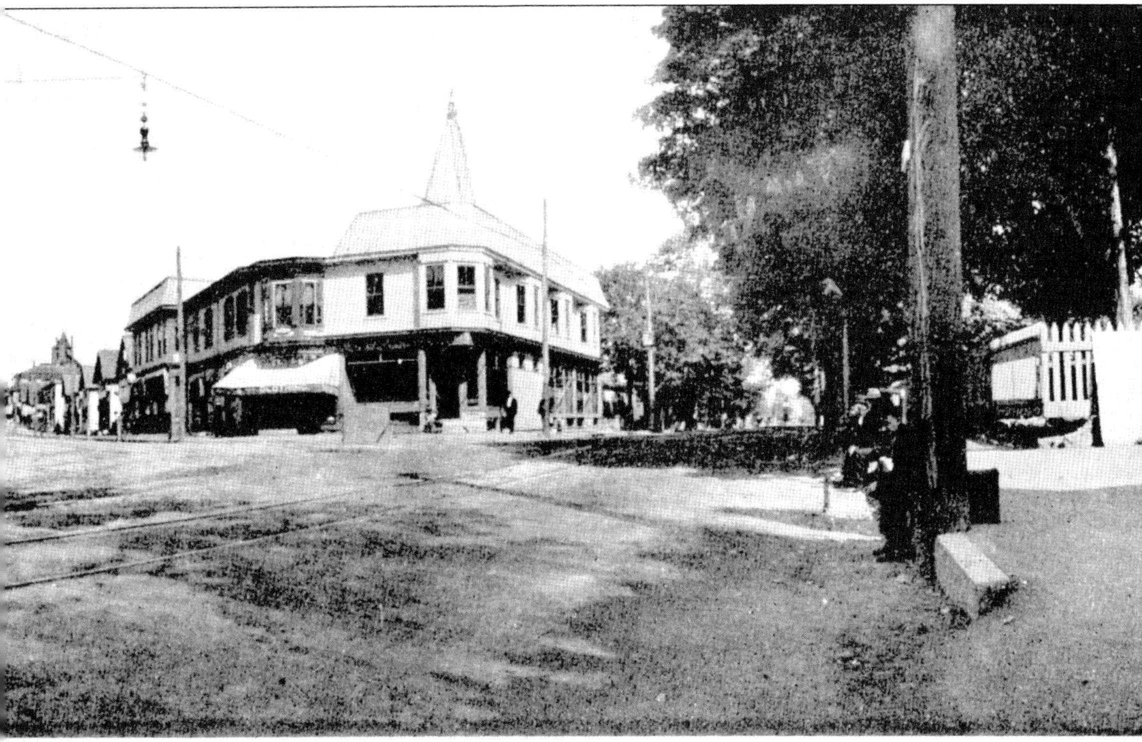

St. Ry. connects with Lowell, Acton & Maynard Line

right is the Naylor Block, which burnt to the ground in February 1917 and was replaced in 1938. Today it is the location of the Boston Bean House.

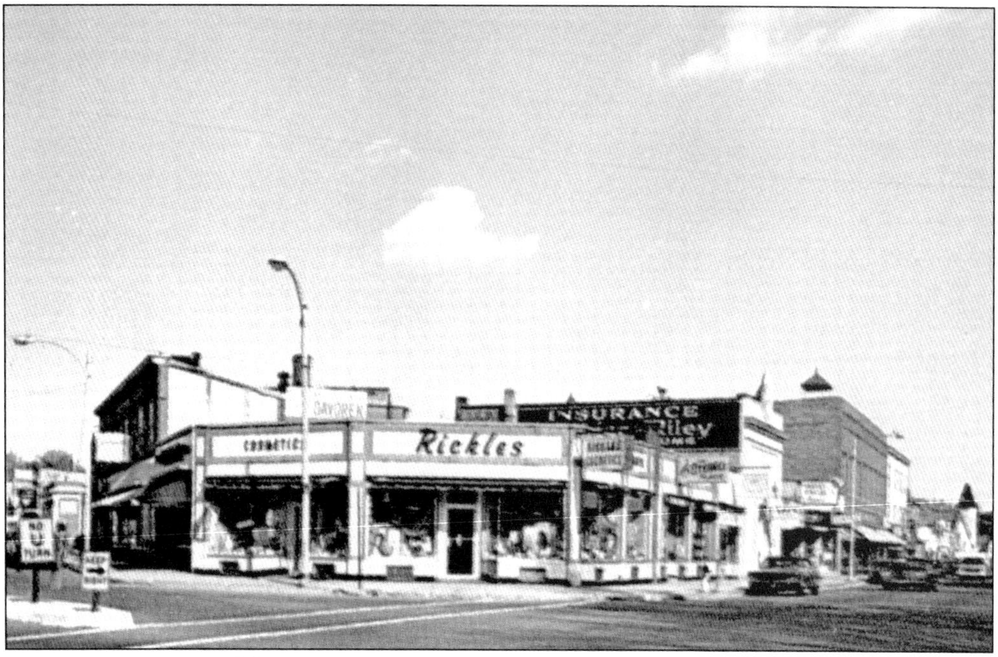


**NAYLOR BLOCK.** Rickles, a cosmetic store, was located in the center of town at the corner of Nason and Main Streets. For more than 20 years, there was a void in the center of town.

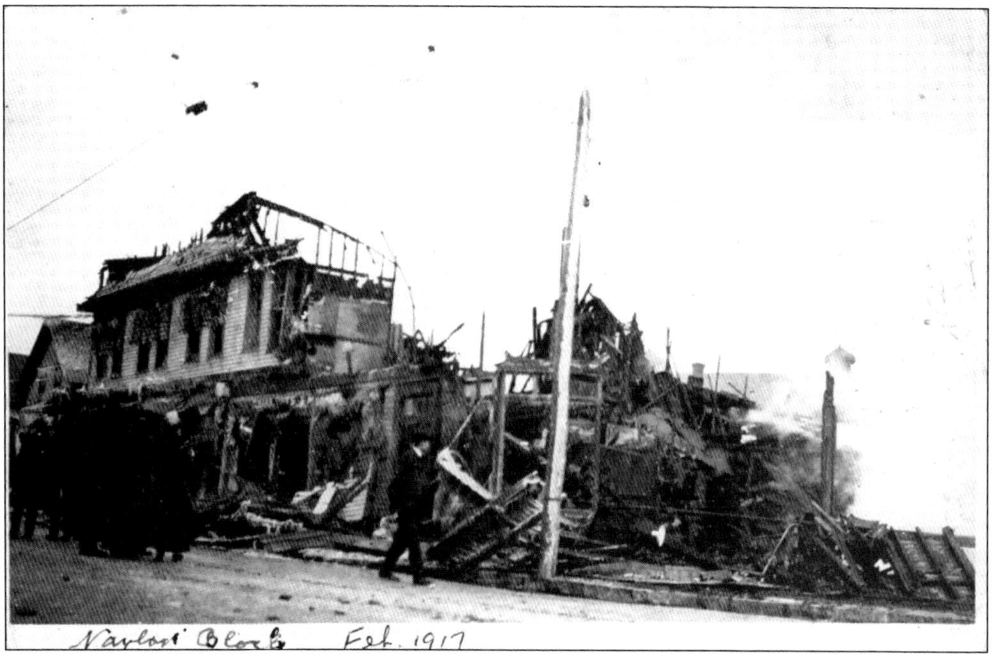


**NAYLOR BLOCK FIRE.** The block of buildings on the corner of Main and Nason Streets were destroyed by fire in February 1917. Today this is the site of the Boston Bean House. (Courtesy of MHS.)

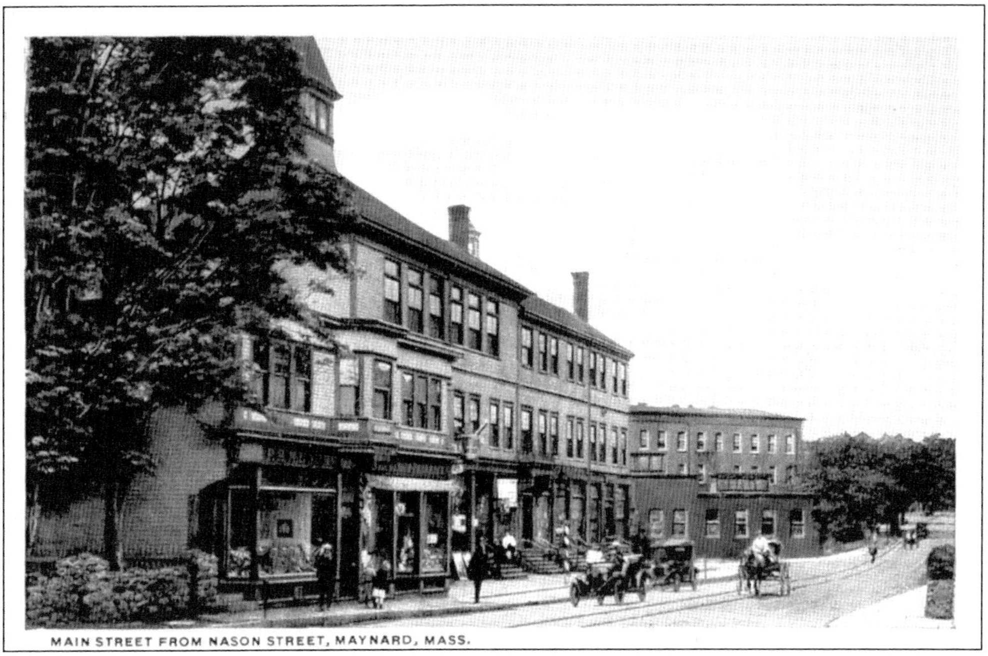


**MAIN STREET LOOKING WEST.** The building on the left burnt in the late 1950s. As seen in both images, both automobiles and horses were still in use; however, the automobile eventually won out as the choice means of transportation.

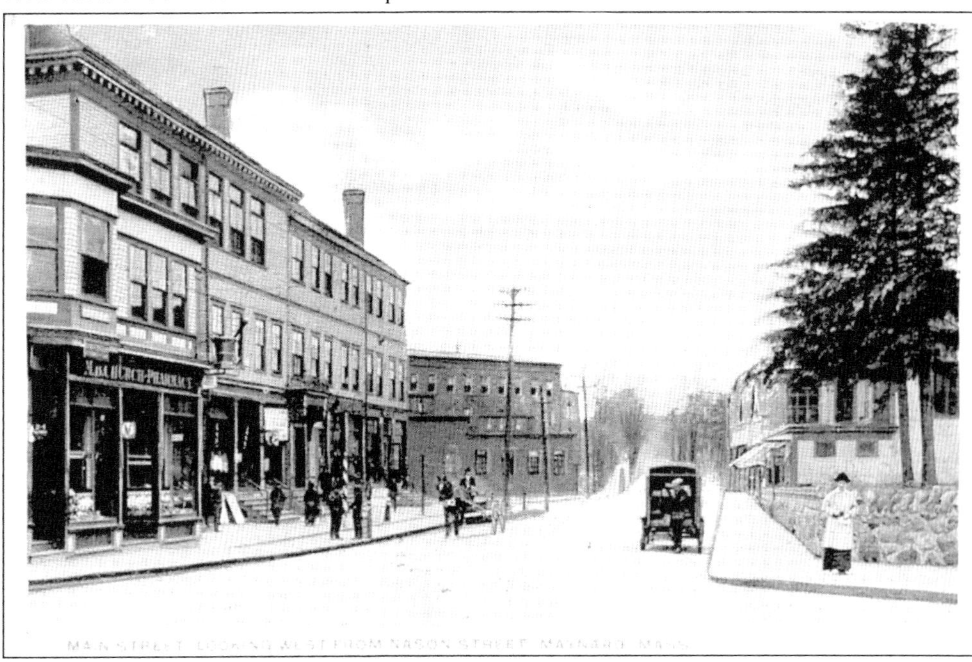

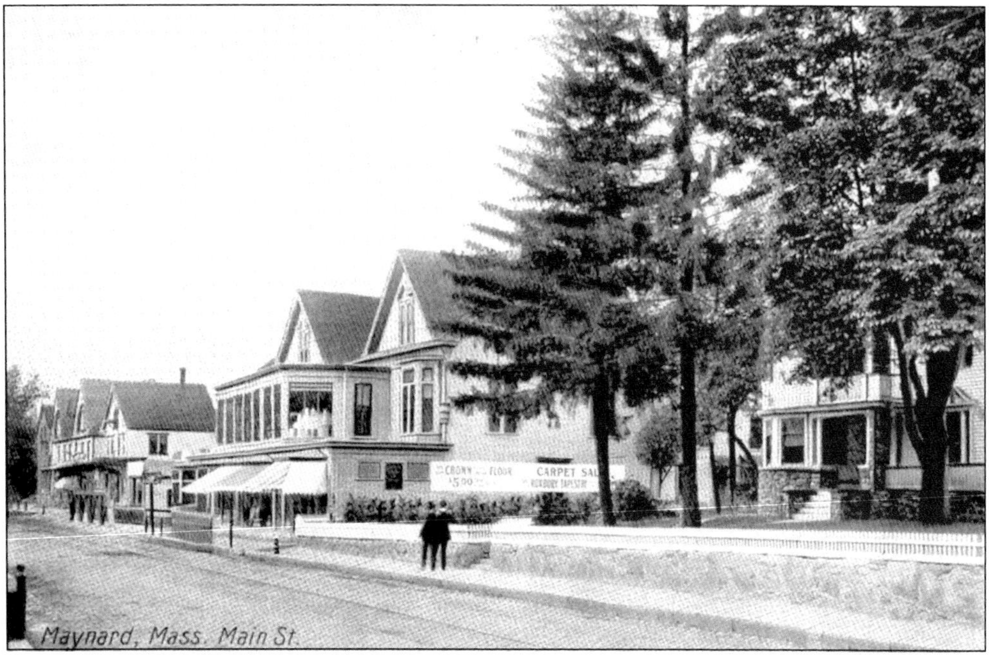


**RIVERSIDE HALL.** In 1872, Maynard held its first town meeting and elections at this hall. It was built in late 1869. Today it is known as Gruber Furniture. There was a movie theater (the Rialto) on the second floor, which burnt in 1936. Amory Maynard II's home is seen on the right.

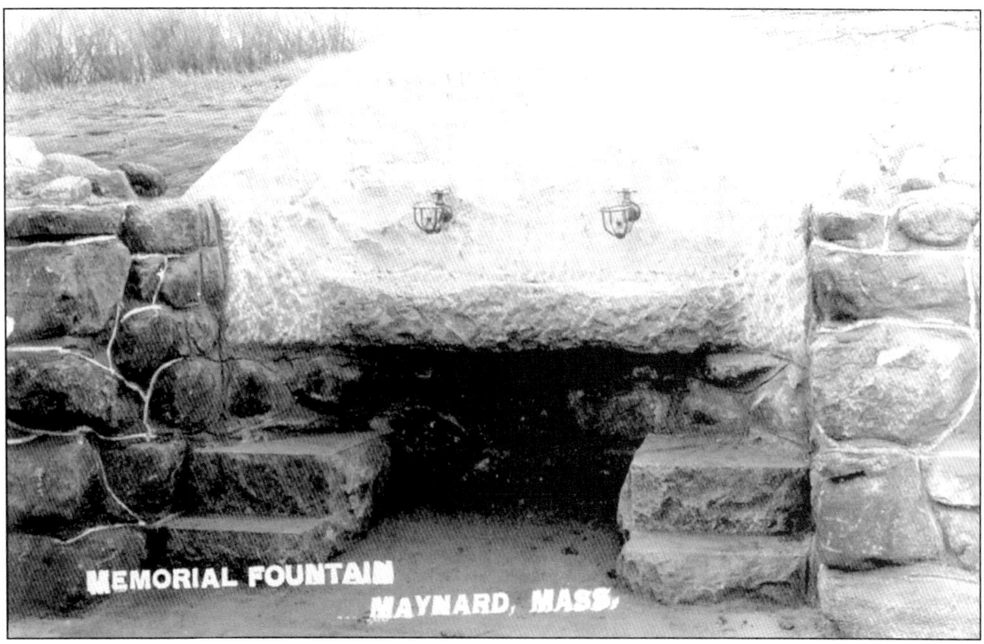


**THE DRINKING FOUNTAIN.** Memorial Fountain, located in front of the Congregational church, was given to the town by Mary J. Brooks in memory of her husband Luke. Local ice dealers split the year, providing ice to cool the drinking water. (Courtesy of Jack Malcolm.)

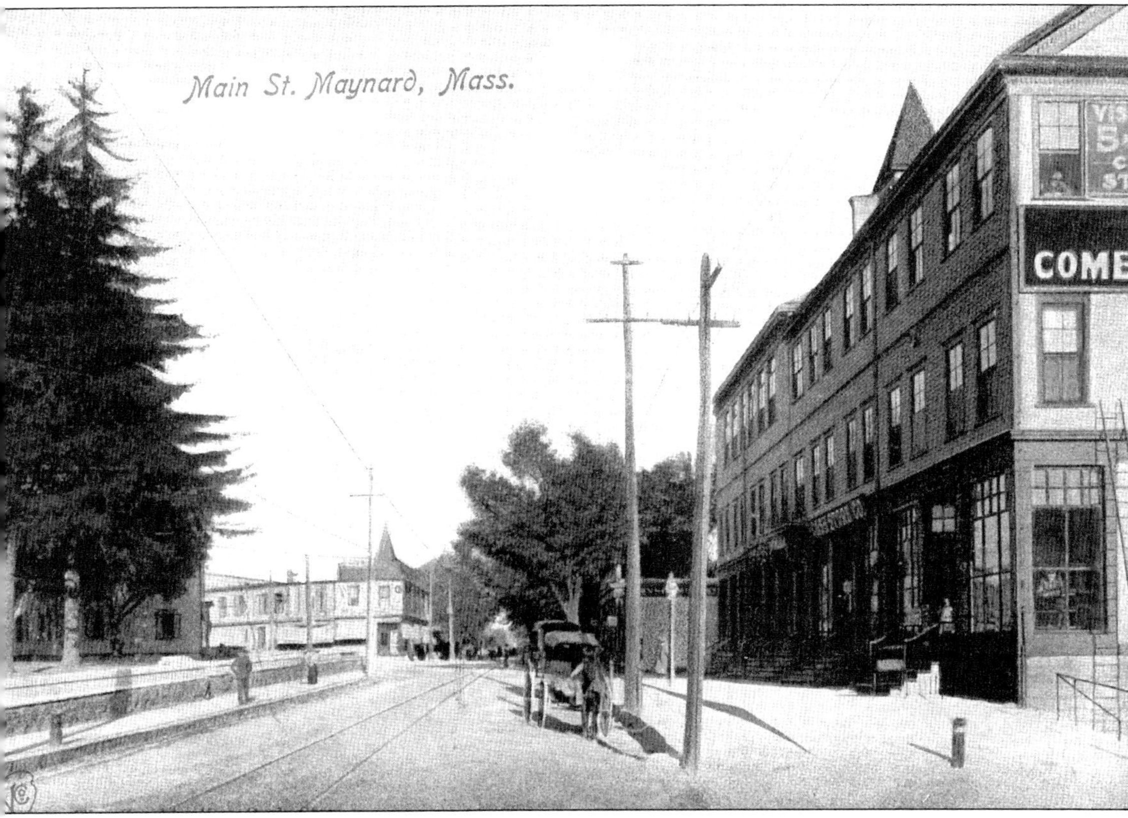


**W. B. CASE STORE.** This store was located in the Masonic building prior to moving to its new building on Nason Street. The Palmaccio family operated O'Berg's Shoe Store for many years in this building. Today the Masonic building is the site of the copy center and several other stores and restaurants.

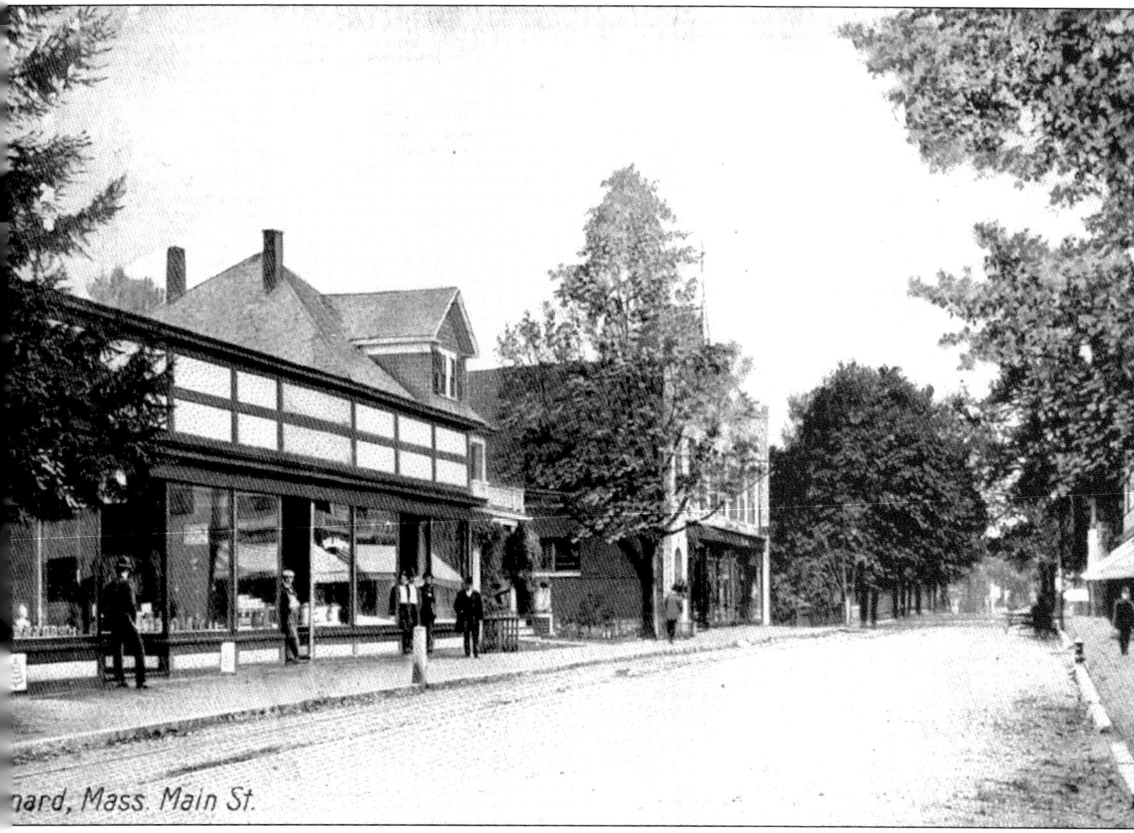


**MAIN STREET LOOKING WEST.** Laid out between 1848 and 1849, Main Street was the first official street in the town. The house on the left was razed to make way for further expansion of the co-op society.

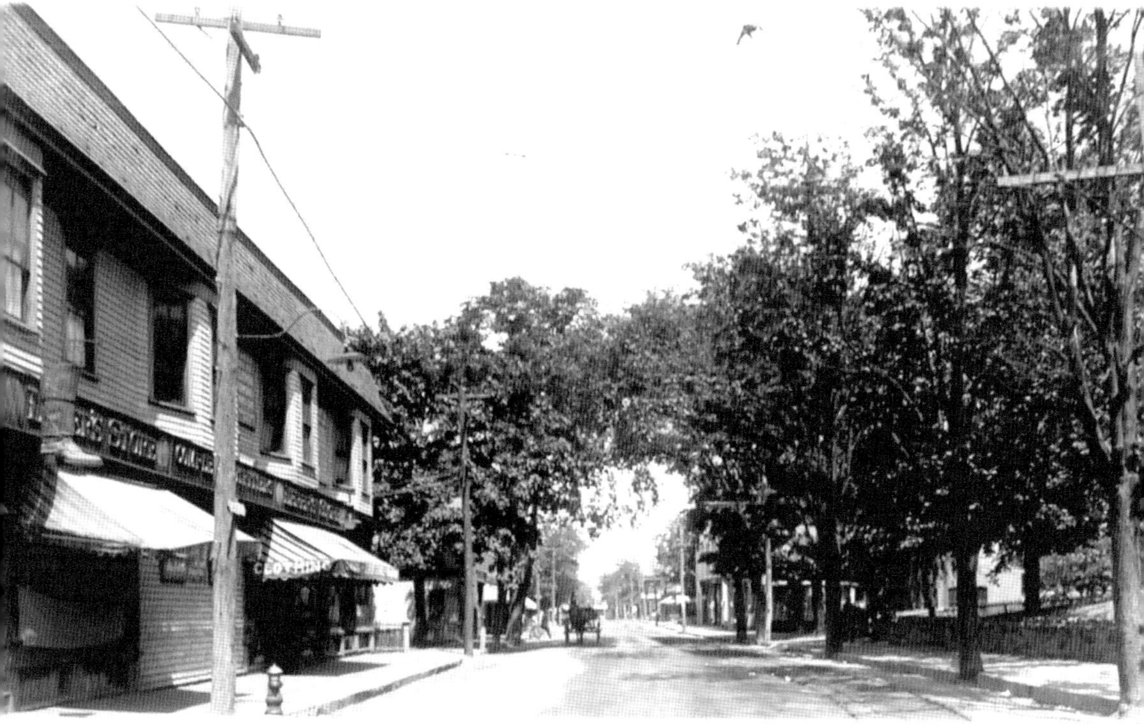


P7325 Main Street from Square, Maynard, Mass.

**MAIN STREET FROM THE SQUARE.** In 1892, the Assabet Manufacturing Company was granted the right to erect poles and run electric wires through certain streets in town. (Courtesy of Paul Polewacyk.)

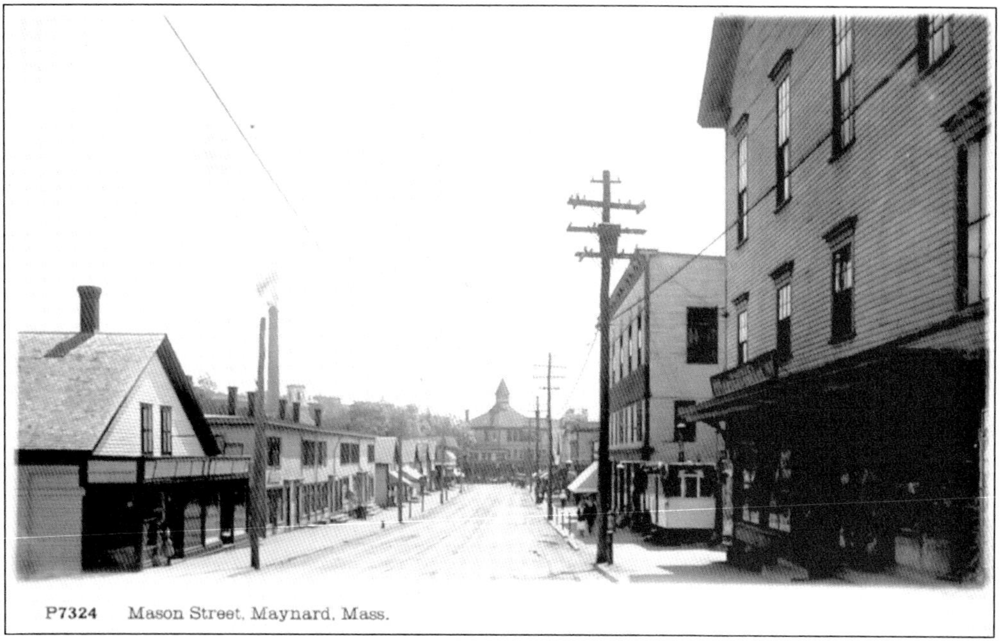


**Nason Street.** The building on the left is the present site of Citizens Bank. The diner and the Knights of Columbus buildings are on the right.

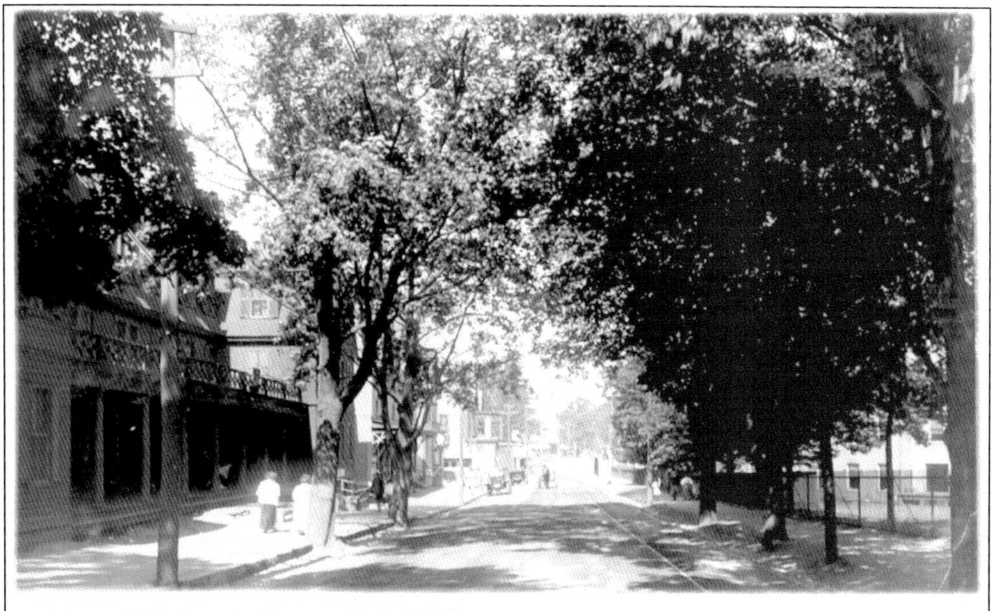


**Main Street.** It may sound strange, but when Amory Maynard came to town, there was no Main Street. But the rapid growth soon made necessary a road through the valley and a bridge across the river. (Courtesy of Paul Polewacyk.)

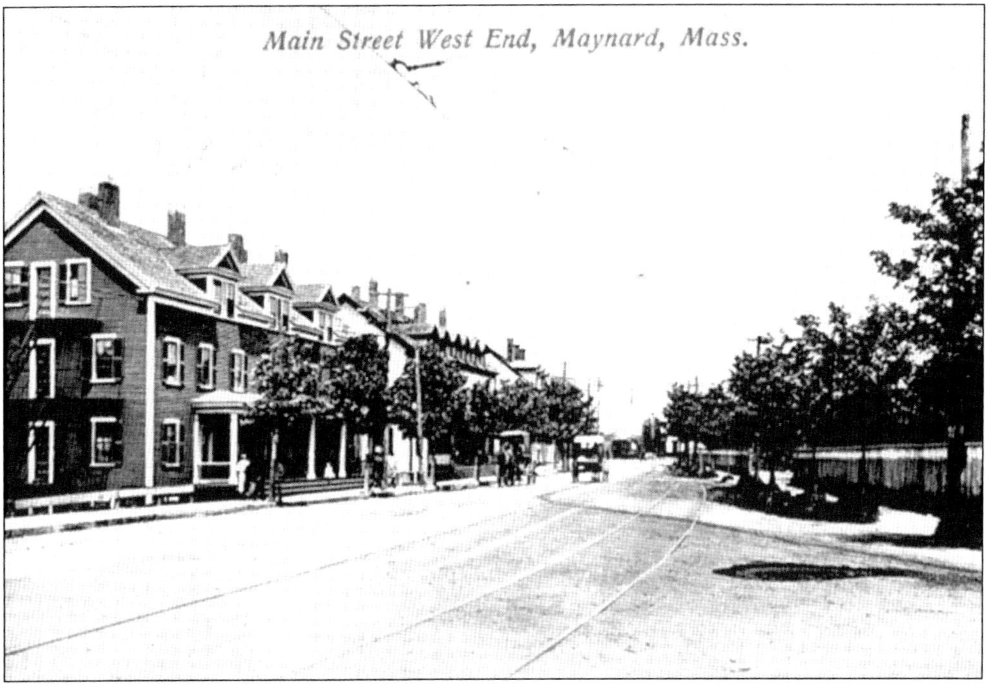


**MAIN STREET, WEST END.** The West End House is on the left. The pond on the right was filled in for parking. The remains of the mill chimney, which was damaged in the hurricane of 1955, was used as fill.

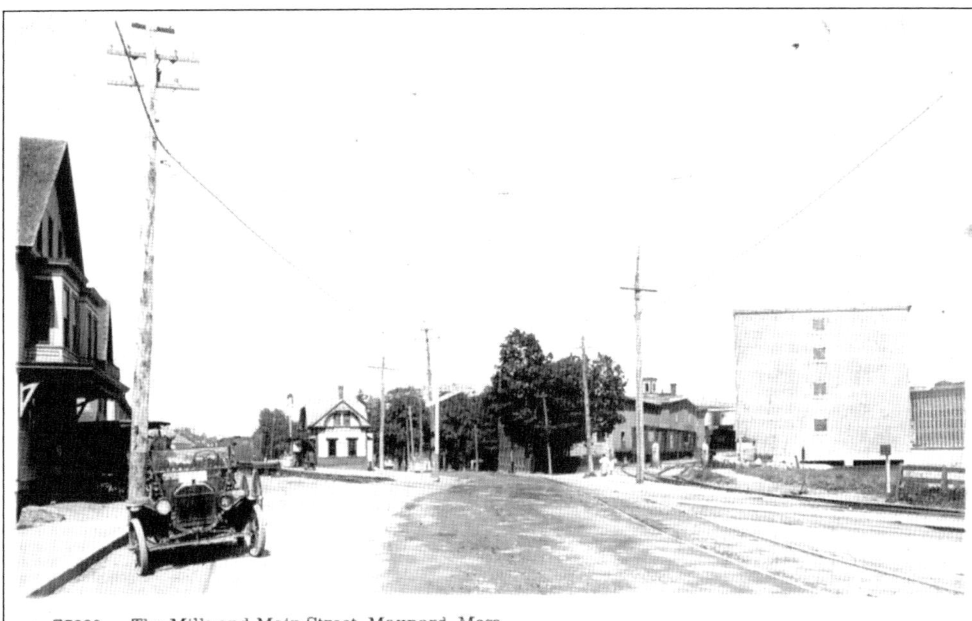


**THE MILL AND MAIN STREET LOOKING EAST.** The railroad station, located near the center of this picture, was eventually torn down by Edward Gately to build a gas station. (Courtesy of Paul Polewacyk.)

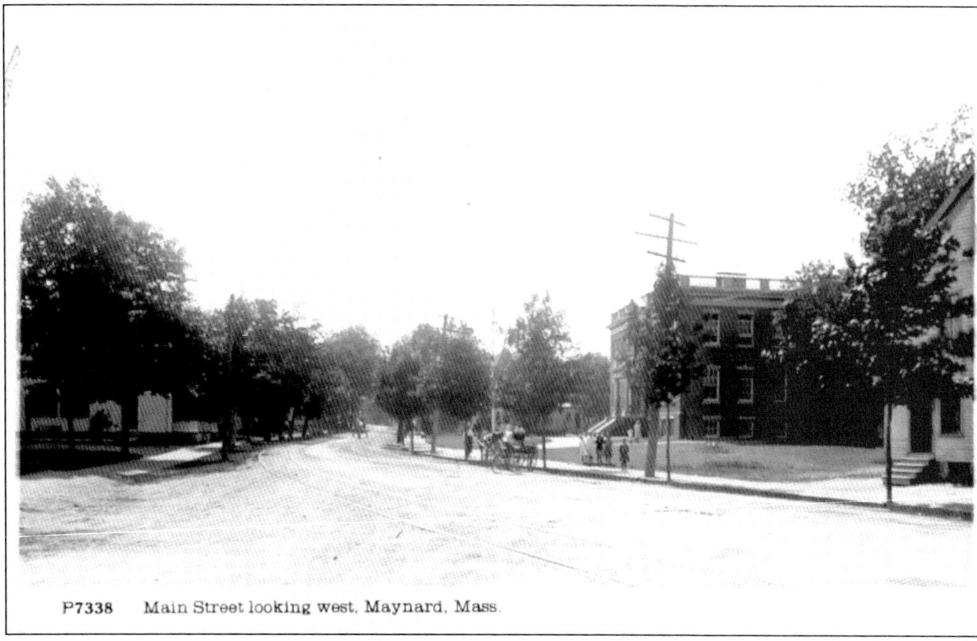


**Main Street Looking West.** On the right is the Main Street School, which later became the site of the Maynard Town Hall. Today the Russell Variety Store is at the right.

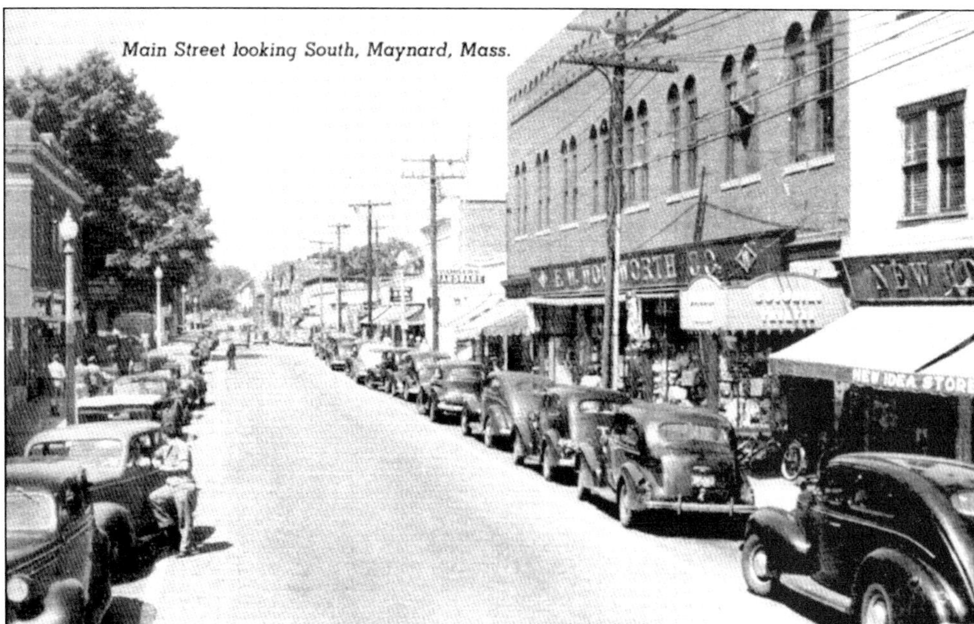


**Colonial Hall.** On the second floor of the F. W. Woolworth building on Main Street, Colonial Hall was built by the Naylor family and opened in February 1914. It was used for many years as a moving picture theater and for all types of functions, such as bazaars, dances, political rallies, graduation exercises, shows, musicals, and so forth.

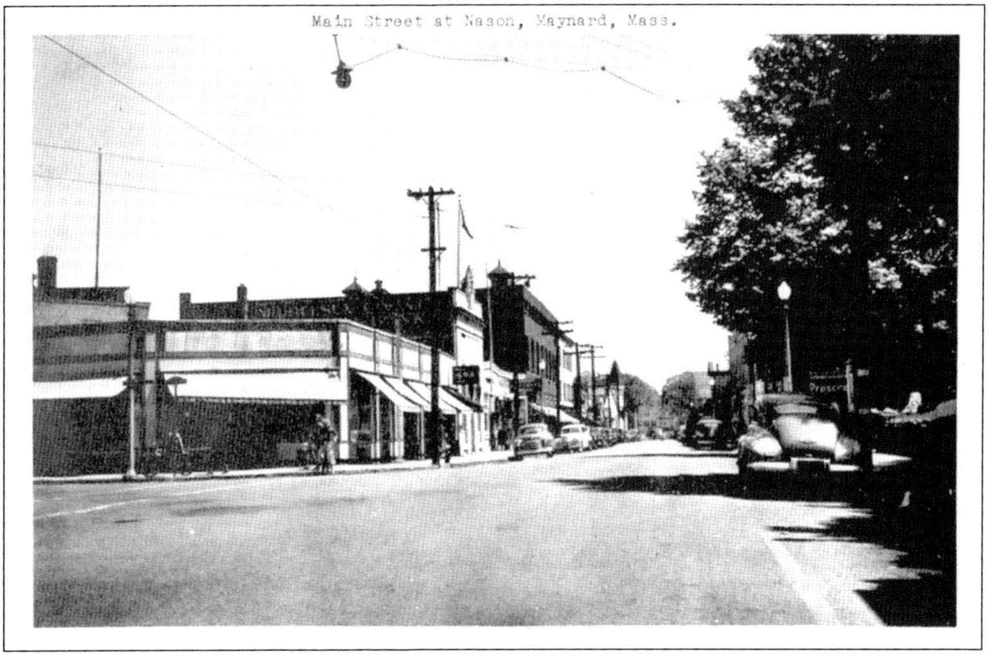


**MAIN AND NASON STREETS.** The electric streetlight showing in the top of this picture and others in the town burned only part of the night at the start and were turned off on nights when the moon was full, but in September 1920, a contract was signed for all-night lighting.

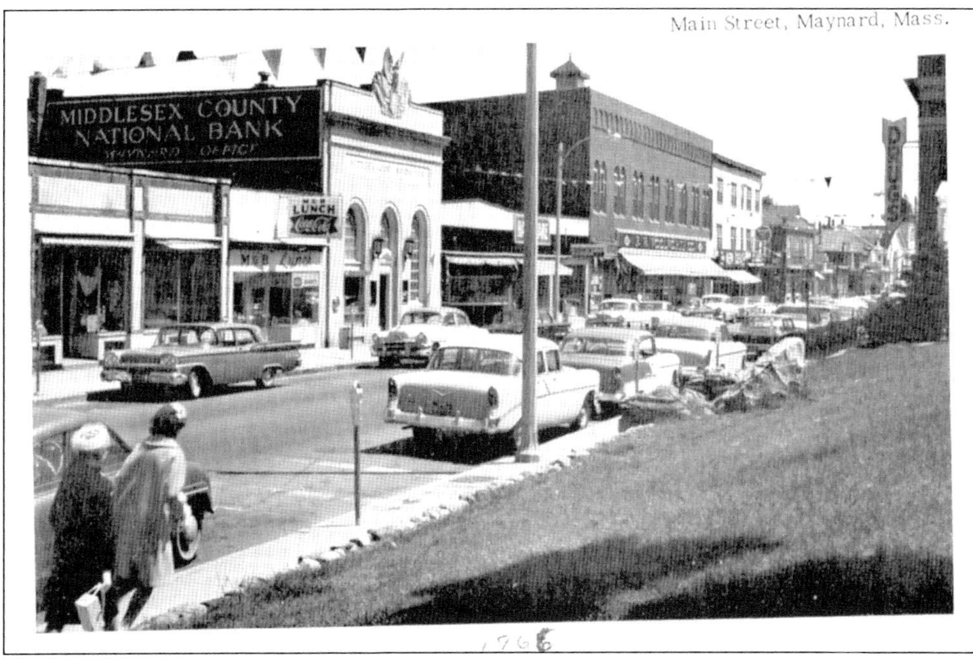


**THE WALL.** The view depicts Main Street from the Congregational church lawn. In the 1950s, teenagers would congregate on what was called "the Wall," located in the front of the church. (Courtesy of MHS.)

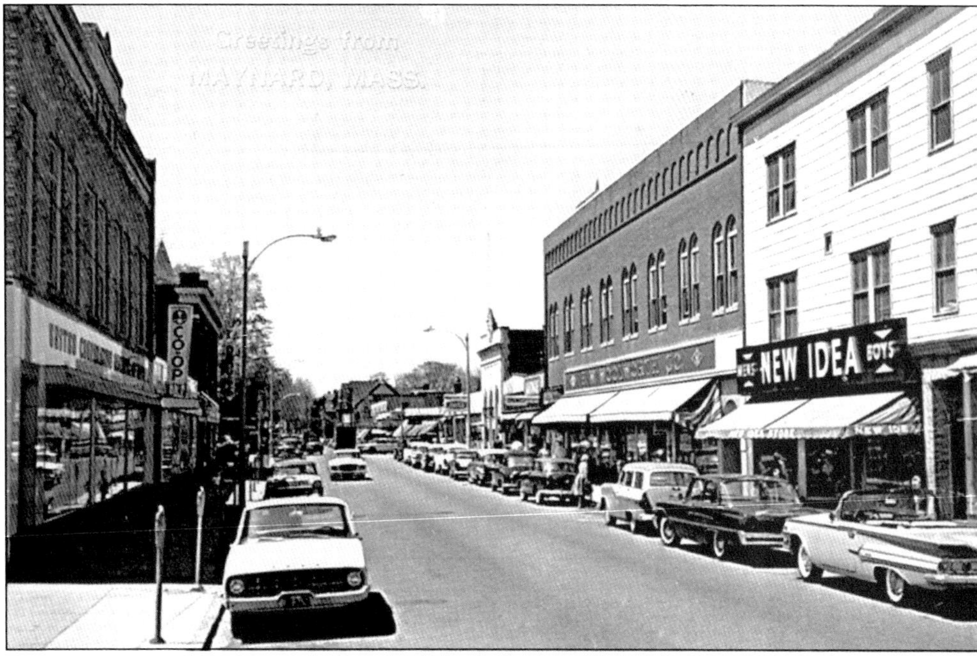


**STUART BUILDING.** In 1891, due to growing needs of the school population, the town found it necessary to lease the Stuart building on Main Street, and the pupils of the third and fourth grades of the abandoned Nason Street School attended school in this building. The Woolworth building (below) housed the Colonial Theatre on its second floor. The Stuart Building ("New idea" in the photograph above) burned in the 1990s.

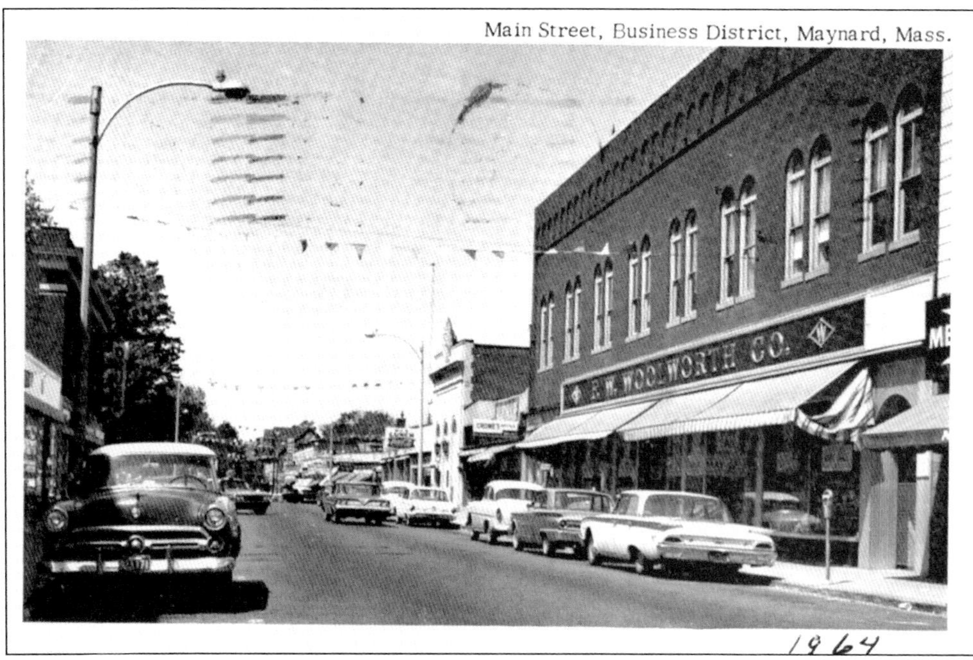

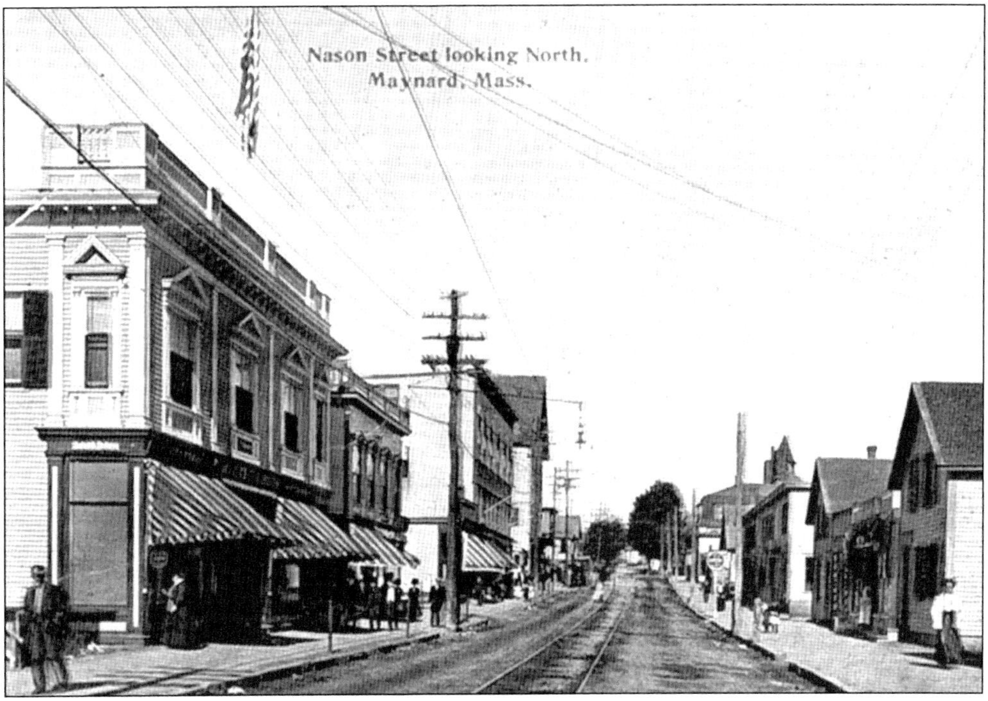


**NASON STREET LOOKING NORTH.** The W. B. Case building is on the left. Case was a longtime businessman in Maynard. Today it is the Maynard Outdoor Store. Homes to the right were moved to make way for the First National Store and a bank.

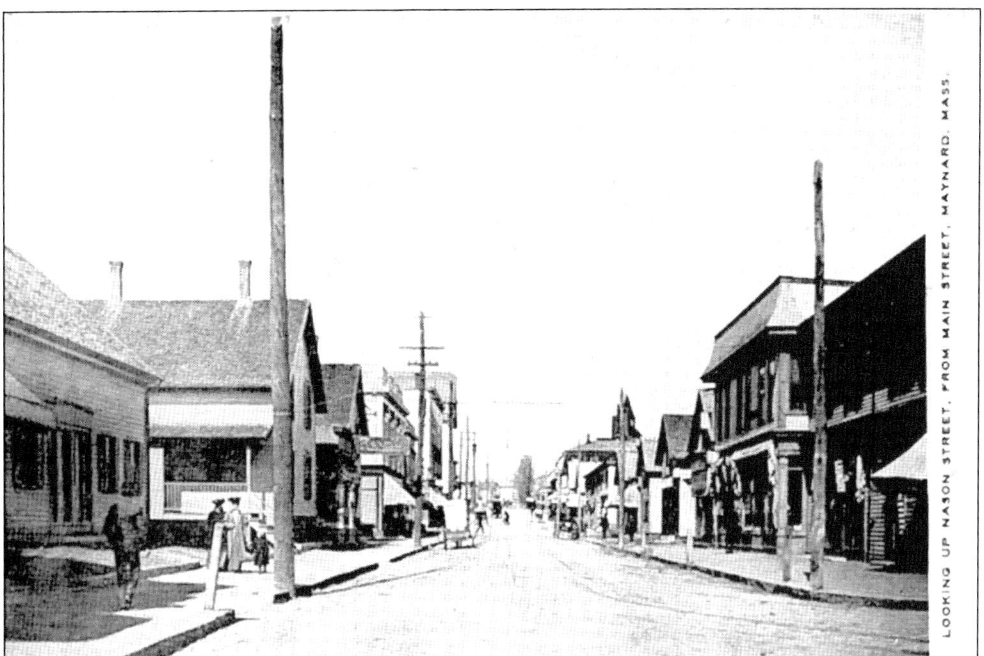


**WE MOVE HOUSES.** This early 1900 scene looks up Nason Street. Notice most buildings on the left have been replaced with commercial buildings. The homes were moved to upper Nason Street.

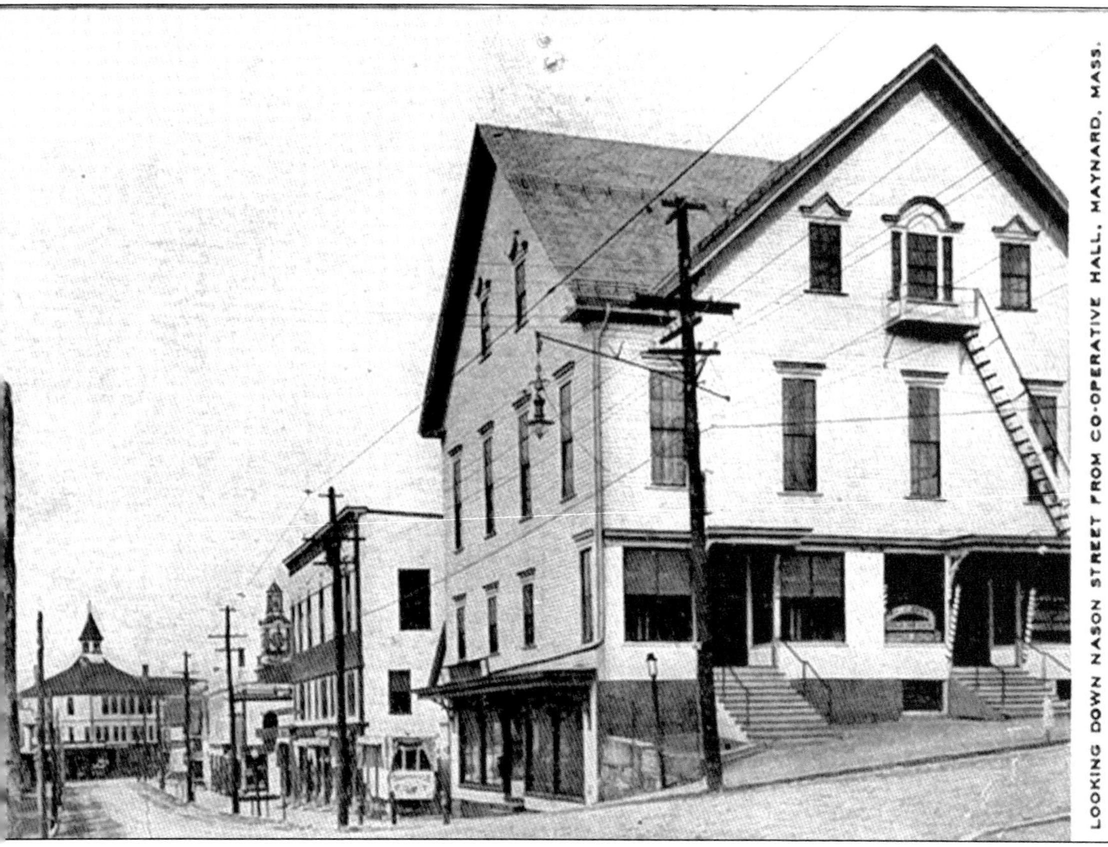


**CO-OPERATIVE HALL.** A cooperative by its very nature is more than a business venture by a large group of people; it is also a cultural, social, and educational institution. The Sovereigns of Industry, or the Riverside Co-operative Association, was organized in Maynard on December 21, 1875, by a small group of English and Scottish textile workers. In 1882, the association bought land on the corner of Nason and Summer Streets, where the Knights of Columbus building is located, and erected a four-story building for $15,000, with the store on the first floor. This became known as Co-Operative Hall. Town meetings, rallies, and athletic and social functions were held there until the two upper floors were destroyed by fire on the evening of January 30, 1936.

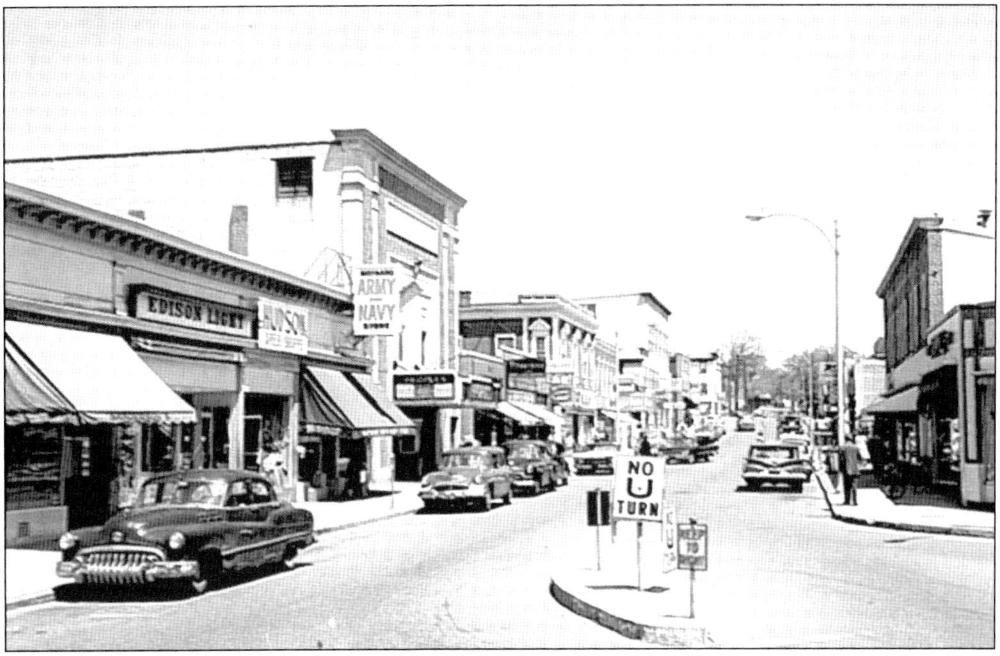


**NASON STREET BUSINESS DISTRICT.** Main and Nason Streets were rebuilt in the 1960s. The Army and Navy Store, now the Maynard Outdoor Store, is located in the Case building. In the 1966 postcard below, banners are flying in honor of Celebration Day.

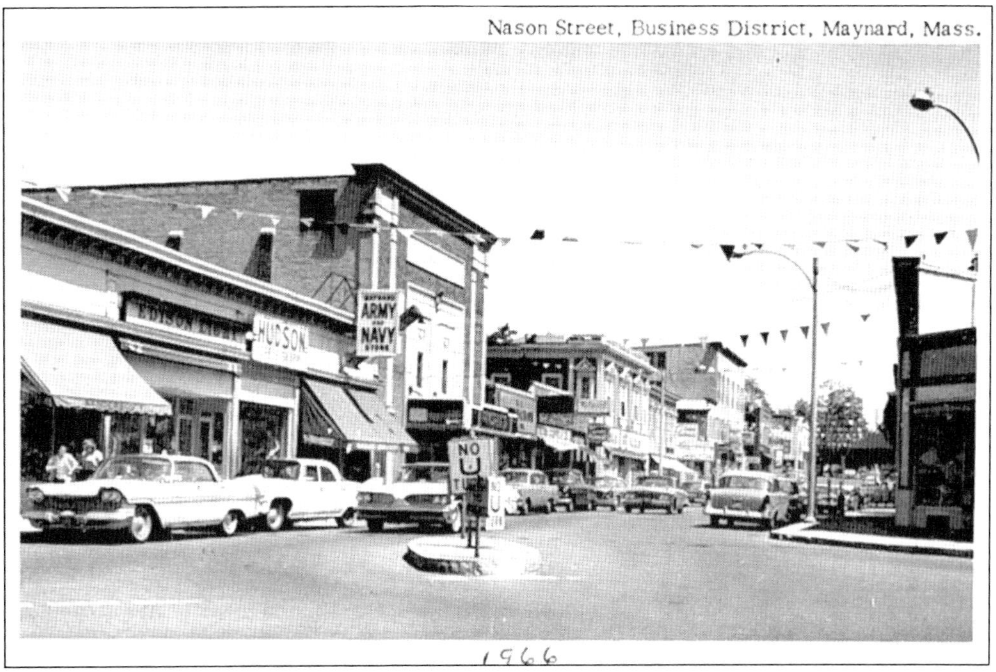

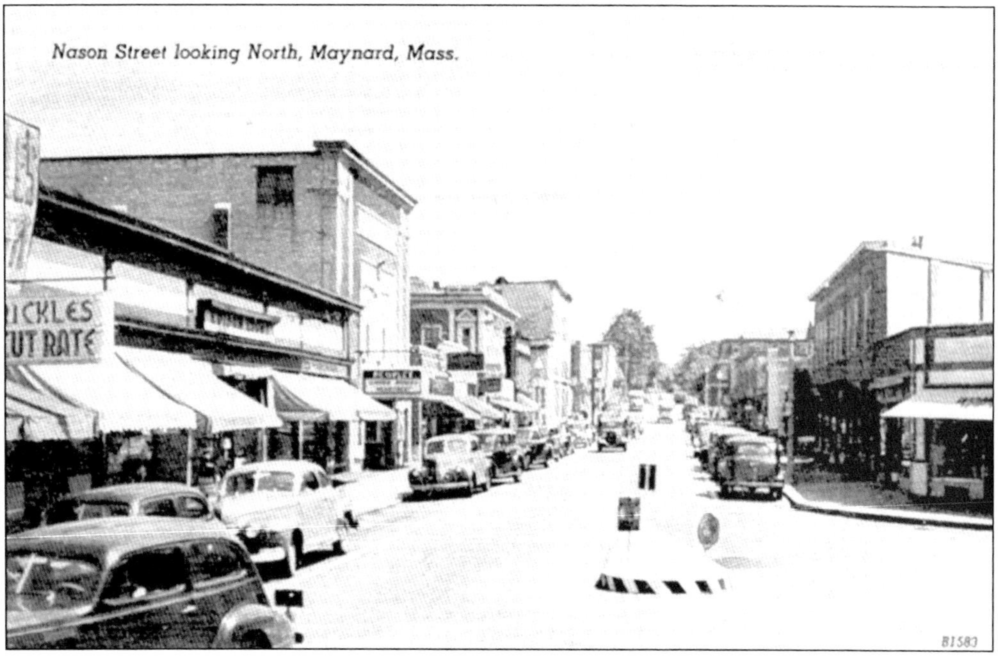


**THE TOWN WELL.** The town had a single well in the center of town. But with an increasing population, a water system became necessary. In 1886, the town began discussion of action to be taken regarding a system of waterworks. On May 25, 1888, a bill was enacted that allowed Maynard to use the water from nearby White Pond for its water system.

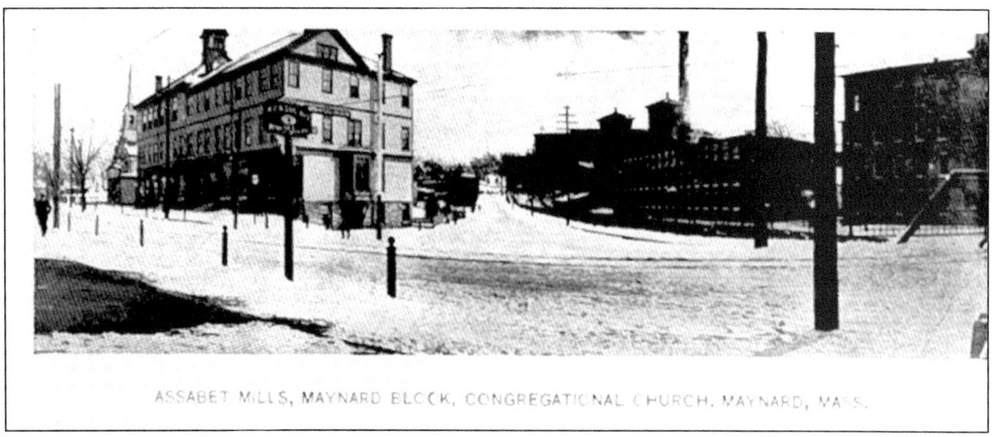


**PANORAMIC VIEW.** The Masonic building is shown on the left, with Walnut Street in the center and the mill on the right. The iron bridge on the right is on Main Street. This intersection is called King Square.

*Four*

# TRANSPORTATION

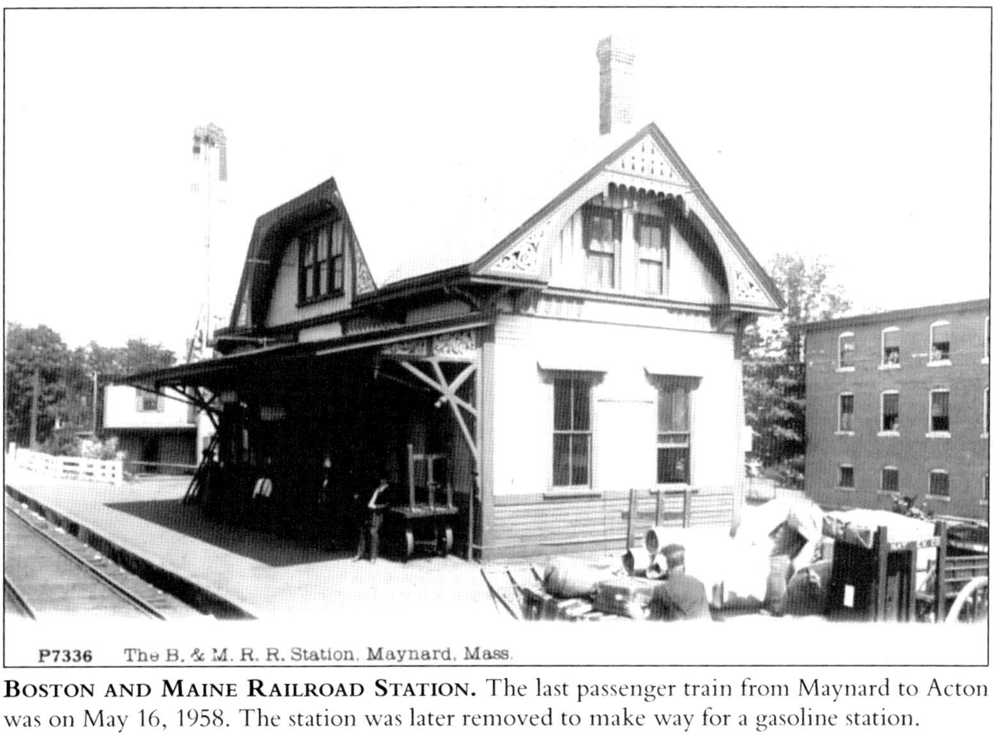


**BOSTON AND MAINE RAILROAD STATION.** The last passenger train from Maynard to Acton was on May 16, 1958. The station was later removed to make way for a gasoline station.

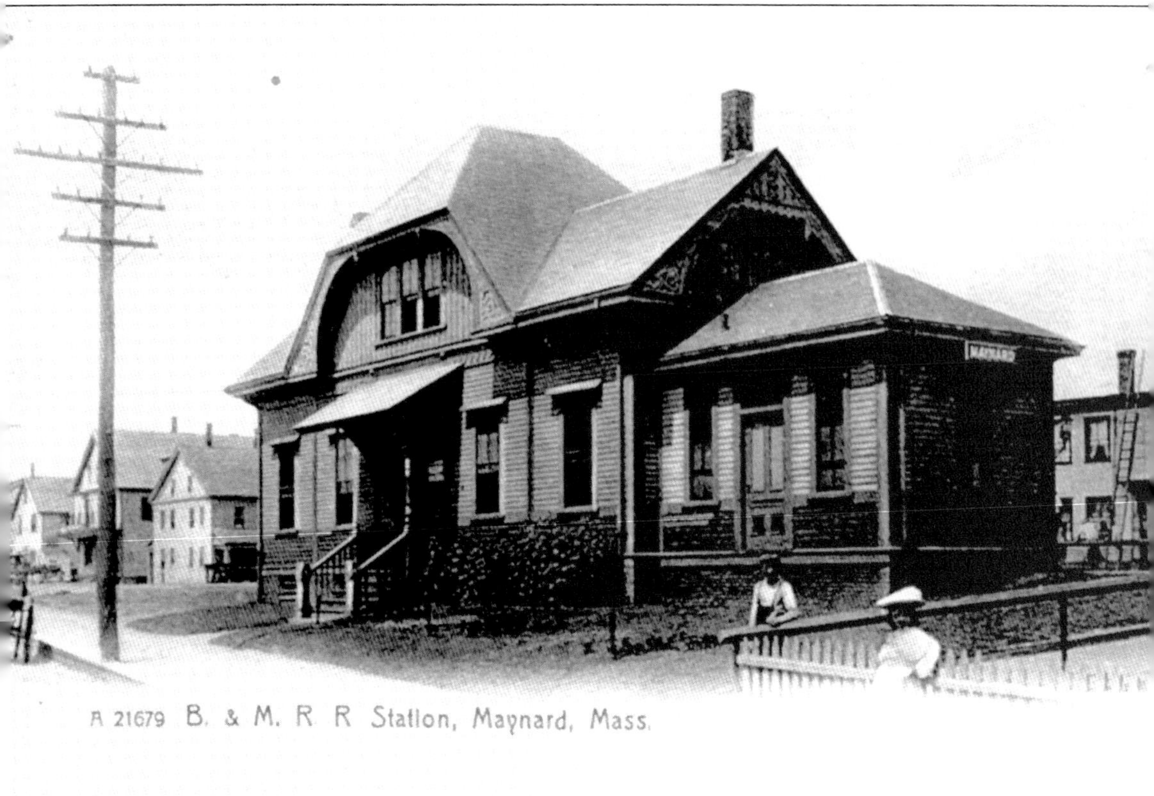

**WAITING ROOM, 1900.** The stationmaster's job at this deceptively small railroad station was enough to wear out the stationmaster within a few months of taking on the job. In addition to serving as ticket master, the stationmaster acted as the freight agent, telegraph operator, and baggage master. The freight business, normally about $3,000 per month, increased to $16,000 because of the extensive building operations under way at the American Woolen Mills. There were 65 cars on the Maynard tracks, 52 at the South Acton station awaiting room in Maynard, and 34 more en route from Fitchburg. Even more traffic came later as work started on the construction of 65 houses the American Woolen Company built in Maynard.

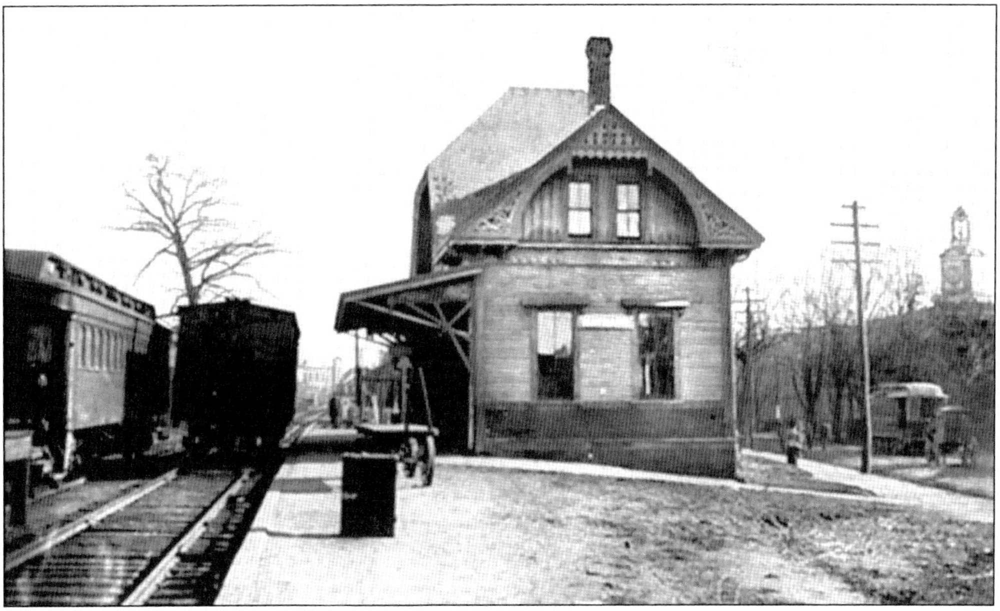

**Maynard Railroad Station.** A freight car waits on the side rail to be picked up. The first passenger train over the line was in July 1850. Rail service from Maynard south to Marlboro was discontinued in 1939, and passenger train service north to Acton was discontinued in 1958. Gasoline was also being sold at the station, as seen in the picture below. Automobiles are already replacing the iron horse as a means to provide Maynard residents local transportation.

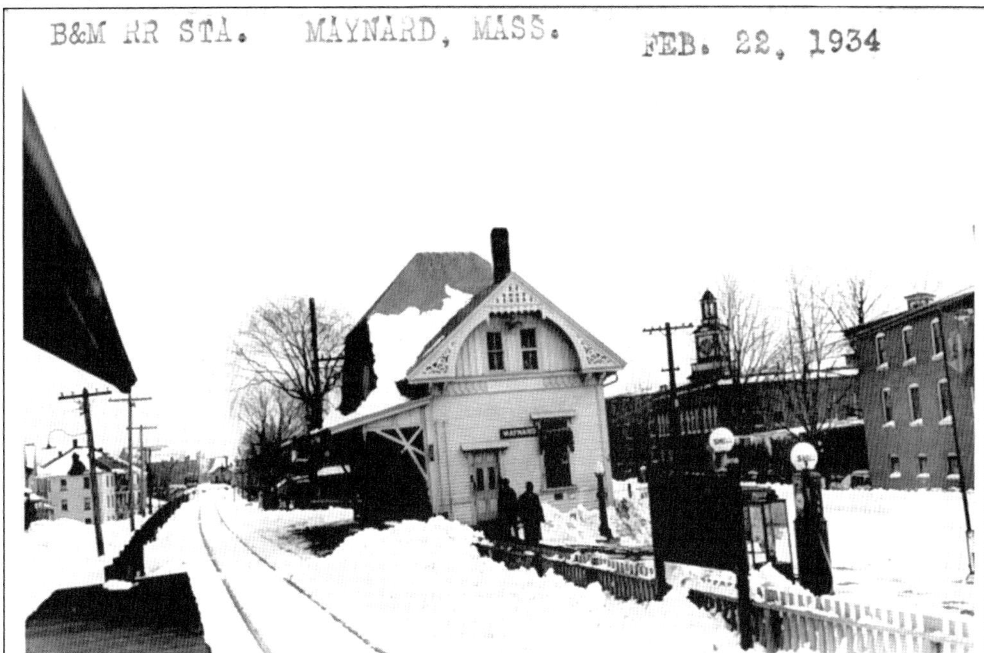

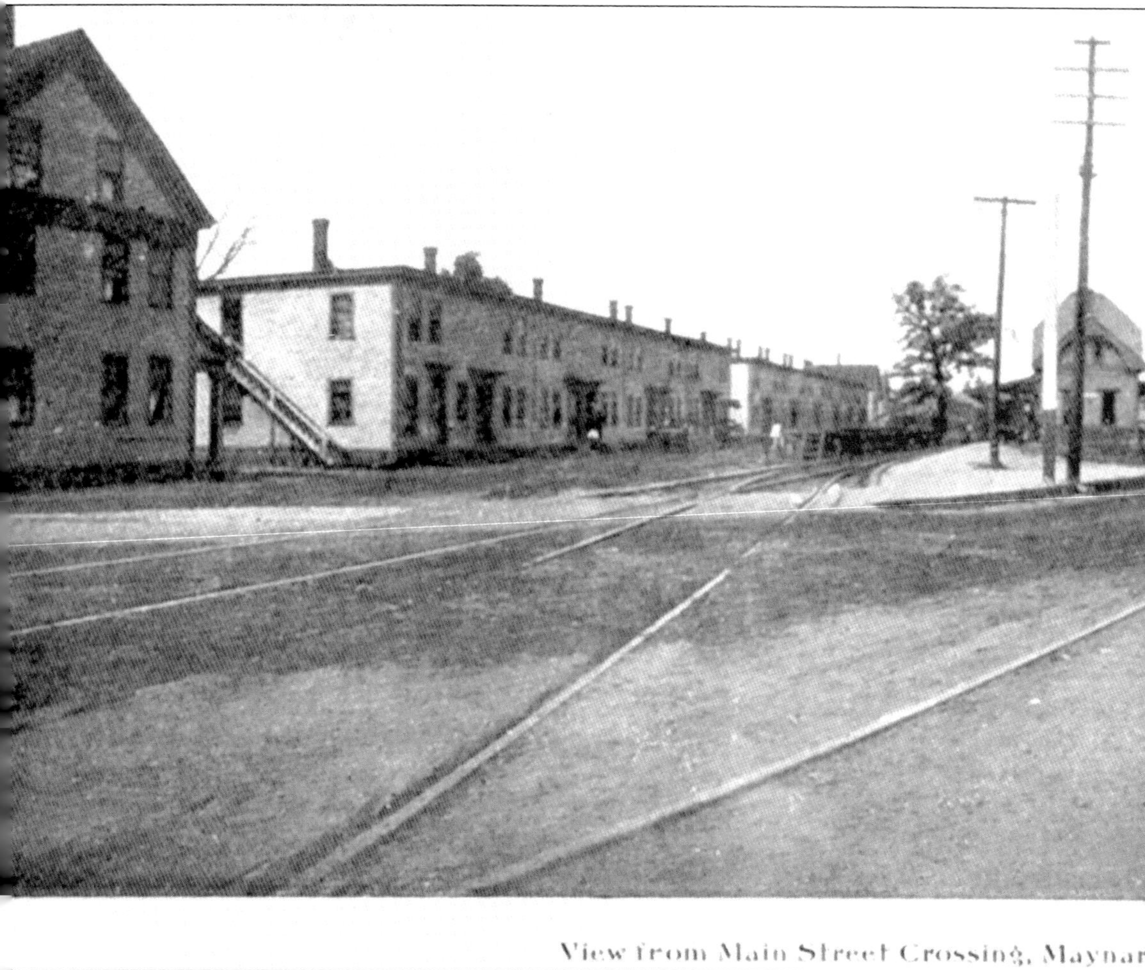


**CROSSING THE RAILROAD TRACK.** This panorama postcard shows a view from the Main Street railway crossing. On the right is a spur rail that enters the woolen mill plant running along the millpond. The tracks near the middle of the panorama postcard are trolley tracks belonging to the Concord, Maynard and Hudson Street Railway Company. On the far left is a row of apartments

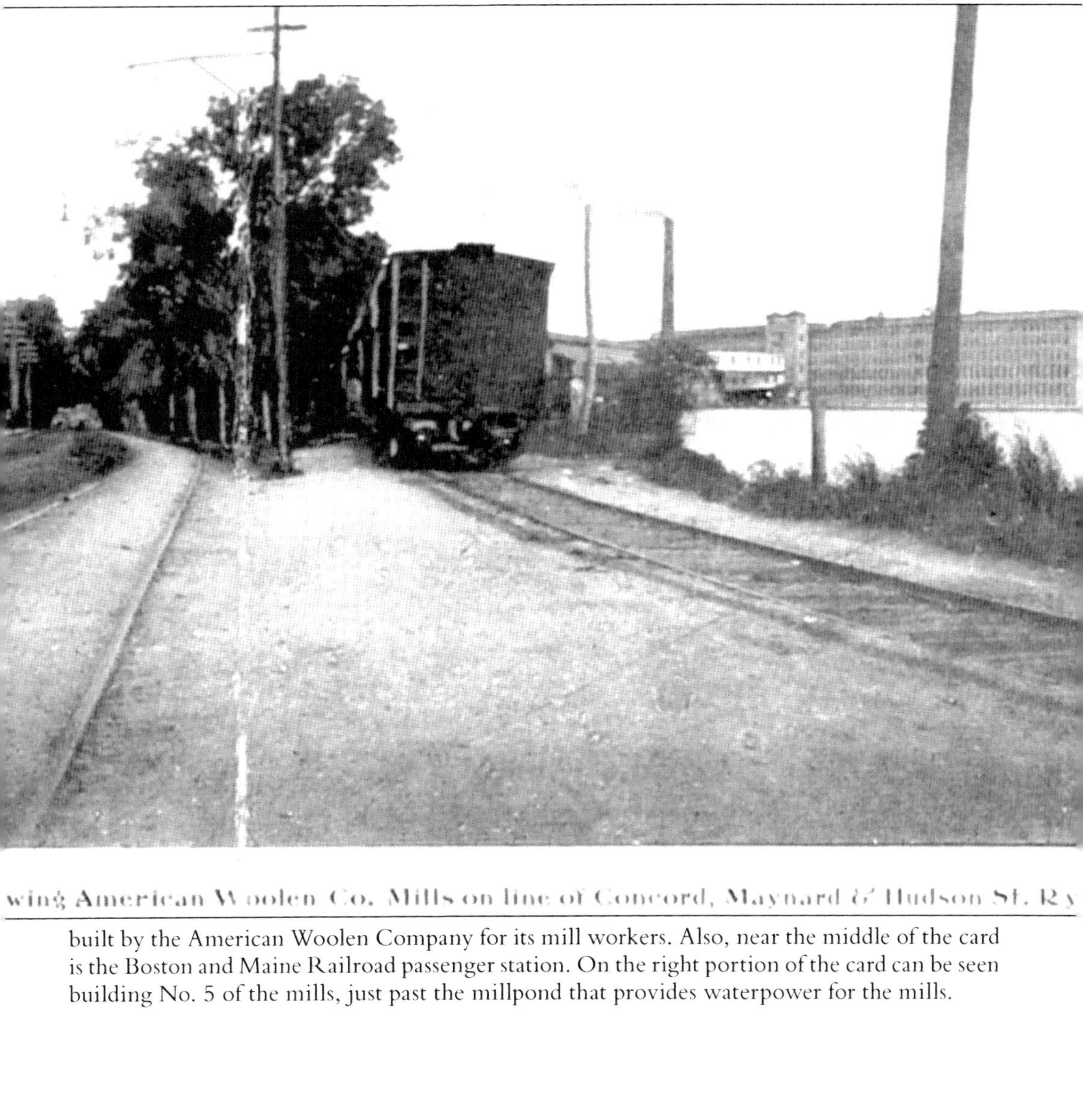


built by the American Woolen Company for its mill workers. Also, near the middle of the card is the Boston and Maine Railroad passenger station. On the right portion of the card can be seen building No. 5 of the mills, just past the millpond that provides waterpower for the mills.

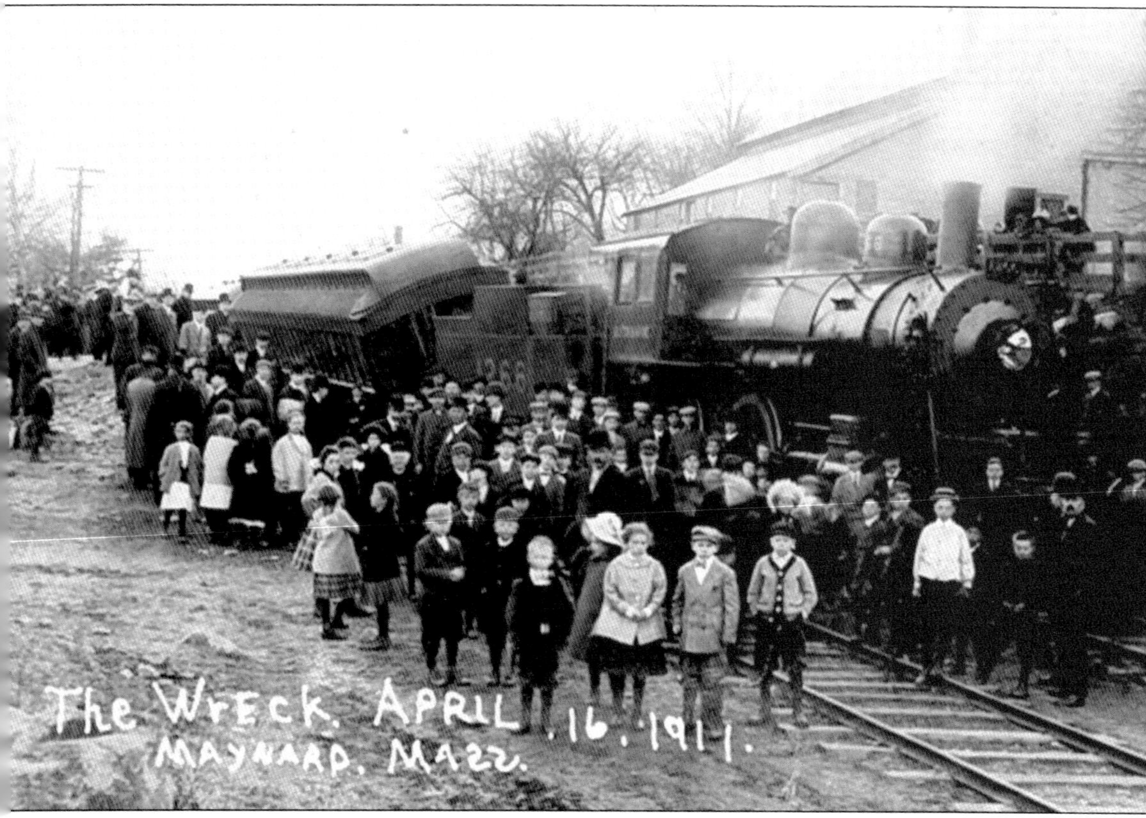


**Train Wreck.** Maynard's only, and therefore greatest, train wreck occurred on Sunday afternoon, April 16, 1911, when the 4:20 Marlboro to Boston local on the Boston and Maine's Marlboro branch rounded the curve from its run along the Assabet River and headed for the Maynard depot just before 5:00. Suddenly, there was a grinding crash of rails, ties, and glass that brought dozing mill workers to their feet, their wives from the kitchens, emptied the many nearby emporiums of refreshment along Main Street, and brought hundreds of others running to the scene.

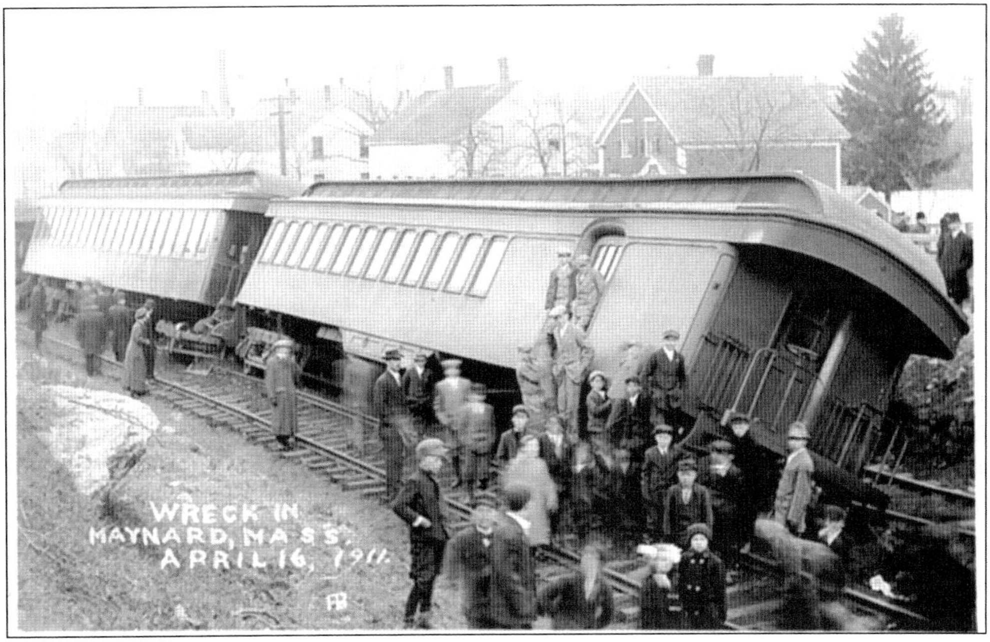


**No Warning.** Nothing but the rarest good fortune prevented a terrible catastrophe at Maynard on Sunday afternoon, April 16, when the tender and two cars of the 4:20 local Marlboro to Boston left the iron about 300 yards west of the Maynard depot, resulting in a most spectacular wreck. There were no fatalities, although a number of injuries were reported.

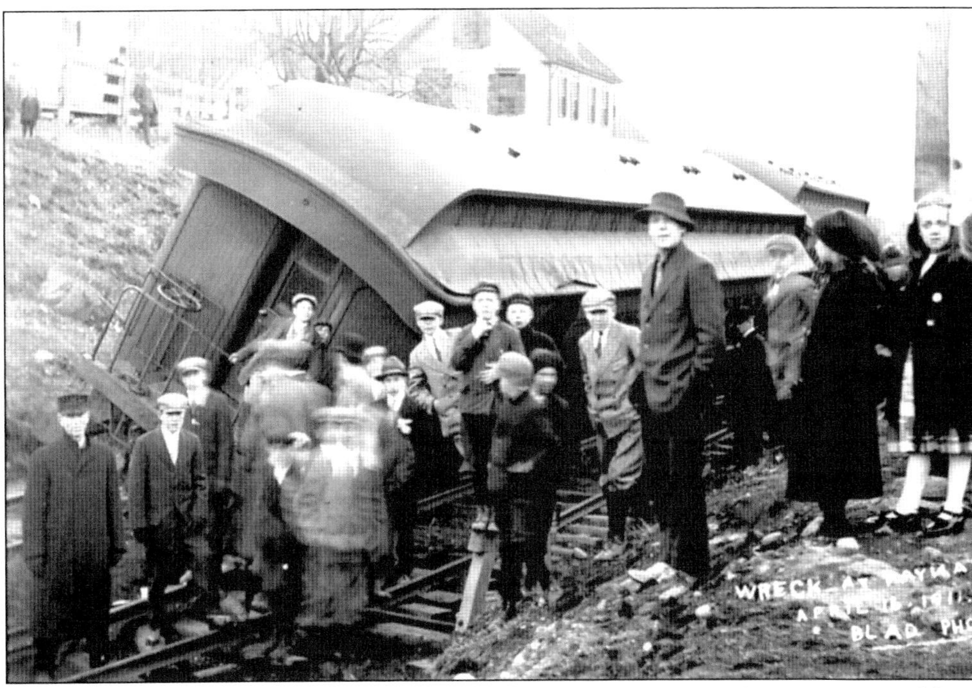

**A Most Unusual Sight.** No cause was given for the accident. A wrecking crew arrived from Boston at 7:15 p.m. and worked until 5:00 a.m. on Monday to clear the wreckage. Trains were run as usual Monday, most of the damage having been done to the side track.

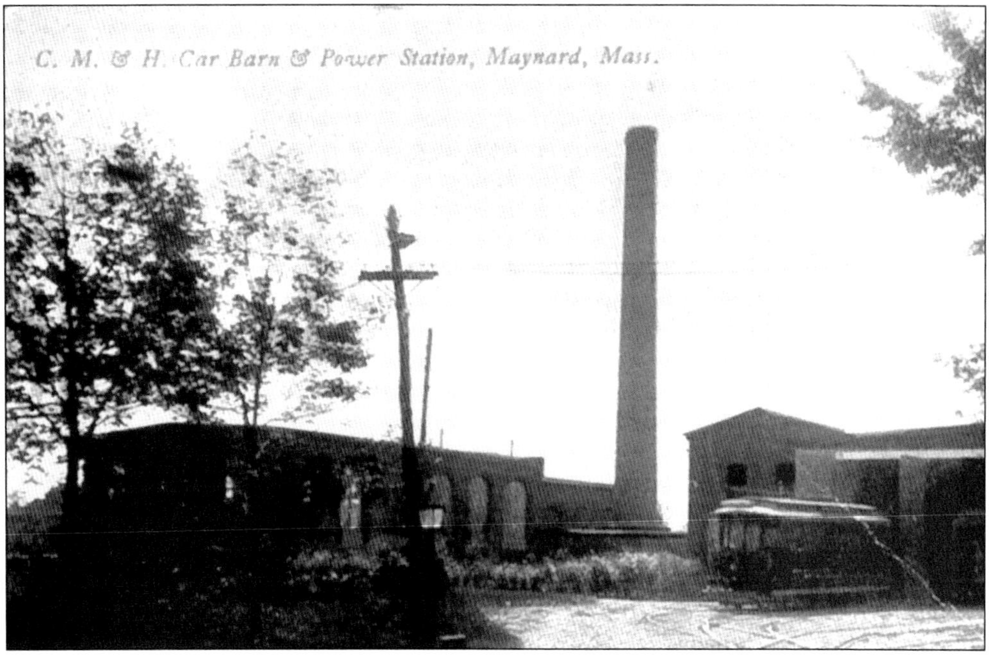


**STREETCAR BARN.** The Concord, Maynard and Hudson Street Railway headquarters on Great Road is shown here, as it existed in 1901. The first car to Concord ran on August 1, 1901, and the first car to Wood Square in Hudson ran on October 1, 1901. In 1903, the line extended from Maynard to South Acton, and in 1909, it extended as far as West Acton. The last car out of Maynard was on January 16, 1923. The power station was sold to the Polish Catholics and became St. Casmir's Church.

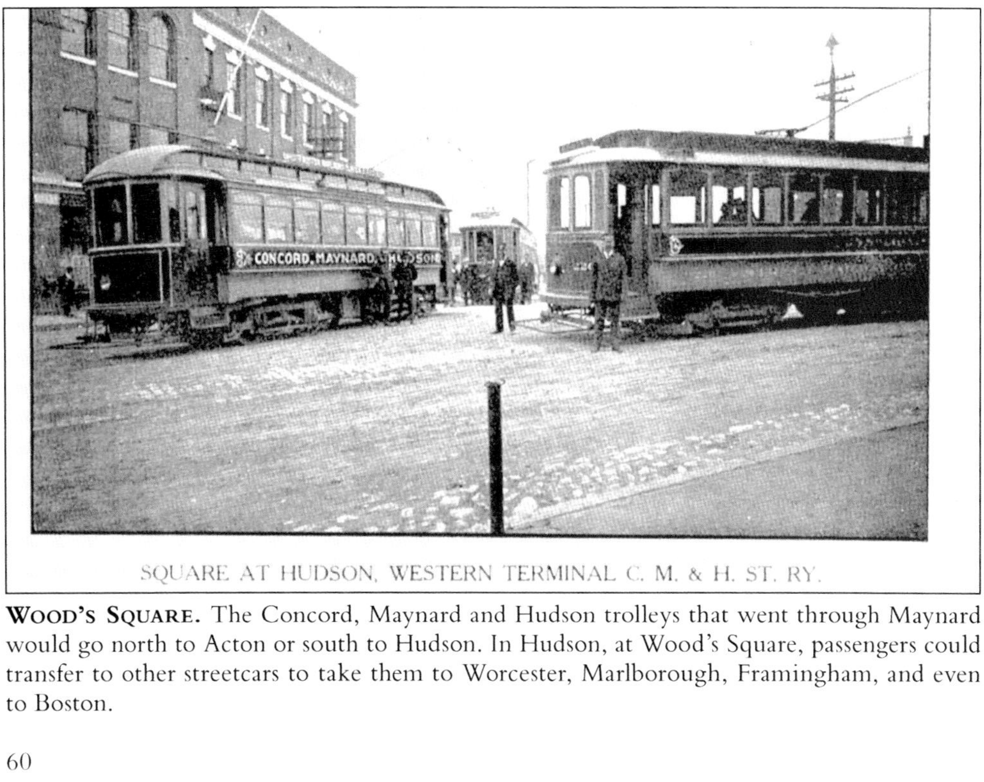


**WOOD'S SQUARE.** The Concord, Maynard and Hudson trolleys that went through Maynard would go north to Acton or south to Hudson. In Hudson, at Wood's Square, passengers could transfer to other streetcars to take them to Worcester, Marlborough, Framingham, and even to Boston.

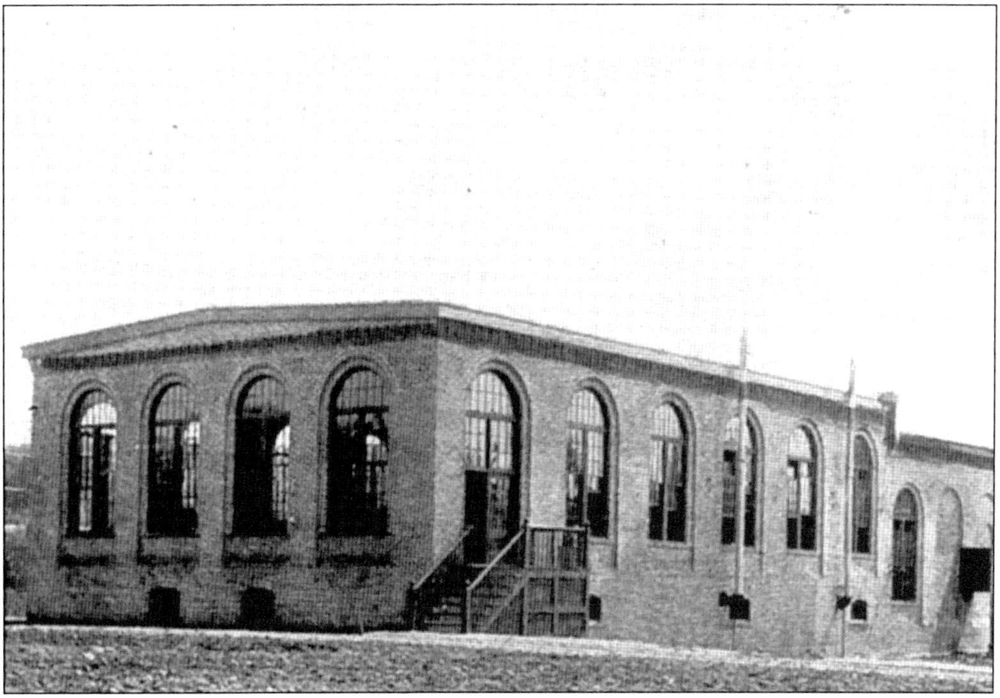

**POWERHOUSE.** The Concord, Maynard and Hudson Street Railway Company built their powerhouse in the center of their line in this building on Great Road. In 1923, the streetcar line closed, and the powerhouse was converted to the St. Casmir's Church.

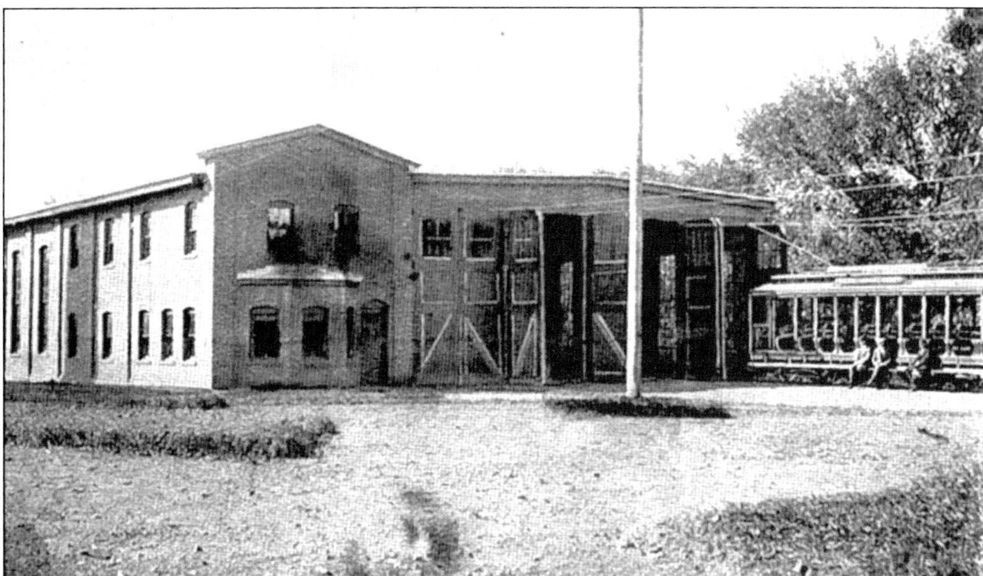

CAR BARN, CONCORD, MAYNARD & HUDSON ST. RY. CO., MAYNARD.

**CONCORD, MAYNARD AND HUDSON CARBARN.** Streetcars were stored, cleaned, and repaired in this large barn next to the power plant on Great Road in Maynard. It was built in 1901 and also housed facilities for the company's business offices and employee recreation rooms.

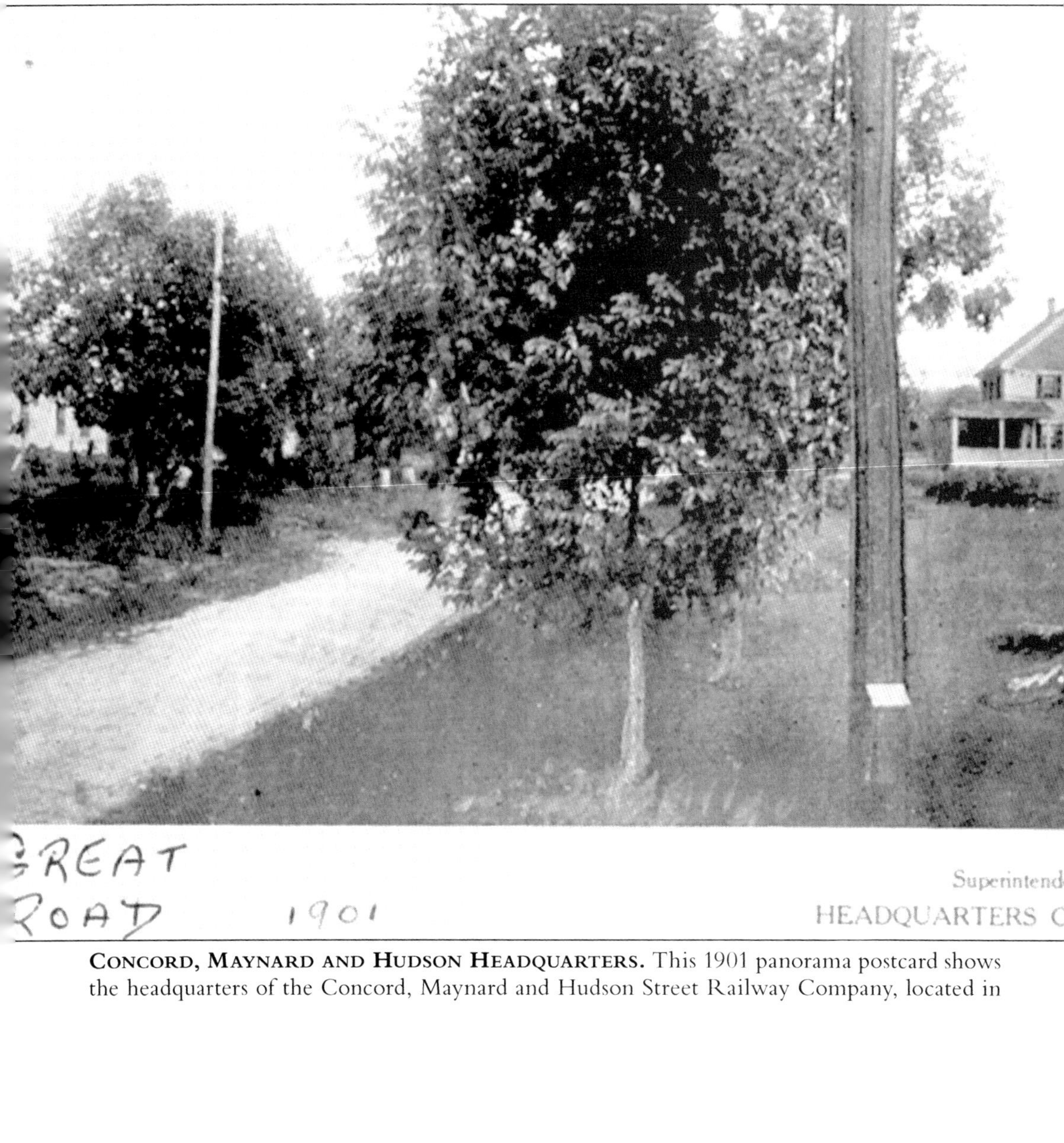


**CONCORD, MAYNARD AND HUDSON HEADQUARTERS.** This 1901 panorama postcard shows the headquarters of the Concord, Maynard and Hudson Street Railway Company, located in

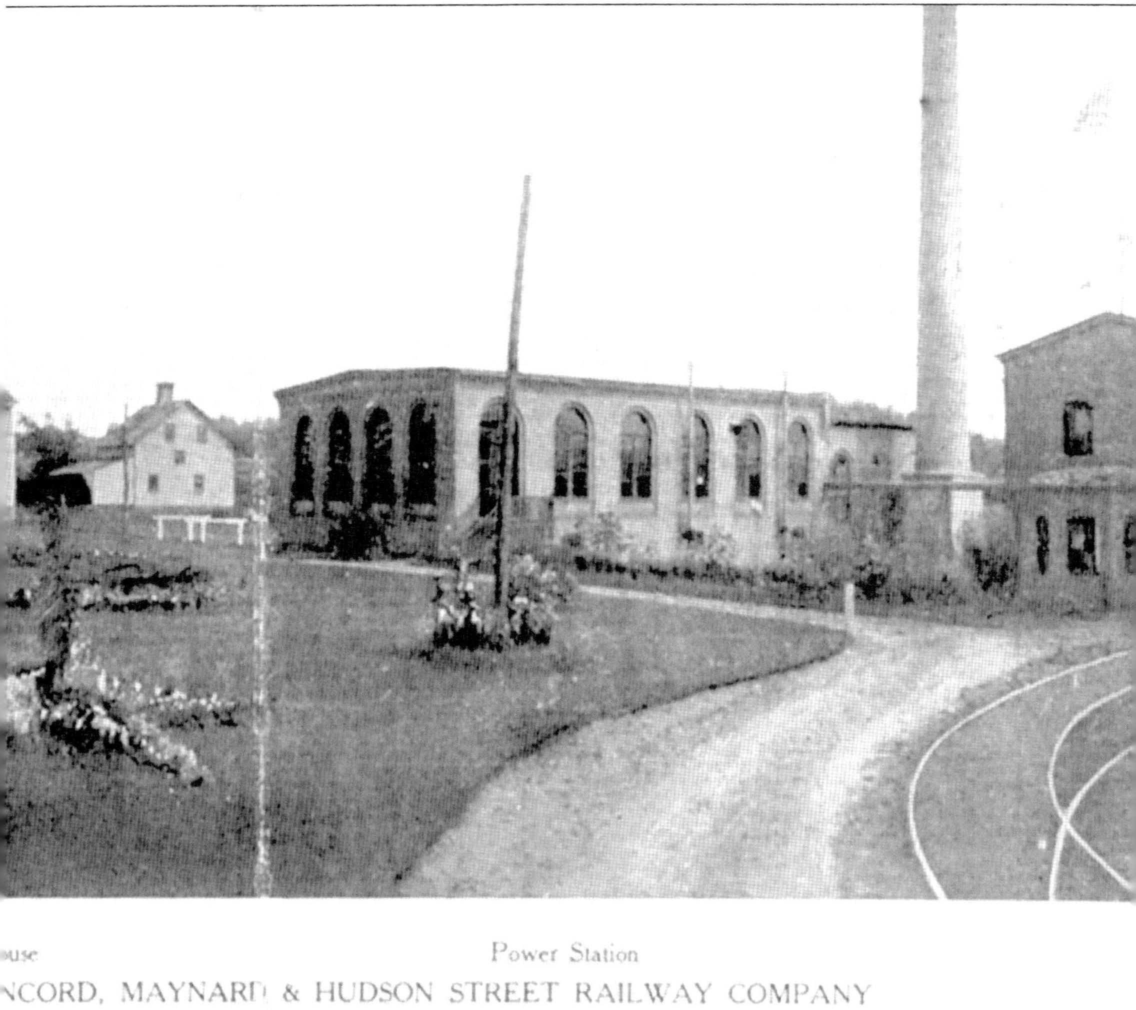


this quiet little house on Great Road next to the power station that is used to generate electricity for the streetcars, which is next to the carbarn that was used to store the streetcars.

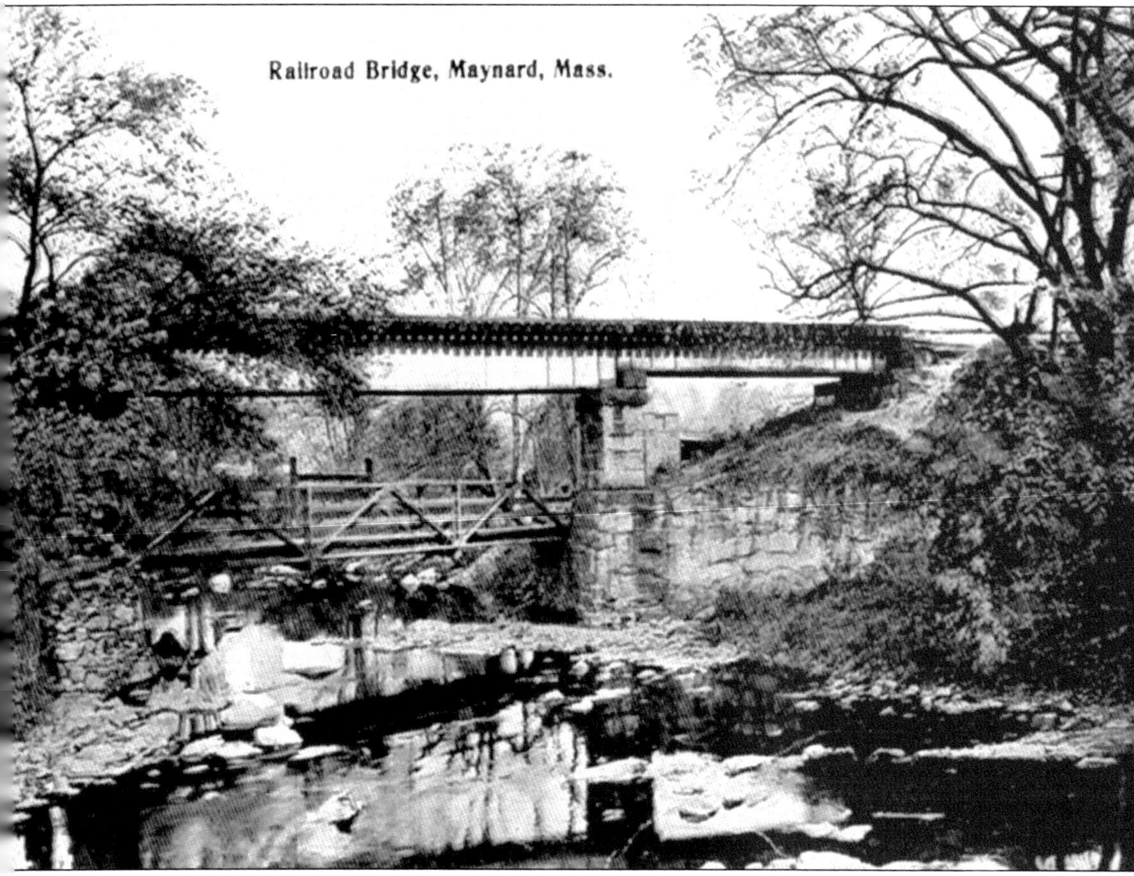


**Boston and Maine Railroad Bridge.** This bridge was built to carry trains of the Boston and Maine Railroad over the Assabet River. It was built in 1848 and dismantled in 1980. The lower bridge was for coal yard use.

# *Five*

# Maynard People

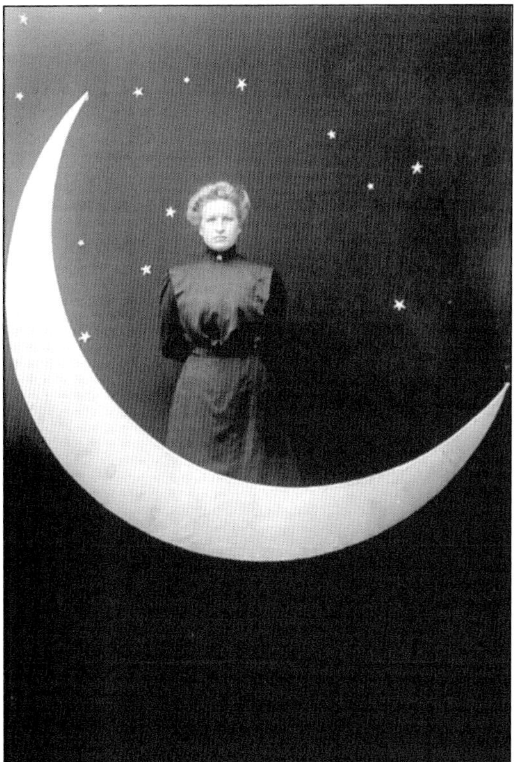

**Pretty Lady.** Arvid Blad, a local photographer, took pictures of local people for family use or distribution. The crescent moon was part of the background.

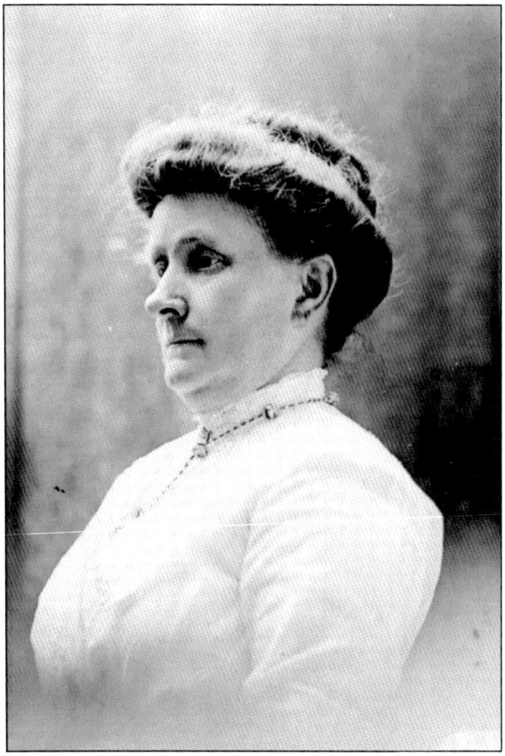

**Prim and Proper.** A Maynard local native in the Taylor family poses for a local photographer. Most pictures of this type are personal.

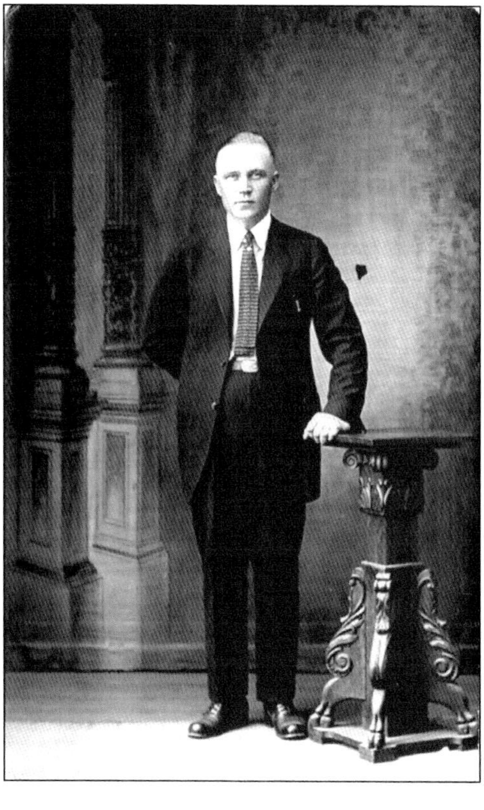

**A Gentleman.** This person was dressed to the hilt, probably for the purpose of a family personal photograph. The Finnish population has given a feel of the style and character of the average person.

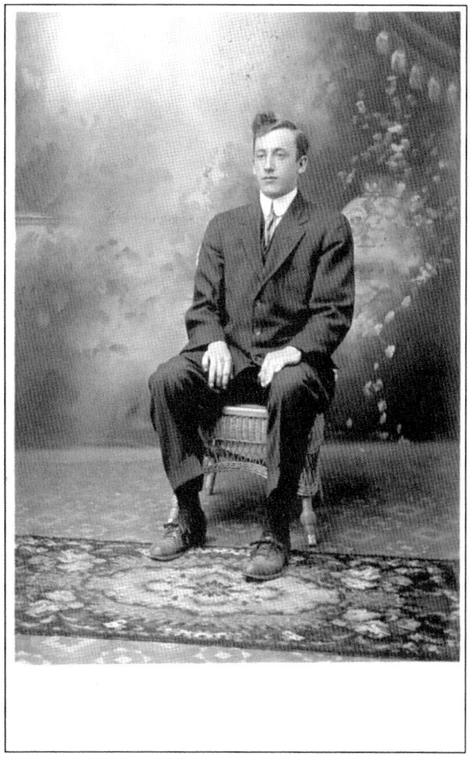

**UNCLE HARRY.** Harry Boothroyd, age 18, was born in England on June 20, 1891, and moved to the United States in 1893 with his parents. He married Mary Dooley on September 11, 1911, worked in the mill as a weaver his whole life, and died in 1979. (Courtesy of Brenda LeSage.)

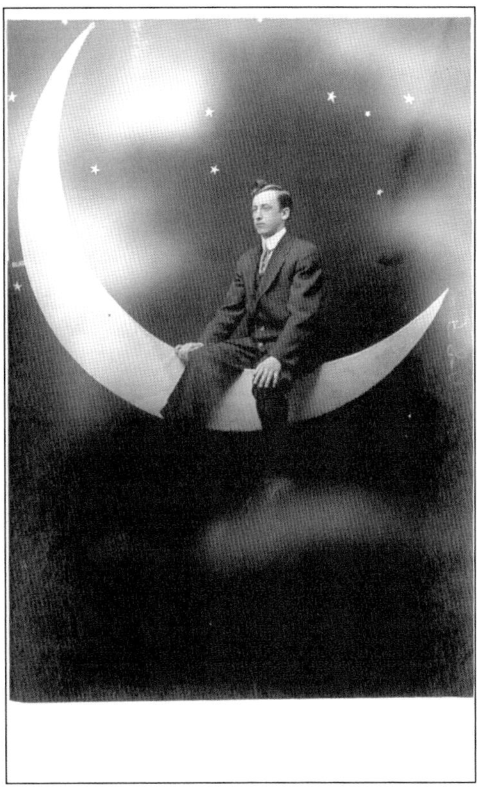

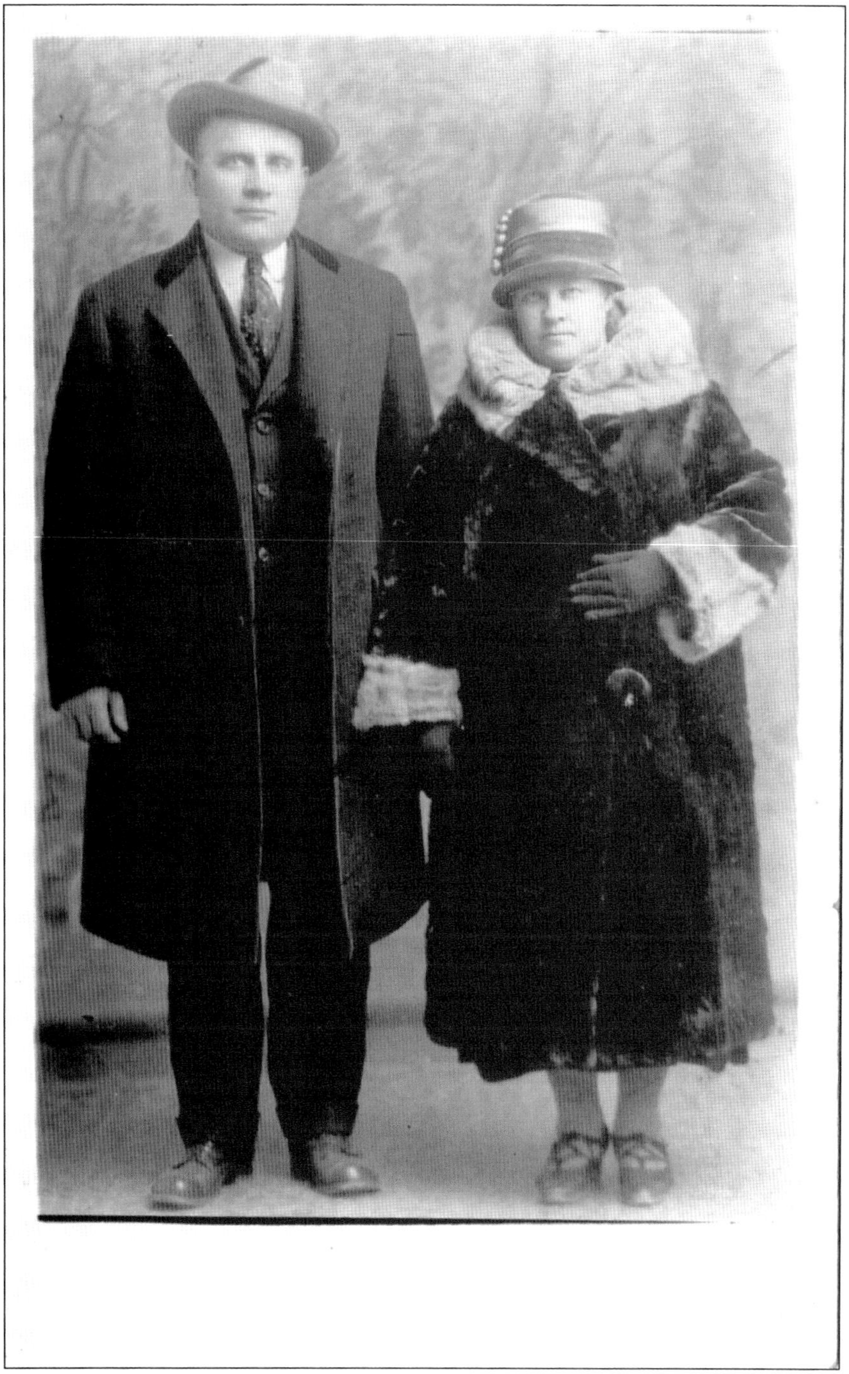

**DRESSED FOR A MAYNARD WINTER.** Because many people in Maynard had European origins, Maynard photographer Arvid Blad was often requested to take family pictures and print them on postcard stock so the pictures could easily be sent to those in their family that were still in the old country. This couple, probably of Finnish origin, put on their best winter clothing to take this formal photograph to let their European family know that all is okay with them here in America. Such postcards were never for public sale and rarely in color.

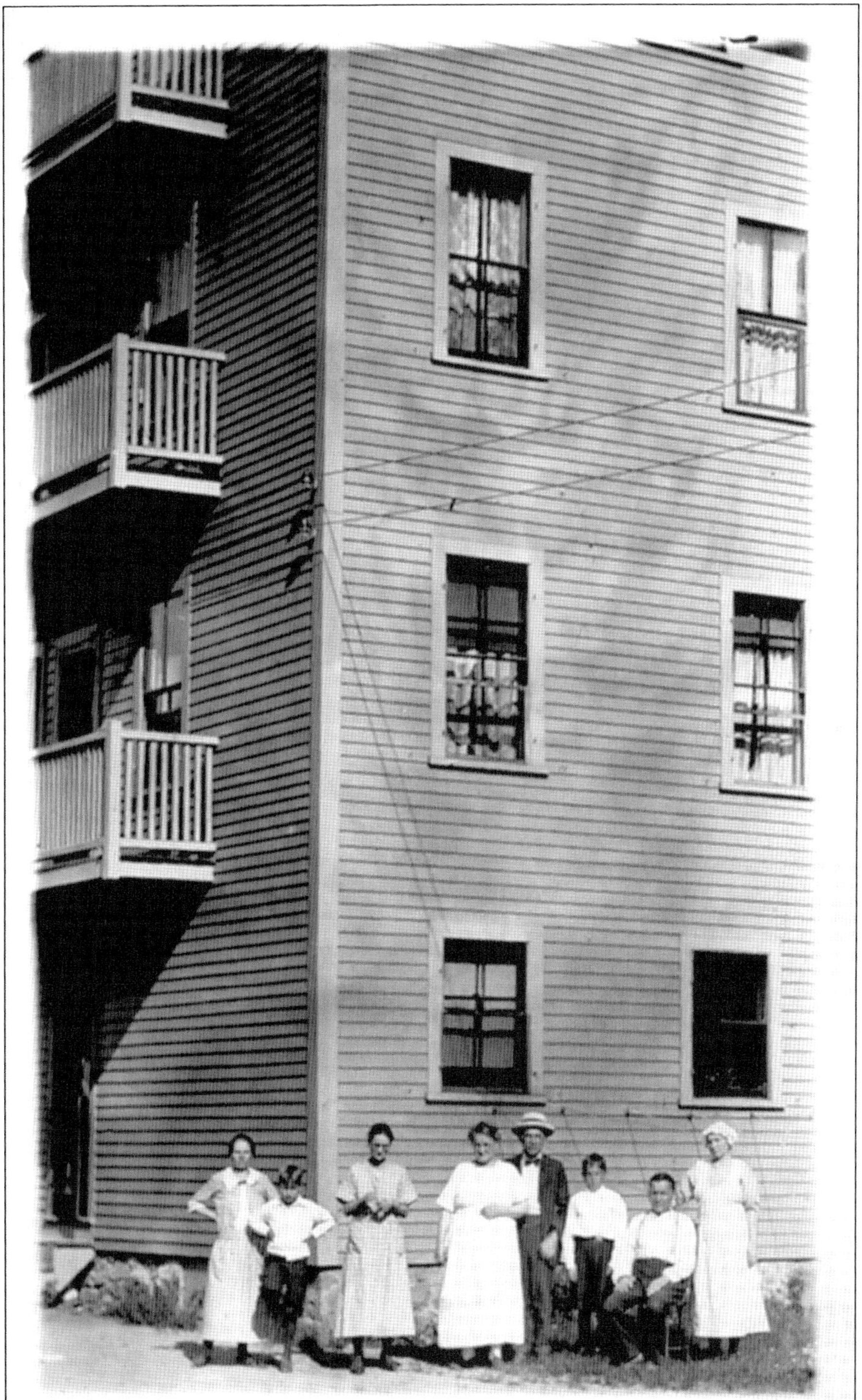

**BOARDINGHOUSE.** The West End Boarding House on Main Street in Maynard has many of its borders posing outside of the rear of the house.

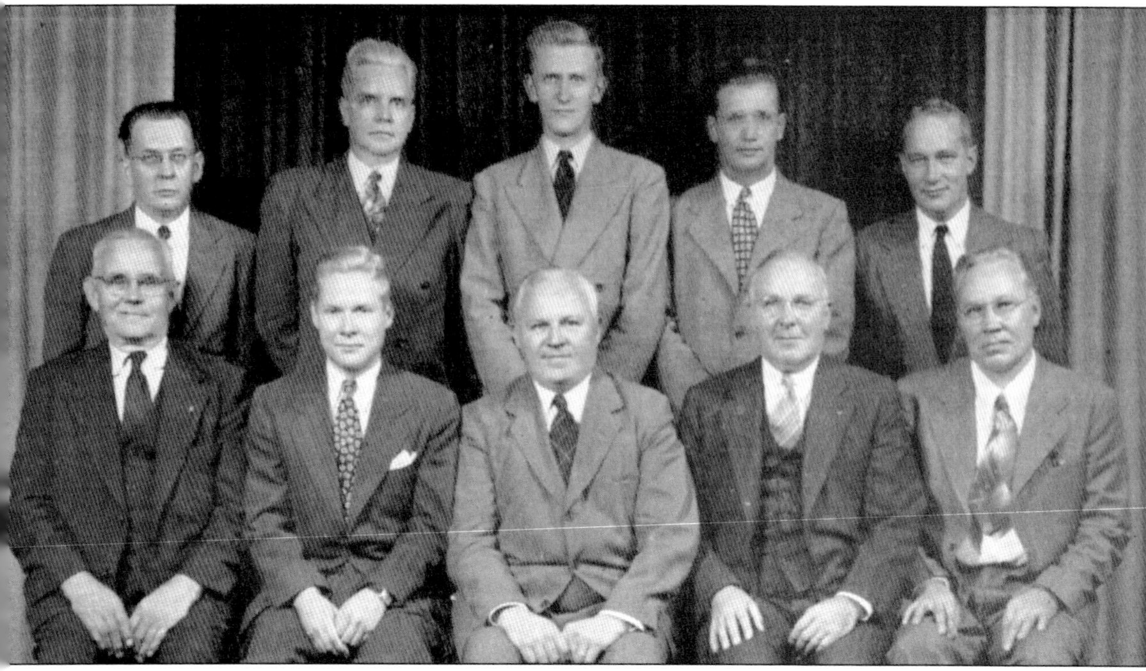

**Board of Directors of the Cooperative.** The board of directors in 1948 are, from left to right, the following: (first row) Anton Anderson (vice president), Elmer Salenlus (secretary), Charles Manty (president), Arvo Rivers (general manager) and ? Palmer; (second row) Waino Parker, ? Kuivila, Rubin Aromaa, Jorma Osmo, and ? Sulkala. Mr. Helander was absent.

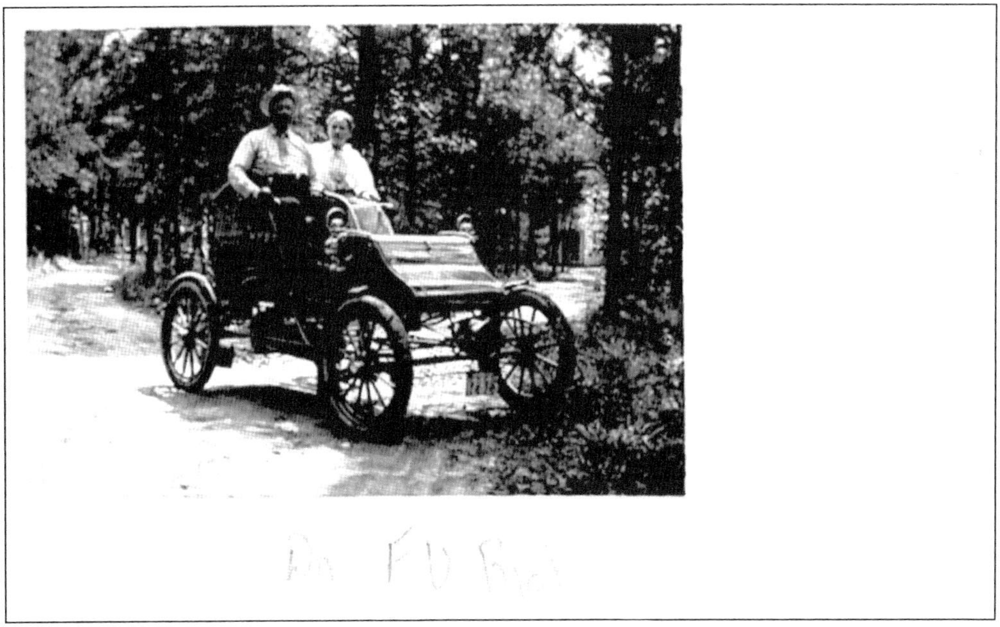

**"First Automobile in Maynard."** This headline is from the *Maynard News*, June 23, 1899. "The horseless carriage is expected to arrive in town soon. It has been ascertained that Dr. Frank Rich was the owner and the first to have an automobile in Maynard." (Courtesy of MHS.)

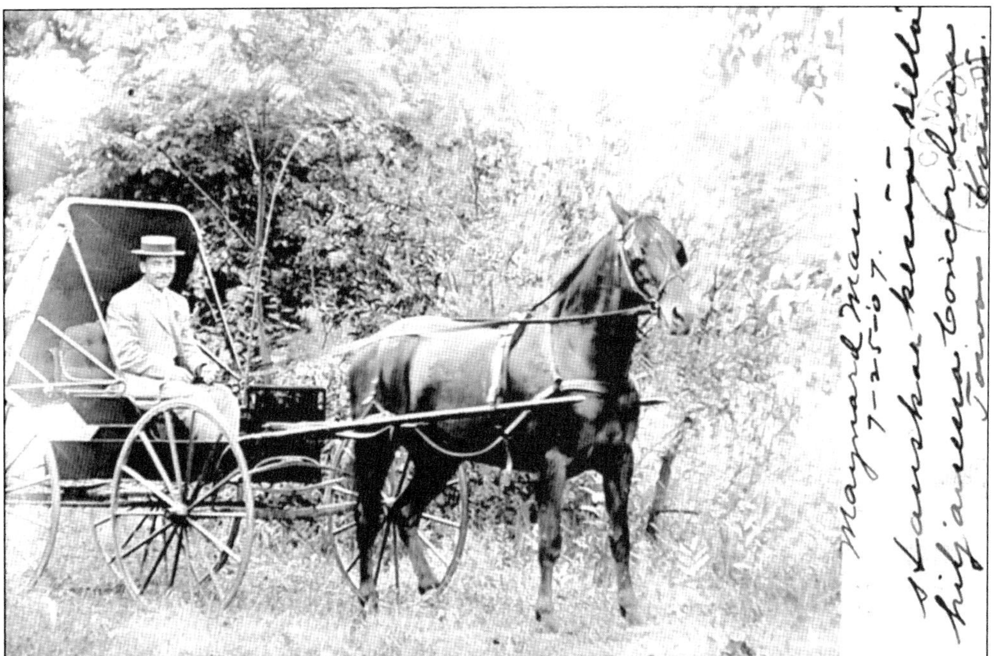

**Horse and Buggy.** In 1907, the main mode of transportation in Maynard was still the horse and wagon. It was soon displaced by the automobile with Henry Ford's Model T car in 1909.

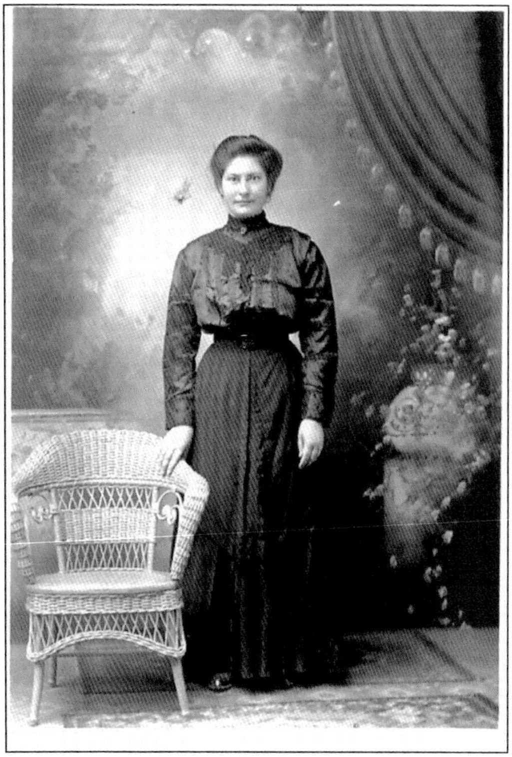

**HER BEST FRIEND.** The message on the back of this lady's postcard read, "Hello Ida, I shall come to visit you, seeing you didn't come to see me as you promised. I waited many evenings. Best Wishes, Mari. Ida: Please give me a photo of yourself."

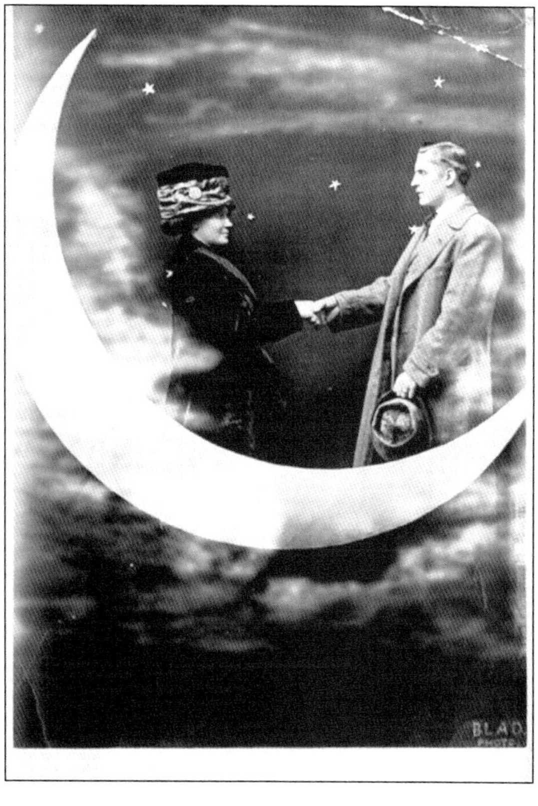

**GOOD FRIENDS.** A special occasion got this man and woman to pose for a local photographer who used a crescent moon as a prop.

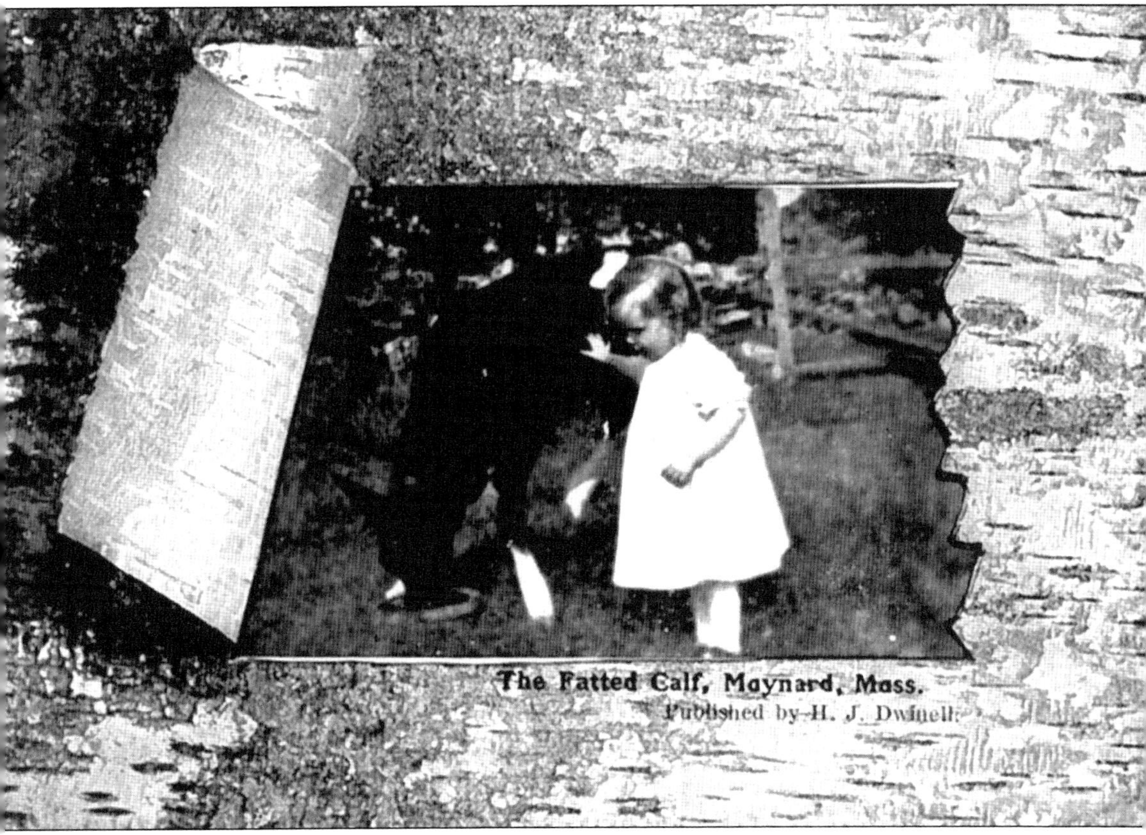


**FATTED CALF.** The young lady with the calf is from Littleton. She posed for this picture and was the daughter of a local farmer. Clara Yapt took this photograph, and it was made into a postcard by H. T. Dwinel.

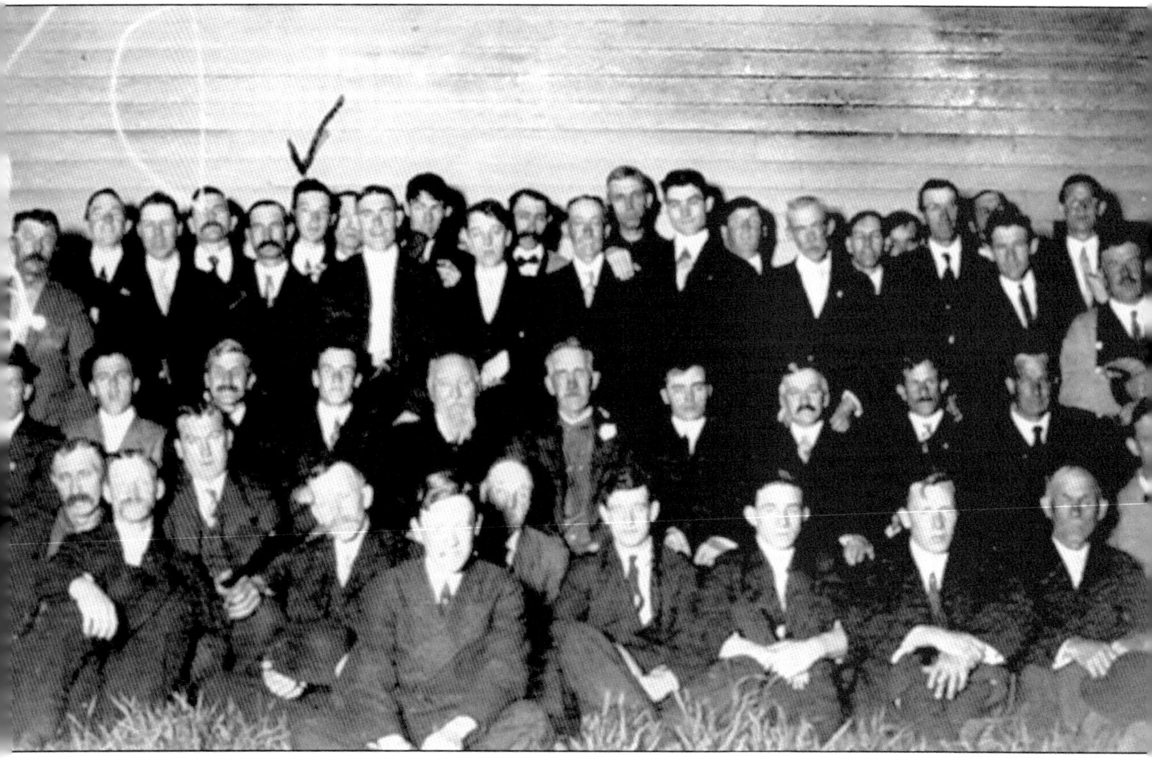

**SURPRISE PARTY.** Sam Wilson was given a surprise party in May 1911 in honor of his 40 years with the American Powder Company. Identified here are A. Lhyzus, Jim Moynihan, Frank Rand, J. Moynikers, N. Jensen, Wilfred Hooper, G. Goodsell, Joe Crotty, Ed Mahoney, Bill Drisdale, Jim Goodson, Bill Tobin, L. McCarthy, Bill Hooper, M. McCarthy, G. Rogers, Sam Wilson, G. Veronariet, Frank Winslow, George Hird, Frank Brackett, Lou Evers, F. Keith, Joe Dineen, Tom King, Pete Alson, H. Olson, Wink McGarry, Lee Donahue, Andy O'Brien, T. Murray, W. Olson, M. Murray, F. Farrell, Nick Driscoll, G. Naraskus, Ilan Splaine, J. Sullivan, W. Loveing, Jim McCarthy, J. O'Brien, B. Ingham, and Jerry Buckley. (Courtesy of MHS.)

*Six*

# Let's Celebrate

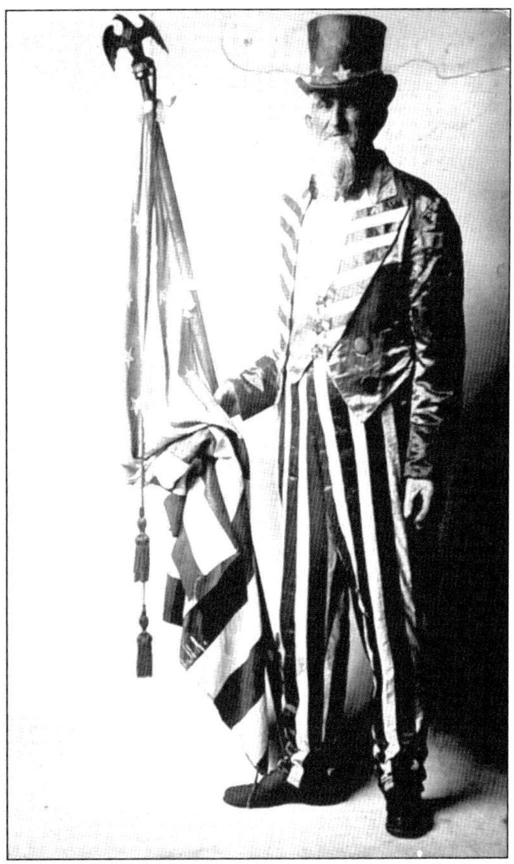

**Uncle Sam.** George W. Young helps to celebrate the Maynard Fourth of July celebration.

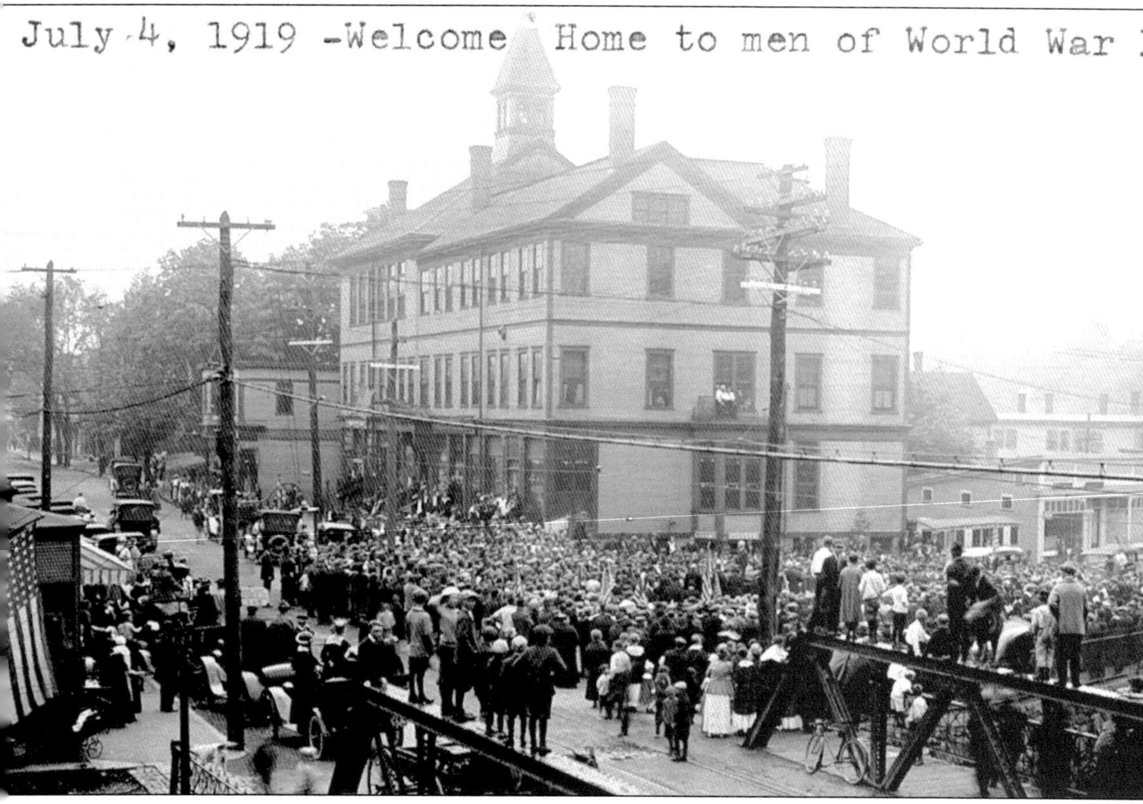


**END OF WAR.** On November 2, 1918, a rumor spread throughout the country that an armistice had been reached. Church bells rang, whistles blew, and an impromptu parade was organized; but the rumor proved false, and the town settled back to its wartime routine. But it had only one week to wait because on November 11, word was flashed to the townspeople that the conflict had ended. Again, the church bells rang out, the fire whistle and the mill whistle blew, whistles on the railroad trains were tooted, schools were dismissed, the Assabet Mills closed, businessmen closed shops, and all gathered at Walnut and Main Streets for a huge parade.

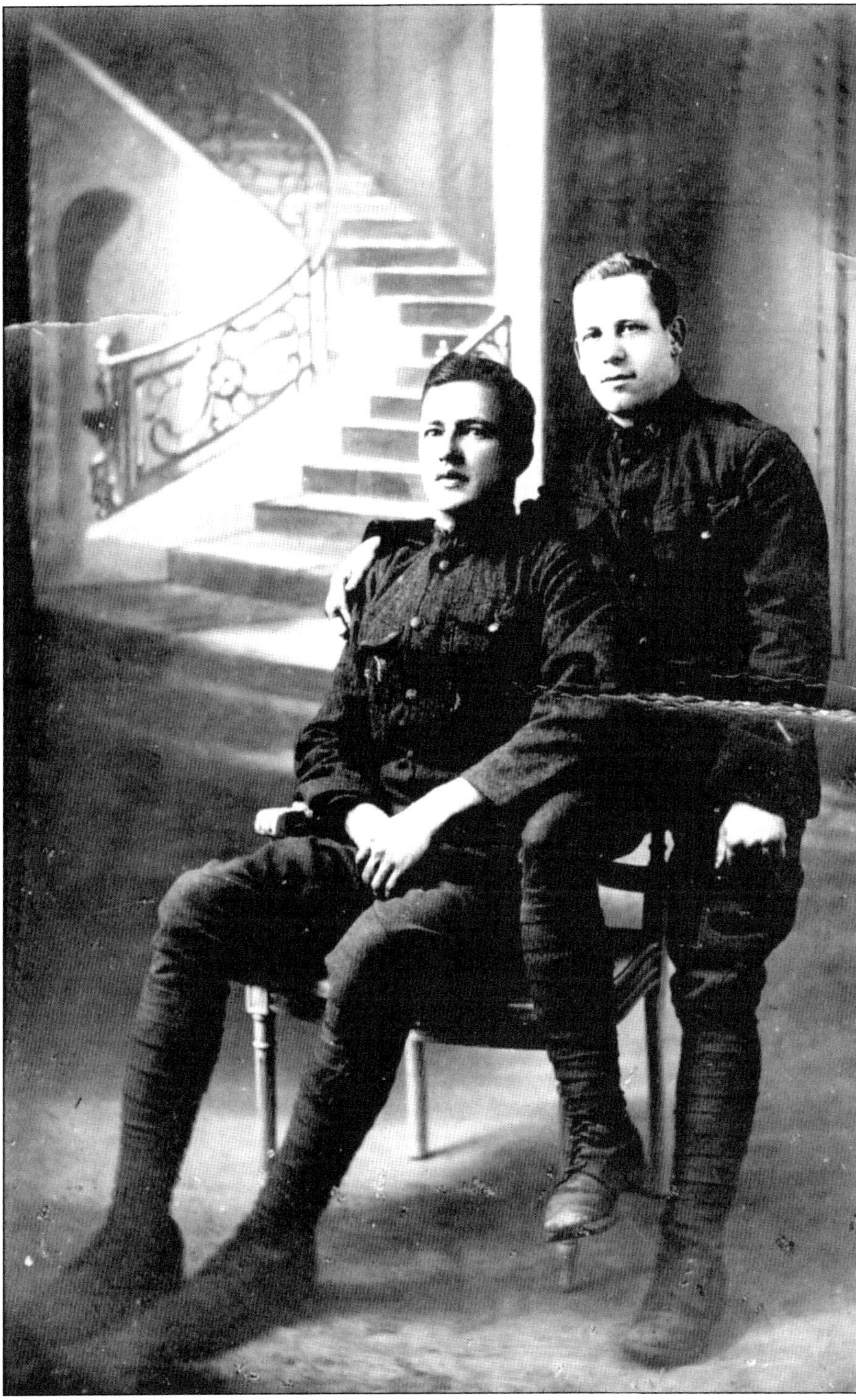

**DOUGHBOYS.** Joseph Boothroyd, on the right, in 1918 wears a World War I doughboy's uniform with an unidentified buddy. During World War I, which America entered into on April 6, 1917, Maynard furnished 340 men, seven of whom died serving their country.

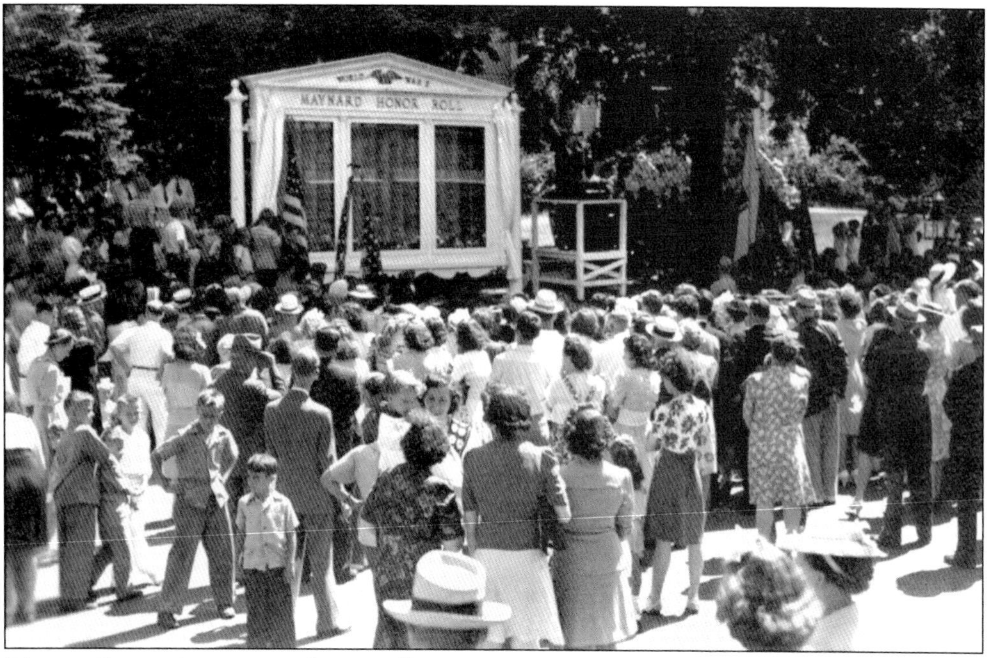


**HONOR ROLL.** A temporary honor roll was erected by Nellie T. Fowler on the lawn in front of the Union Congregational Church. It was dedicated Sunday, September 8, 1918.

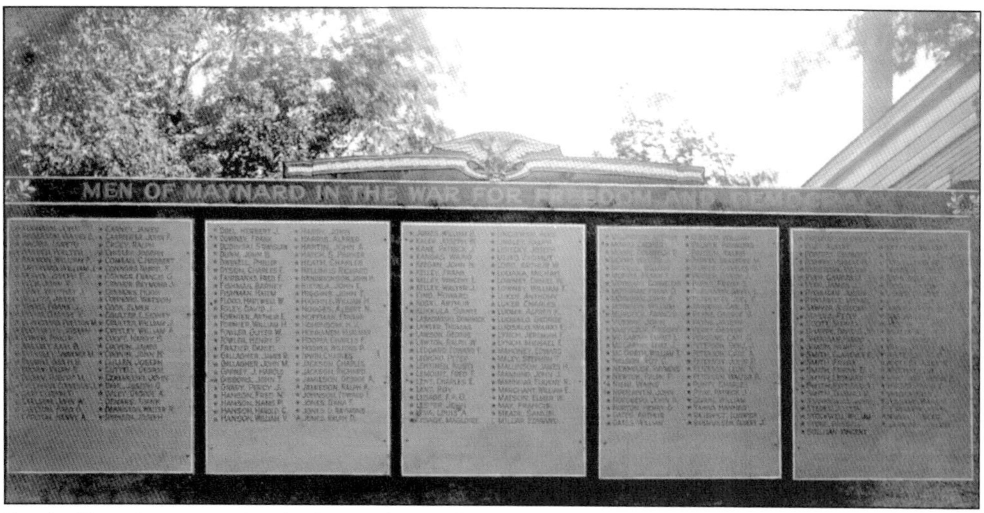


**LET'S NOT FORGET.** On the home front, the citizens kept the Assabet Mills running day and night; harvested their victory gardens; sent five Liberty Loan drives over the top; put up with food shortages, heatless days, and wheatless days; removed every other streetlamp; turned the lights off at midnight; and registered 804 men in the draft of June 5, 1917, and 1,115 men in the final draft of September 12, 1918.

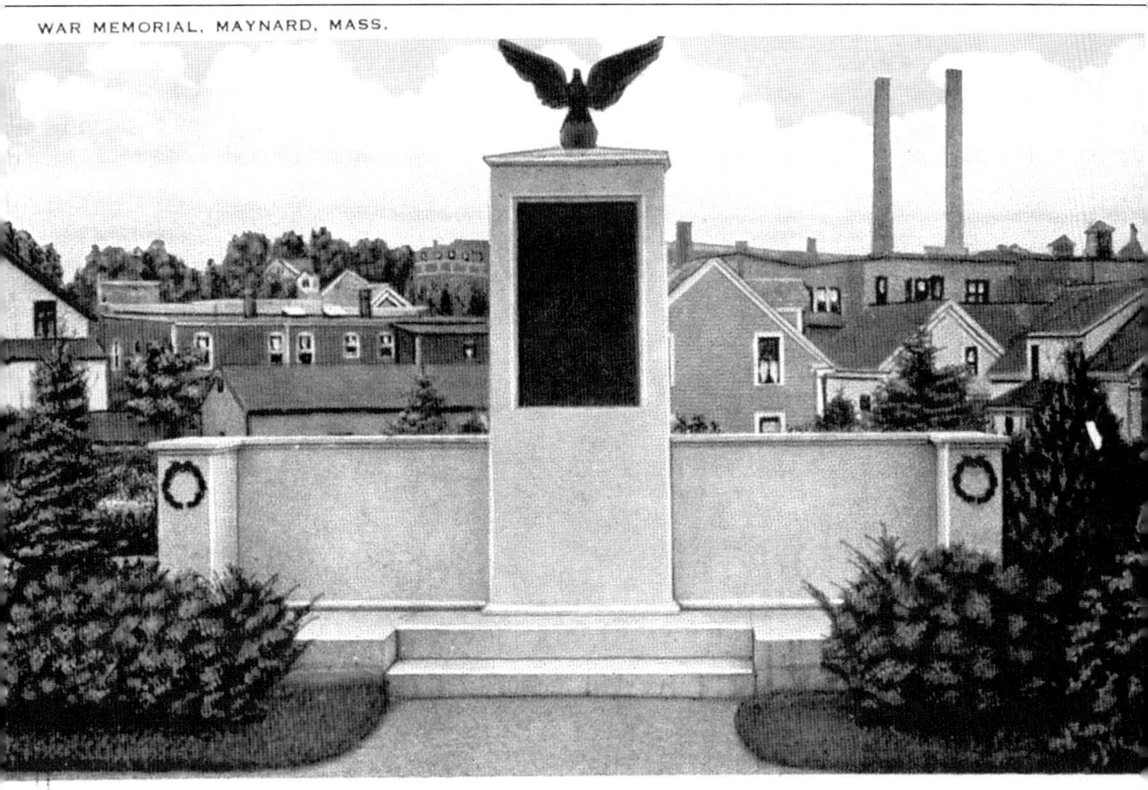


**MEMORIAL PARK.** In 1922, the old Maynard Hotel property on Summer Street was purchased for $10,000, and in 1925, $4,000 was appropriated for grading and improving the lot. A contract was awarded for a soldiers' monument to be erected in the new park. The park and monument were dedicated on Sunday, November 15, 1925, as Memorial Park, with Congresswoman Edith Nourse Rogers of Lowell as the speaker. A flagpole was erected from contributions received from the public and several fraternal organizations. In 1926, three trustees of Soldiers' Memorial were elected for the first time.

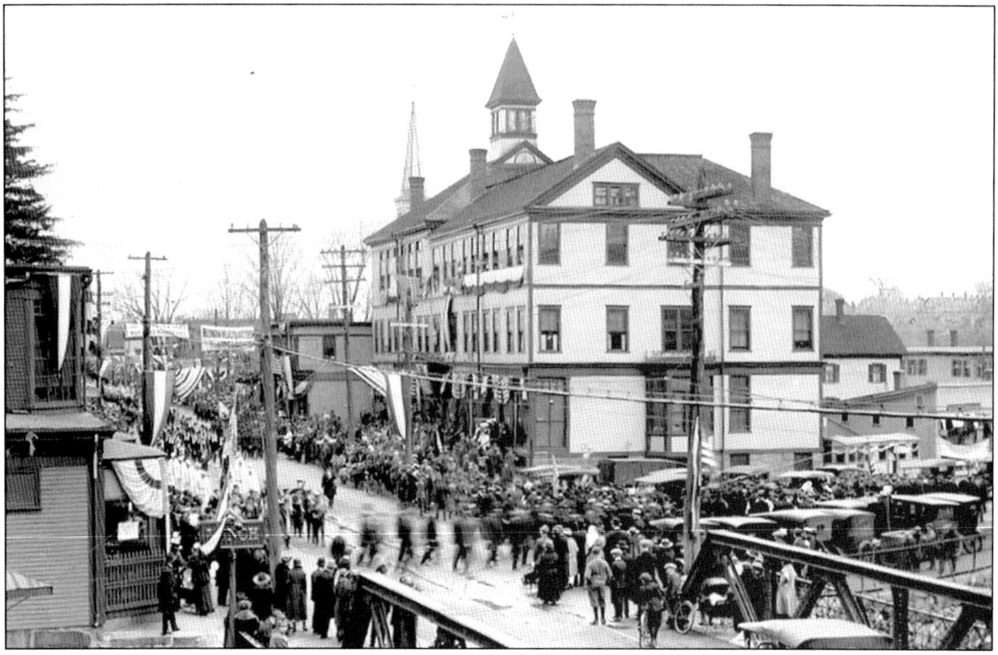

**THE 50TH ANNIVERSARY.** At the annual town meeting, March 7, 1921, it was voted to celebrate in an appropriate manner on April 19, the 50th anniversary of the founding of the town. Moderator Horace F. Bates and clerk Frank E. Sanderson were instructed to appoint a committee of 21, who were to meet and add to their number sufficient to create a good working force and carry out a definite program.

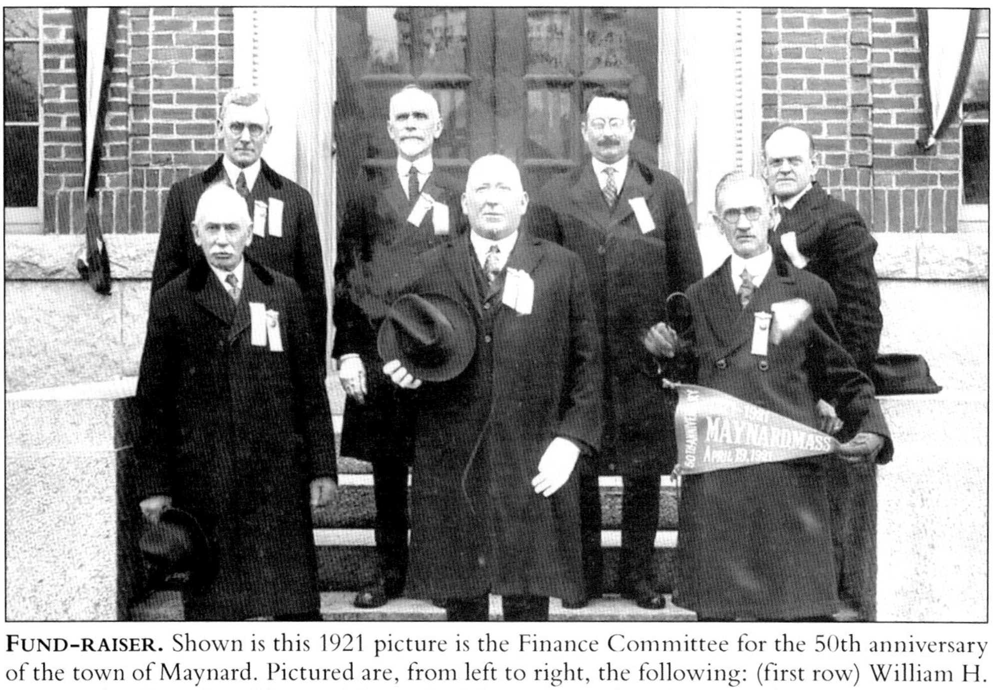


**FUND-RAISER.** Shown is this 1921 picture is the Finance Committee for the 50th anniversary of the town of Maynard. Pictured are, from left to right, the following: (first row) William H. Guttenridge, B. J. Coughlan, and G. H. Greighton; (second row) T. F. Parker, P. J. Sullivan, H. H. Young, and George D. Elson. (Courtesy of MHS.)

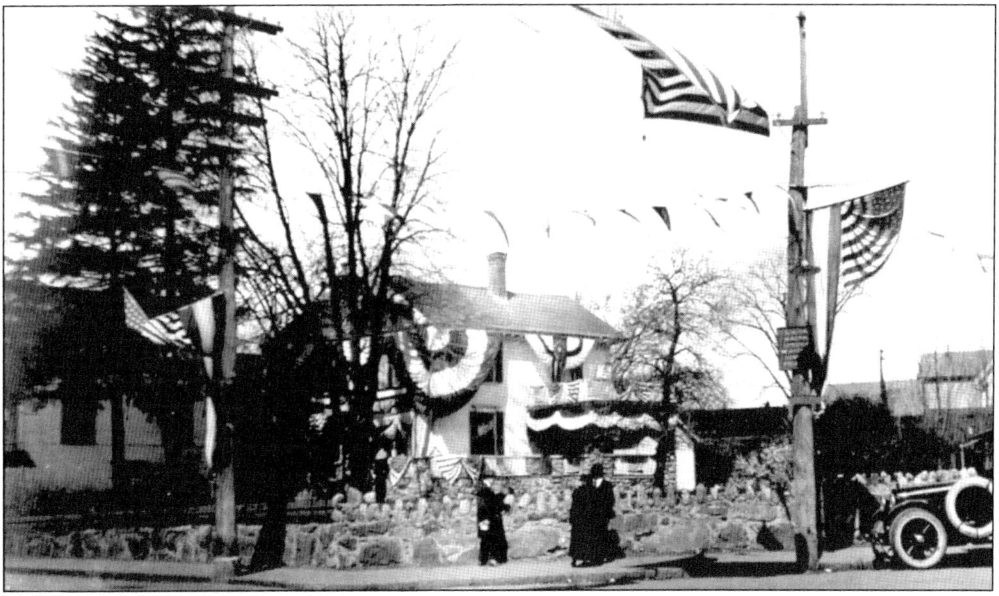

**Home of Amory Maynard II.** This home, all decorated up for the 50th anniversary of the birth of the town of Maynard, is located at the westerly corner of Nason and Main Streets.

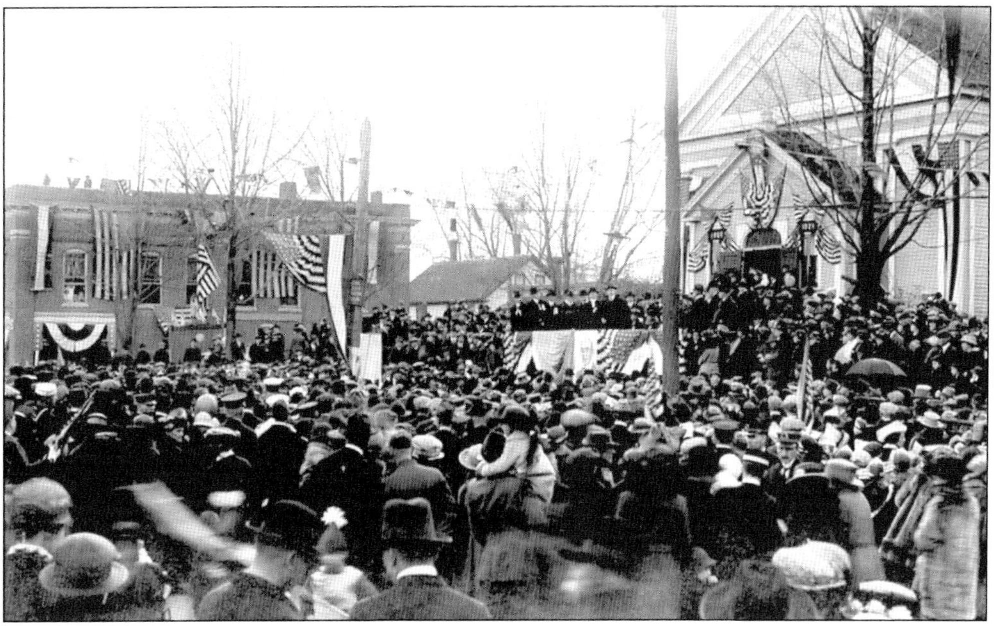

**Let the Celebration Begin.** On the reviewing stand constructed on the front lawn of the Congregational church in Maynard are the speakers gathered to address the crowd at the 50th anniversary of the town in 1921.

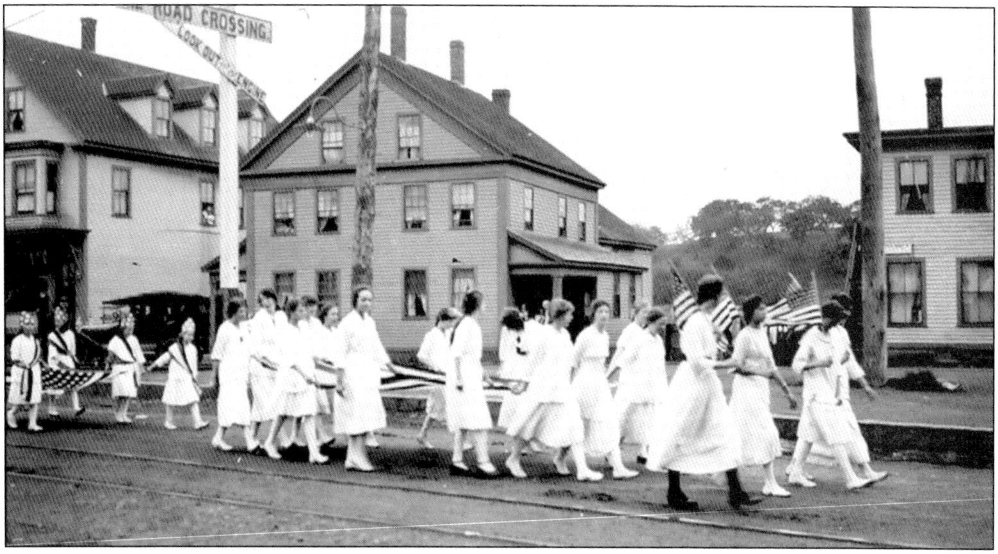


**MAYNARD TEMPERANCE SOCIETY.** The ladies of the Maynard Temperance Society are participating in the 1921 parade celebrating Maynard's 50th anniversary. They are marching down upper Main Street. (Courtesy of MHS.)

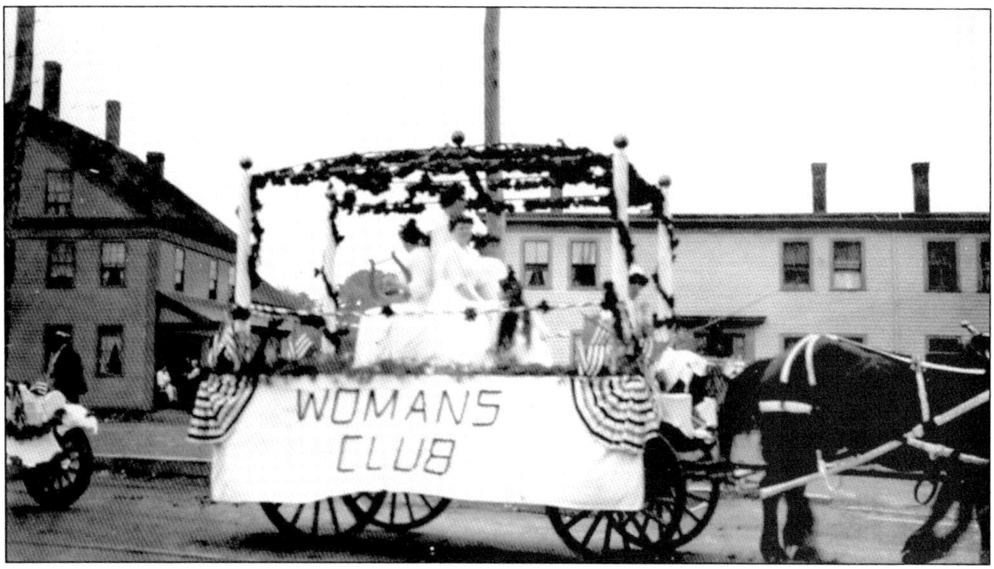


**MAYNARD WOMANS CLUB.** The club was organized in March 1904 with 69 members as a philanthropic, educational, and civic organization. Meetings were held in the Masonic hall, George Washington Auditorium, Knights of Columbus Hall, and Fellowship Hall (Union Congregational Church). It is still a very active club.

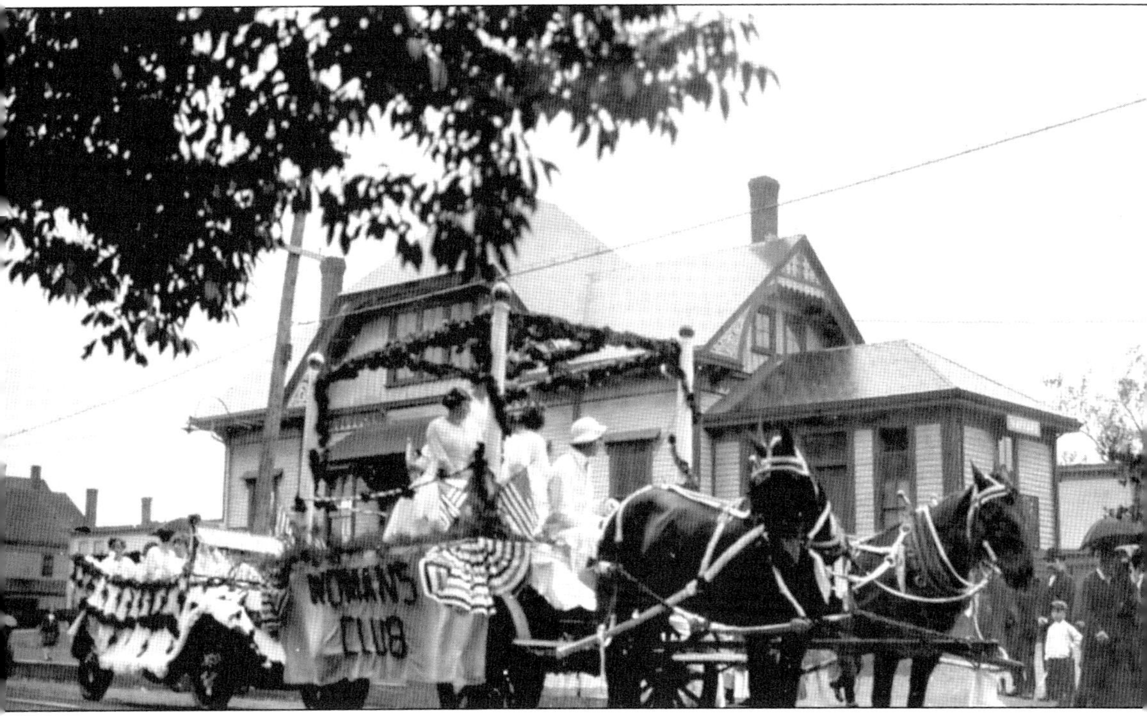


**MAYNARD WOMANS CLUB AND KNIGHTS OF PYTHIAS.** These two floats are waiting in front of the railroad station on Main Street in 1921 for the 50th anniversary celebration parade to begin.

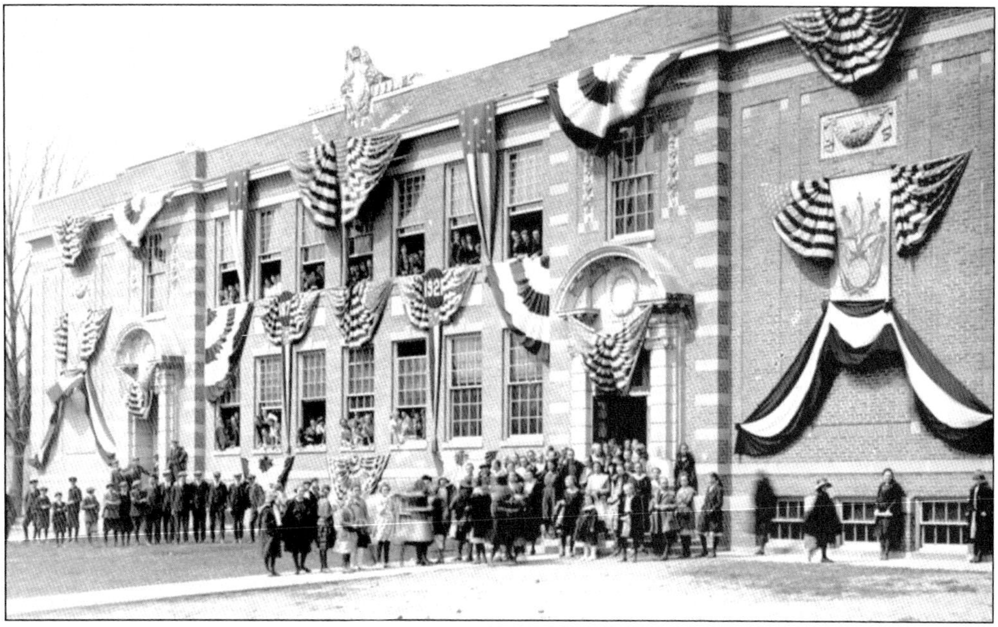

**MAYNARD HIGH SCHOOL.** In 1921, at Maynard's 50th anniversary, the school decorated itself very elaborately to join in the celebration. The school replaced the Nason Street High School, which burnt in 1916.

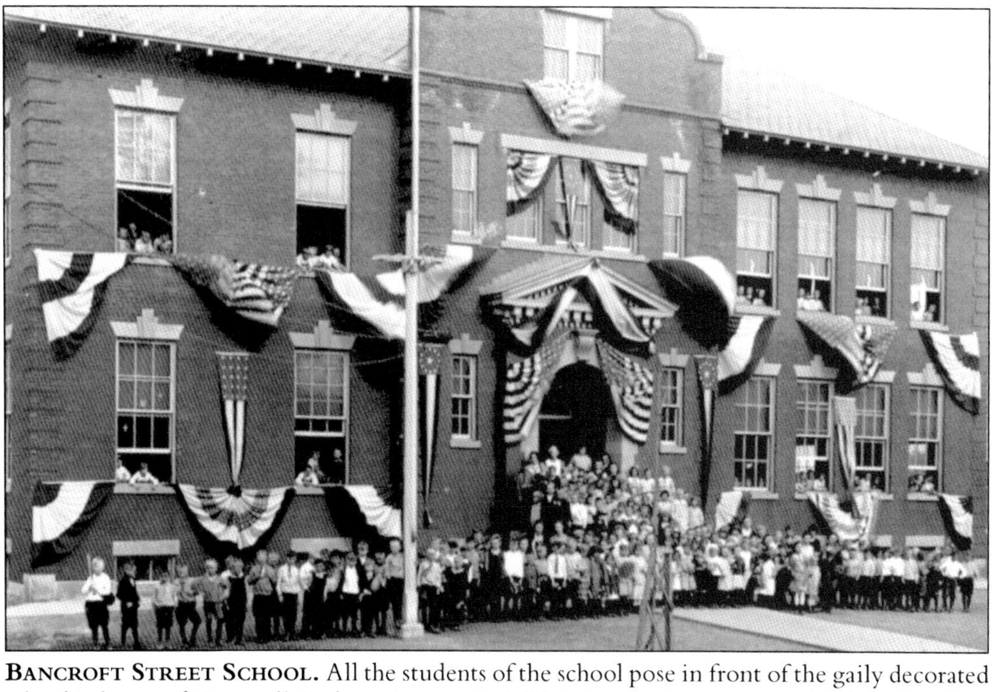

**BANCROFT STREET SCHOOL.** All the students of the school pose in front of the gaily decorated school in honor of Maynard's 50th anniversary in 1921. The school was renamed Calvin Coolidge School in honor of the president.

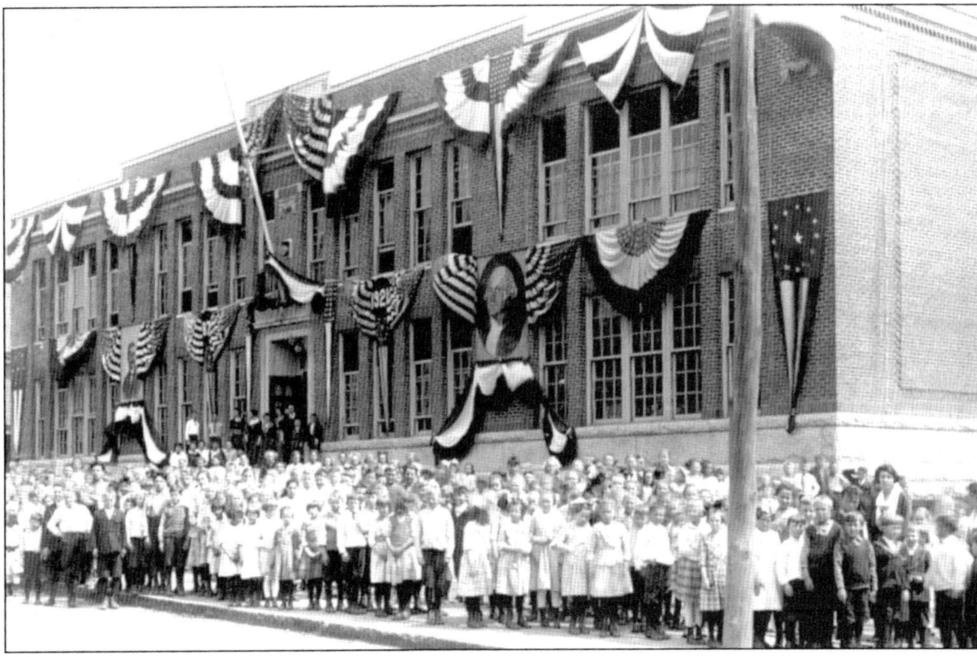

**NASON STREET SCHOOL.** During the 50th anniversary of Maynard celebration in 1921, all the students pose in front of the decorated school. It will soon be the new Maynard Public Library.

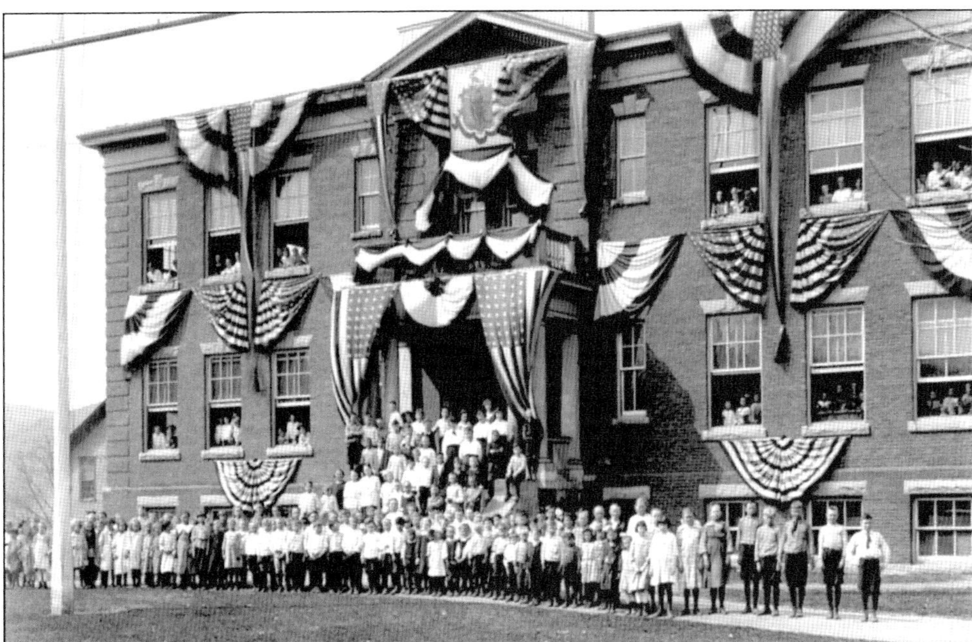

**MAIN STREET SCHOOL.** The school and its students celebrate along with the rest of the town during Maynard's 50th anniversary in 1921. Later the school was renamed the Woodrow Wilson School. It was built in 1902 and burnt in December 1952.

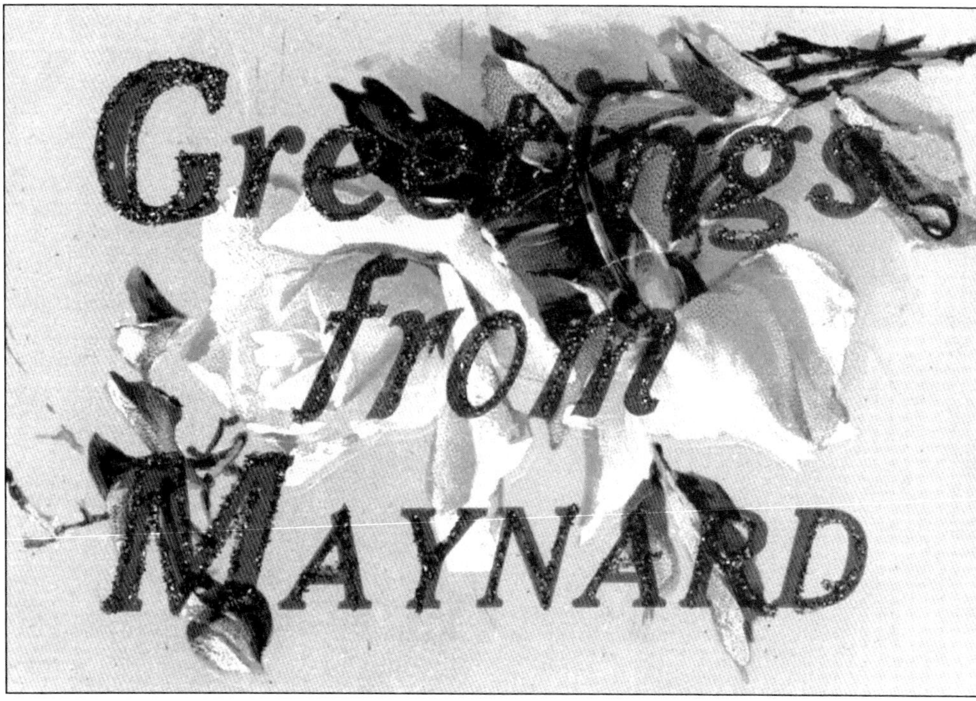


**HOLIDAY GREETINGS.** What better way to celebrate a holiday (Valentine's Day) or just pass on a greeting from Maynard to friends and relatives than to use a postcard.

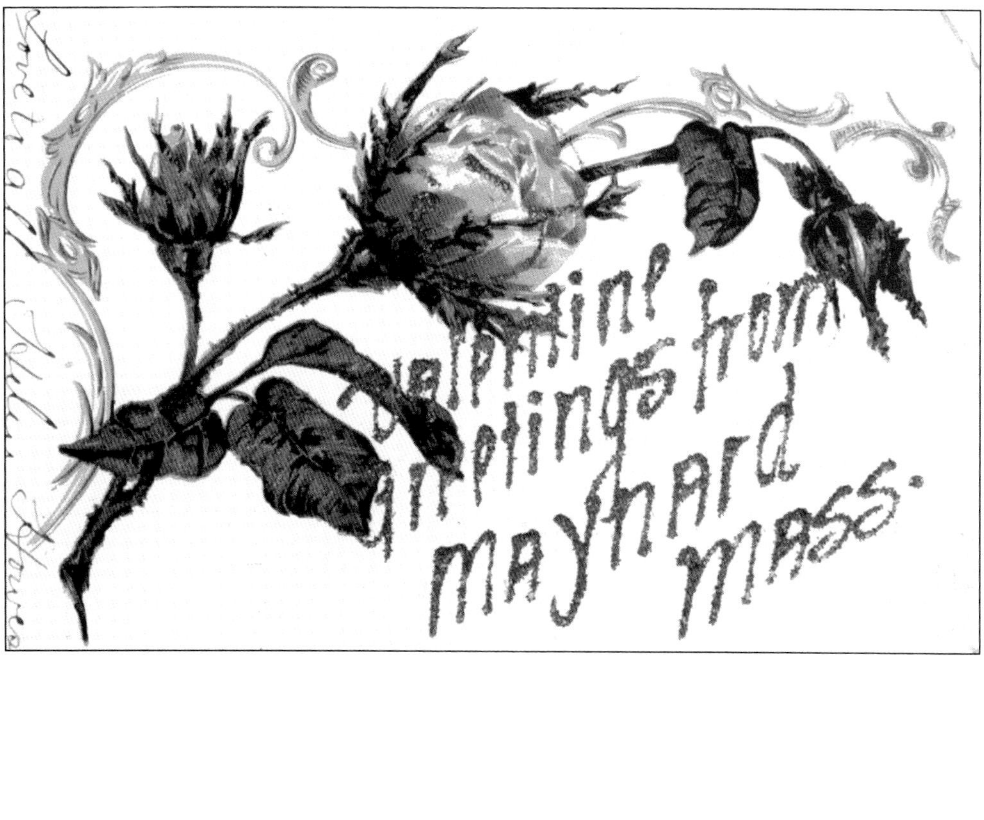

*Seven*

# Commerce

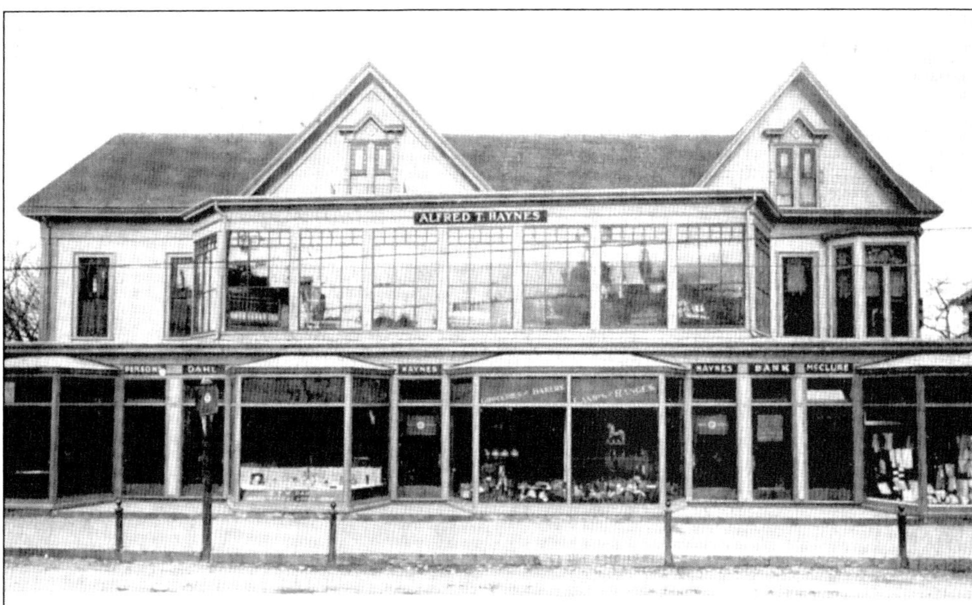


**Riverside Block on Main Street.** This block was built in the late 1860s by the Maynard family. The Assabet Institution for Savings got its start on the second floor in 1904. The upper floor was destroyed by fire on Saturday, July 14, 1934. It is now known as the Gruber's block.

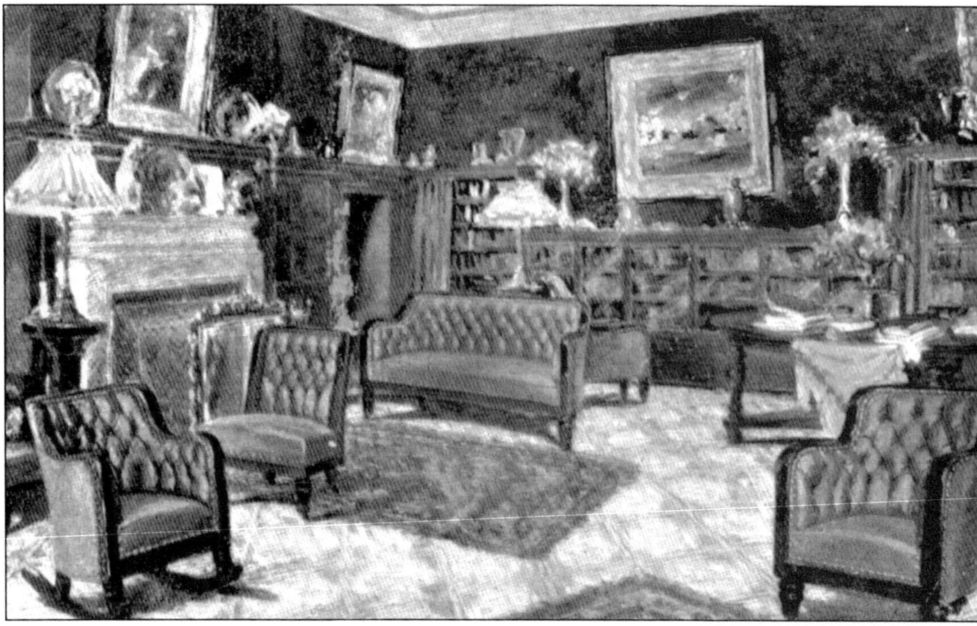

**HAYNES SHOWROOM.** These postcards, mailed in January 1912, were used to introduce some very elegant and expensive furniture to the residents of Maynard by showing them several of the displays in the showroom of the Alfred T. Haynes and Company. The advertising postcards both state that the cost of the furniture is not nearly what you might think.

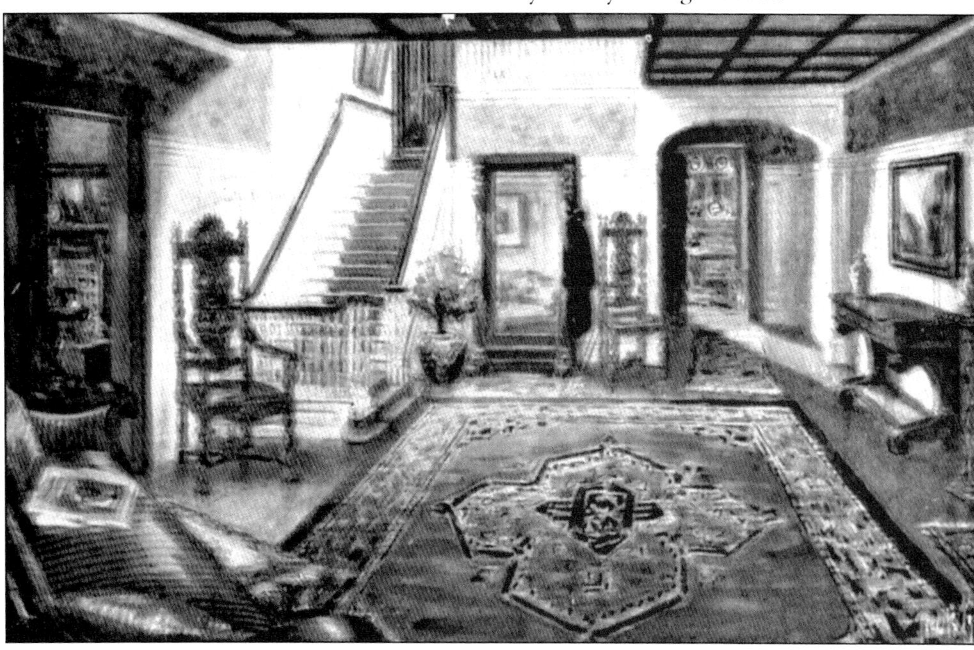

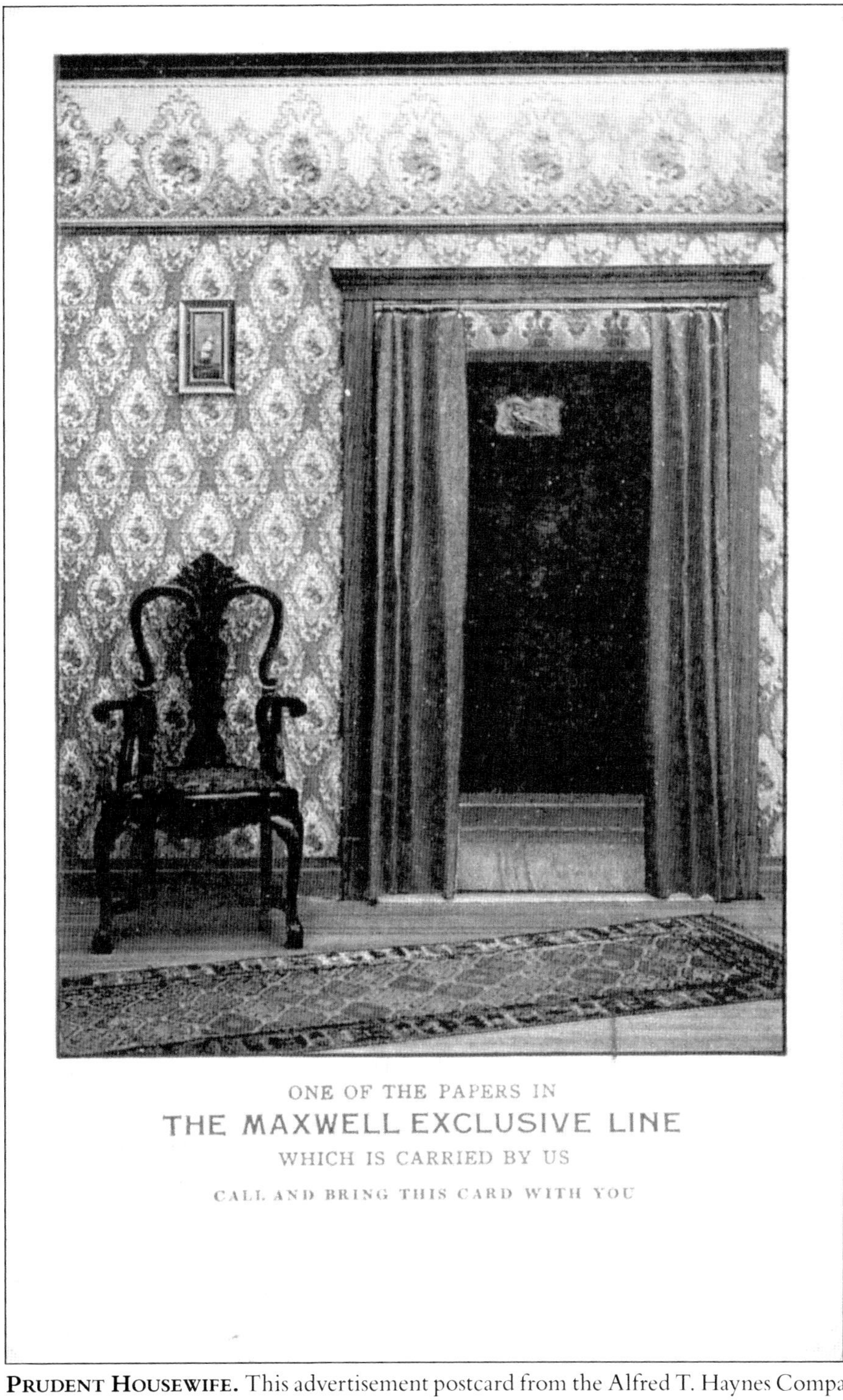


**The Prudent Housewife.** This advertisement postcard from the Alfred T. Haynes Company in Maynard was promoting very fancy wallpaper. Printed on the back of the card is "It is the prudent housewife who is now making early preparations for her Spring decorating and papering."

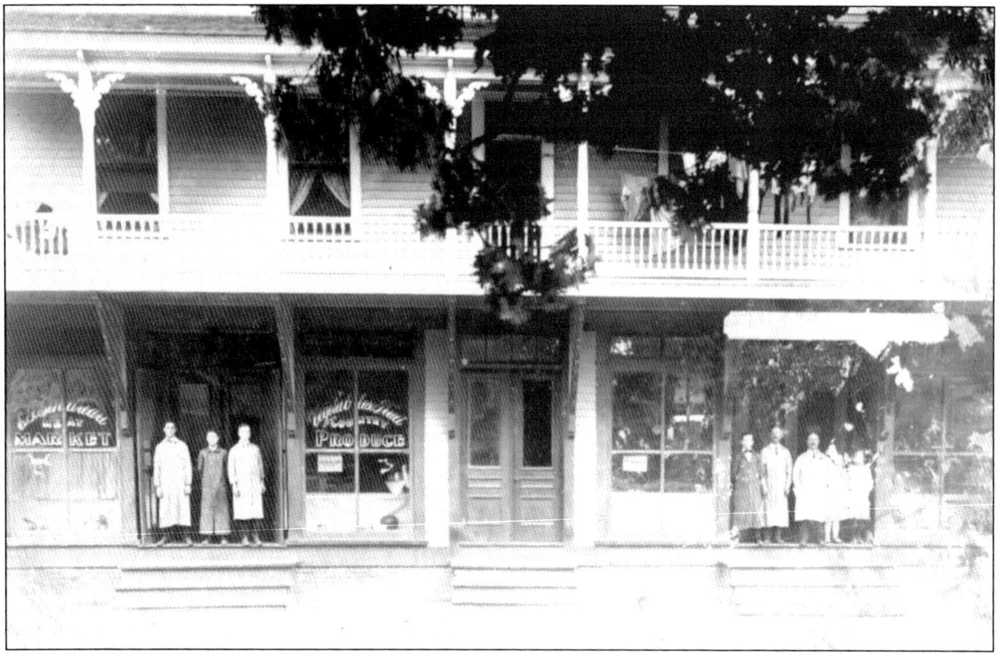


**THE AMORY BLOCK.** This block of stores was built by Amory Maynard and was occupied on the first floor by various types of businesses. Today it is the site of the Blue Coyote pub.

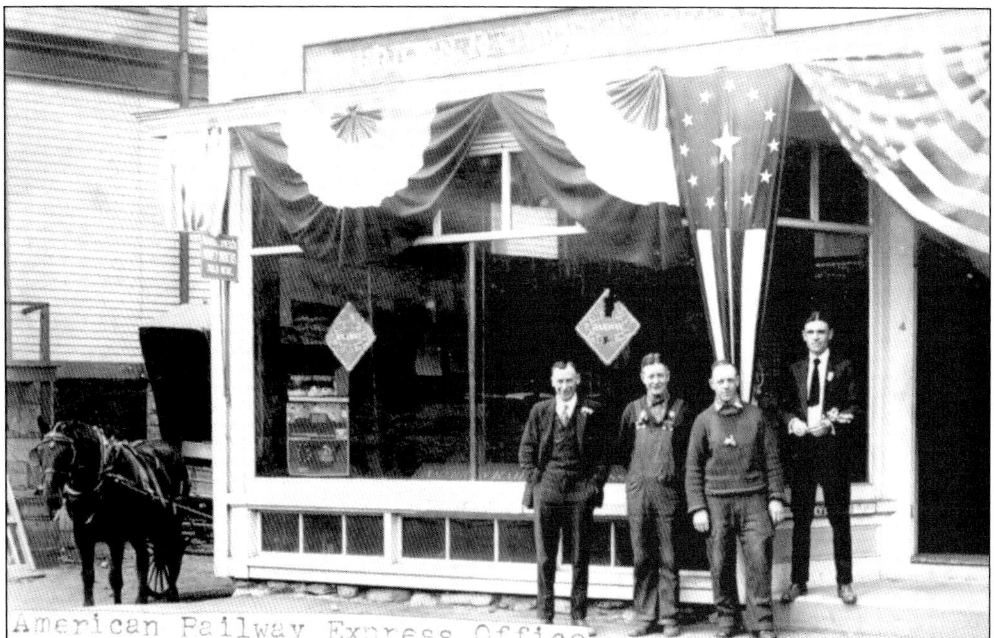


**AMERICAN EXPRESS AND RAILWAY EXPRESS.** The Railway Express office in Maynard is on 51 Main Street, the former site of Paul's Bakery. John Rounds was the agent. In those days, most packages were delivered either by train or by express wagons. (Courtesy of MHS.)

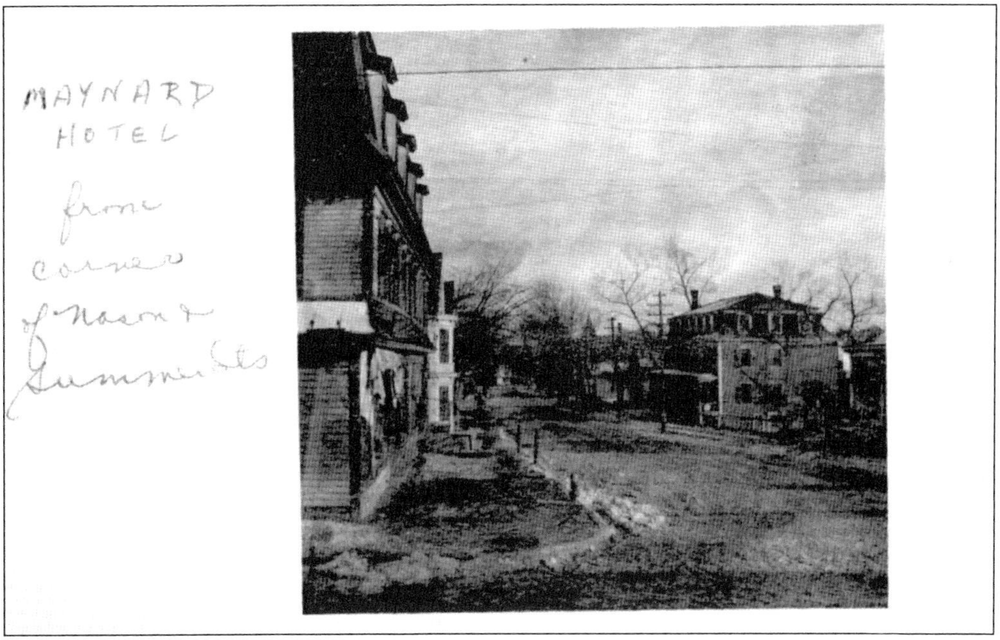


**MAYNARD HOTEL.** The hotel was built in 1867 on Summer Street by Peter Haley. Originally, it was known as the Glendale House, and it had several owners. This was a tavern and hotel. Later the name was changed to the Maynard Hotel. It was owned and operated for many years by Hugh McGrail, then John Desmond, and, finally, by Martin Peterson. The building was destroyed completely by fire on January 29, 1921. (Courtesy of MHS.)

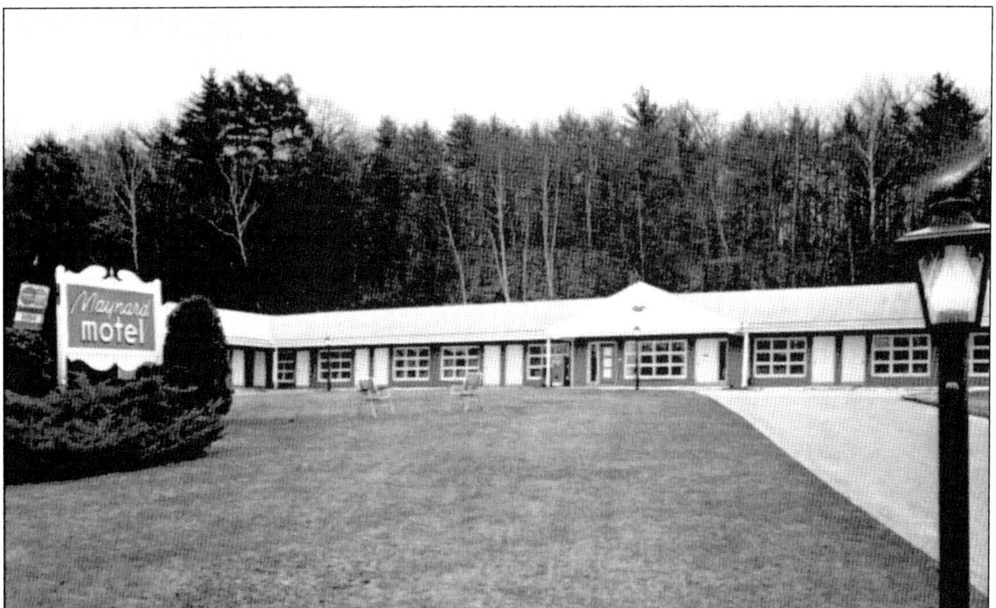


**THE MAYNARD MOTEL.** This modern version of the Maynard Hotel was built at the Acton town line on Powder Mill Road in 1961–1962 by Leon Christian. It consists of 14 deluxe units with modern conveniences. It has recently been replaced by a Wendy's fast food restaurant.

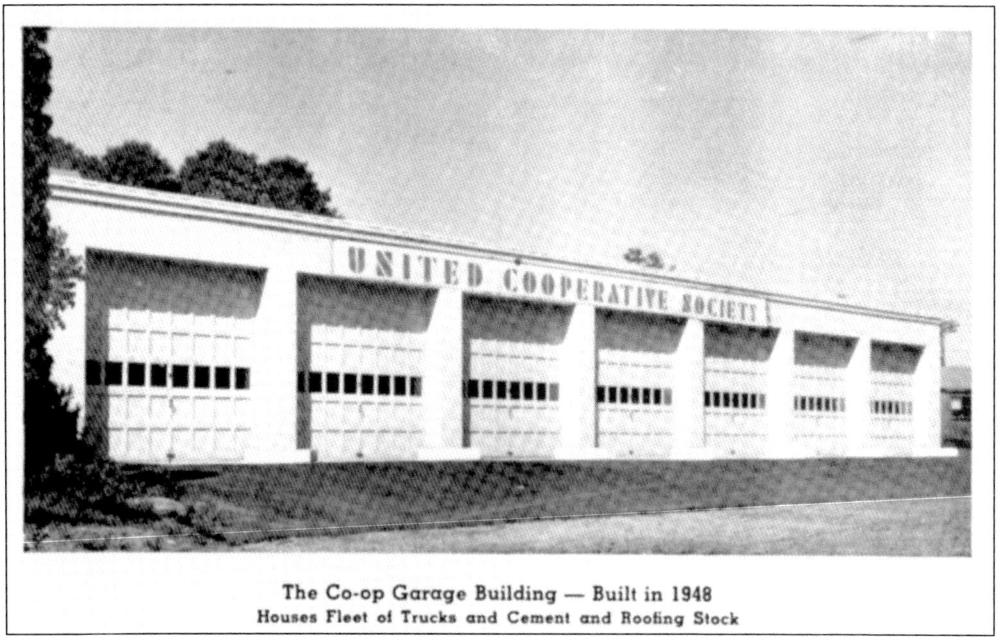


**THE CO-OP GARAGE BUILDING.** Built in 1948 by the United Cooperative Society, this garage was used for their trucks and supplies of building material.

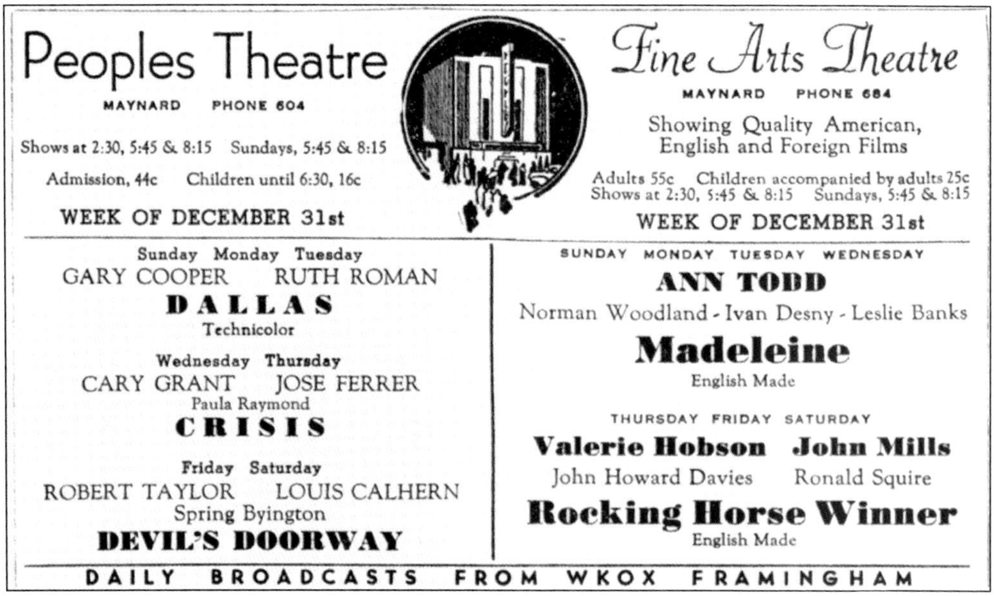


**WHAT'S PLAYING AT THE MOVIES?** On May 6, 1921, Peoples Theatre on Nason Street was opened with a license to show moving pictures. In June 1949, the Fine Arts Theatre, a moving picture house on Summer Street, was opened. A few years later, Peoples was closed, and the Fine Arts became the only moving picture theater in town. (Courtesy of Jack Malcolm.)

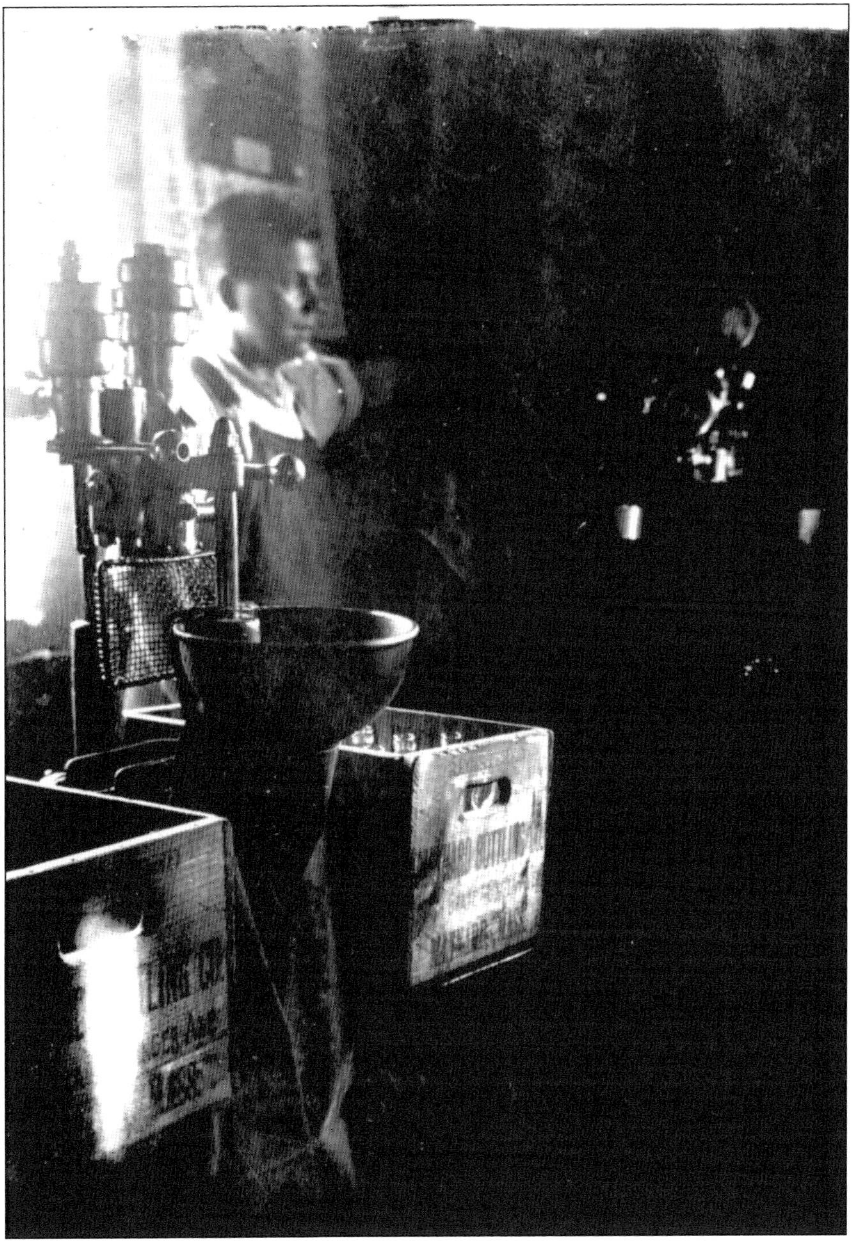

**MAYNARD BOTTLING WORKS.** K. Paul Hilander, a young Maynard man of Finnish origin, formed a partnership with Abraham Pirnes and purchased the Maynard Bottling Works from Waino Keto on April 24, 1914. The company, which had been established in 1899, was located at Florida Road and Euclid Avenue. Hilander soon bought out Pirnes's interest and continued the business as sole owner and manager. Without motorized machinery, he labored early and late to supply customer demands. The ingredients used in the manufacture of his product were the best procurable. As business increased, the company acquired the most modern machinery to keep up with all competitors. (Courtesy of MHS.)

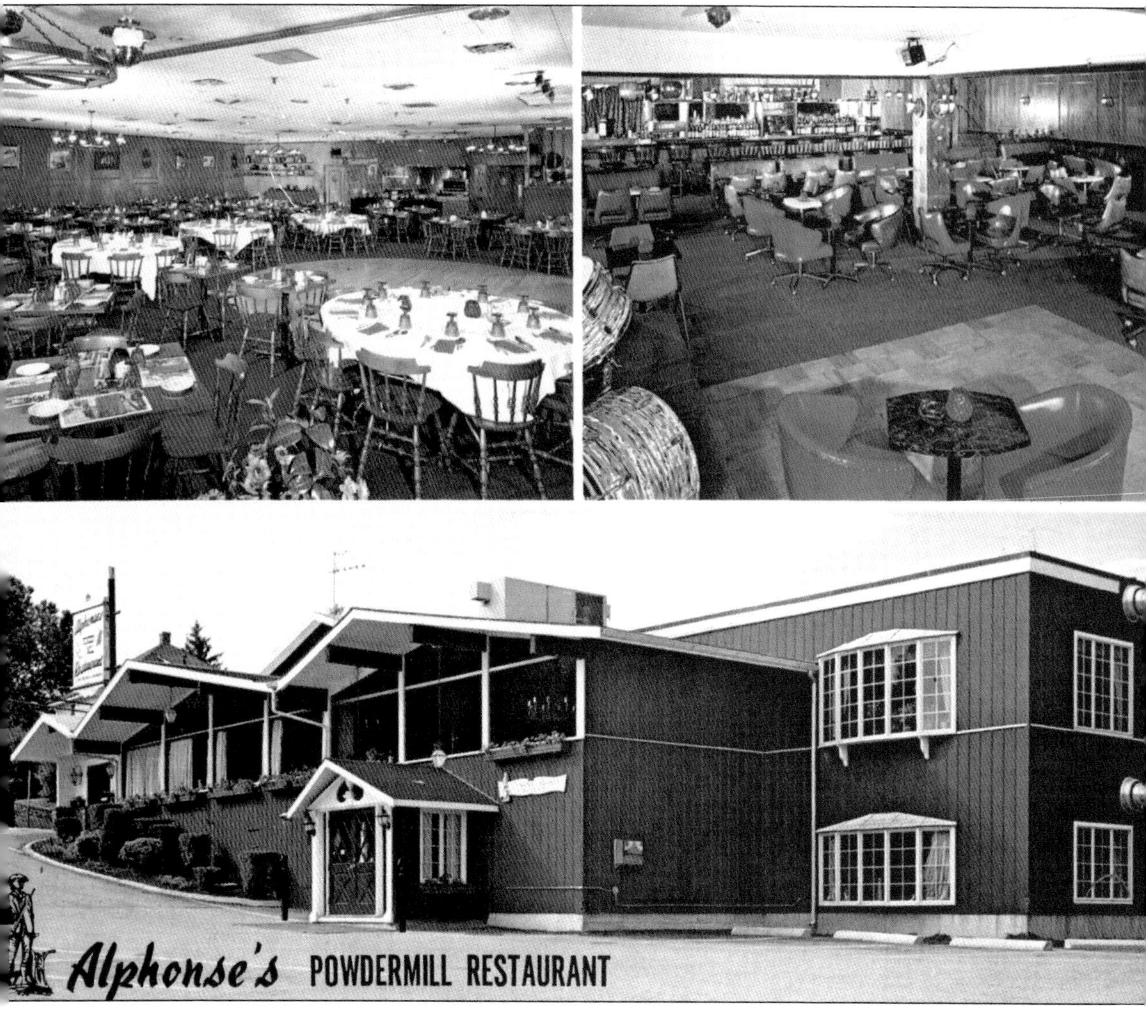


**ALPHONSE'S POWDERMILL RESTAURANT.** This restaurant was named after the famous Powder Mills of Maynard and is famous as a place to entertain 25 to 1,000 guests. It features the Carriage Room, the Hearth Room, and the Minuteman Lounge. This building is now the site of the Elks organization.

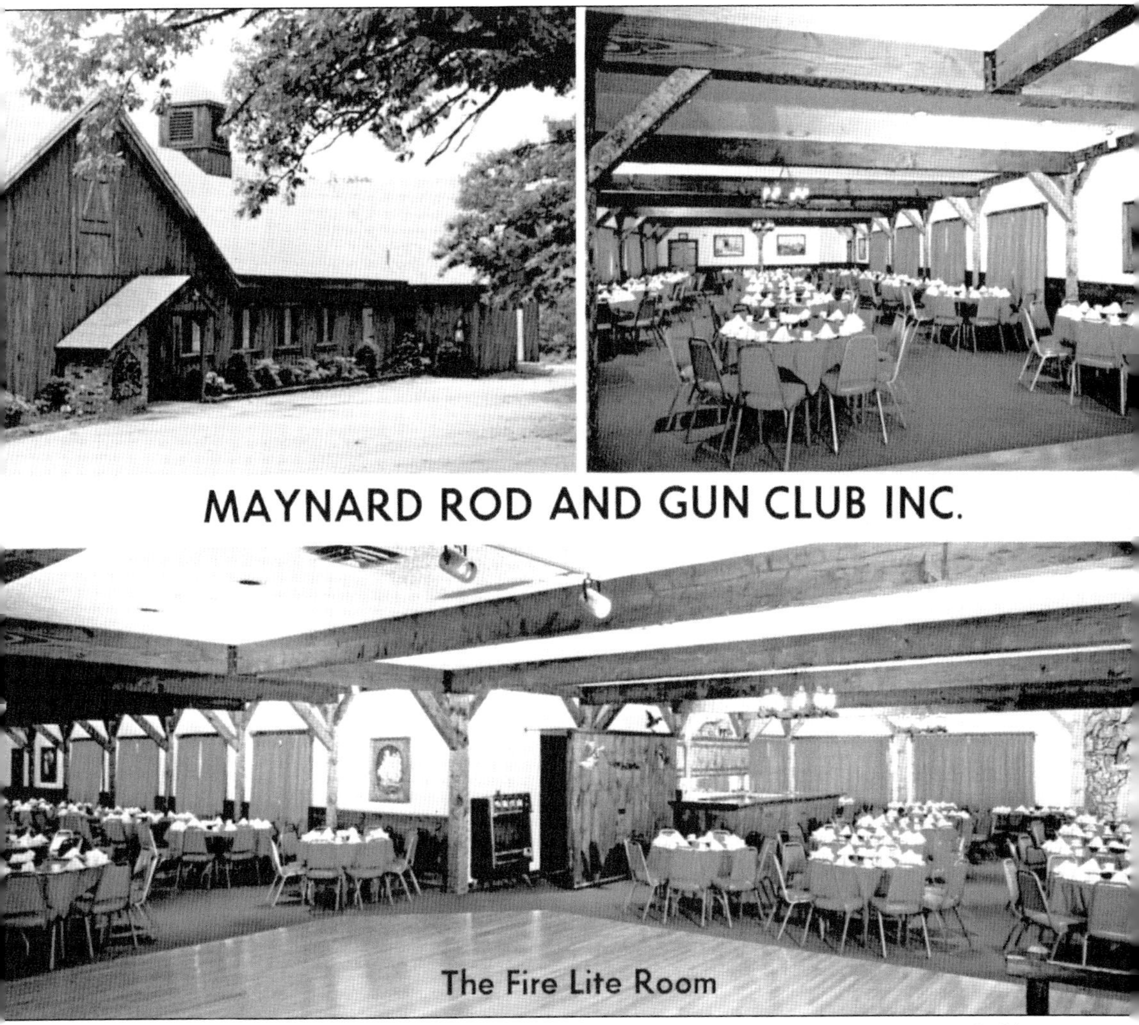


**THE MAYNARD GUN CLUB.** The club was organized July 16, 1915, at a meeting held in the Boston Clothing Store on Nason Street. It was managed by John Peterson, who was the grandfather of Governor Walter R. Peterson of New Hampshire. On June 27, 1929, the club opened a clubhouse at White Pond in Hudson. It was forced to vacate in 1942 when the United States government issued orders there could be no shooting on the grounds adjacent to the then Ammunition Depot. In 1944, the club purchased the present site off Old Mill Road and built a new clubhouse.

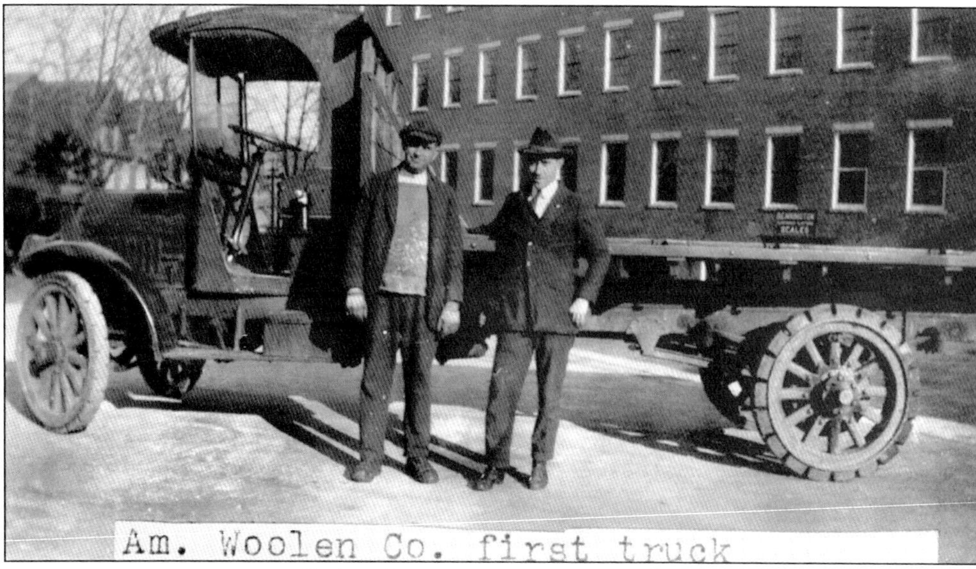


**MILL TRUCK DRIVERS.** Mill chauffeurs Harry Burnham (left) and Roy Gray are standing in front of the American Woolen Company's first truck. Roy Gray later became a popular janitor at the Calvin Coolidge School.

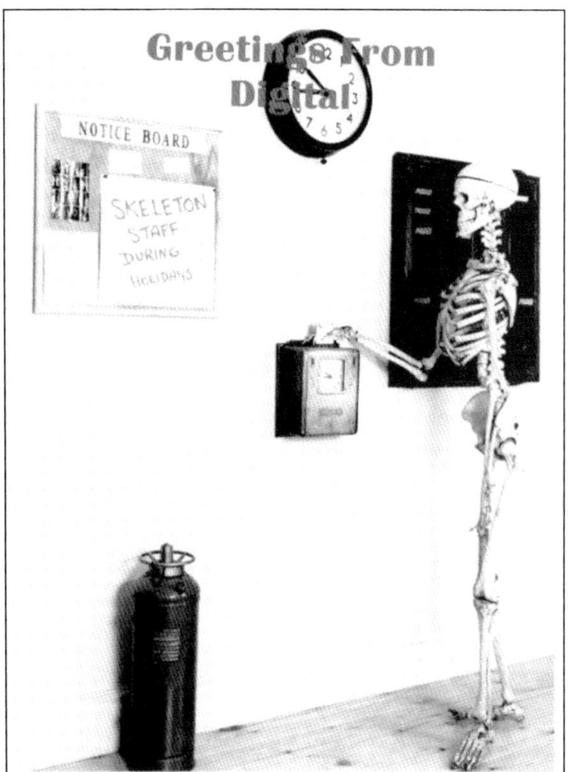


**DYING TO GET TO WORK.** With $70,000 in seed money, three engineers launched Digital Equipment Corporation in 1957. Digital Equipment Corporation occupied 8,600 square feet of space at Maynard Industries No. 12 mill building.

# *Eight*

# Religion

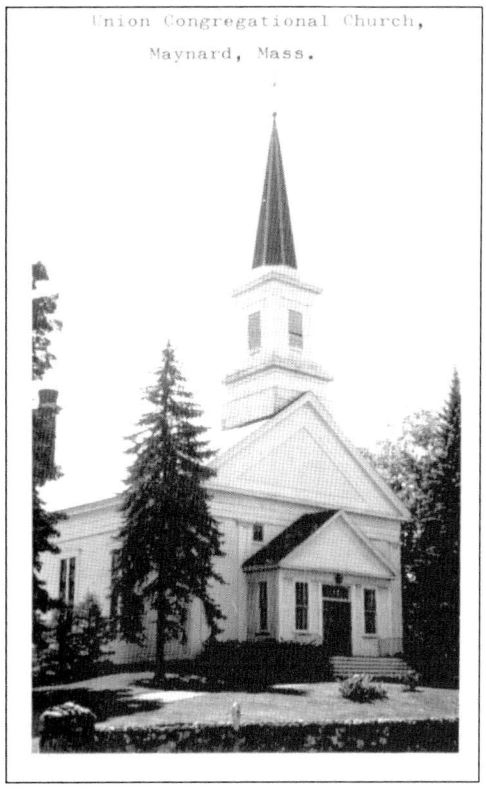


**Union Congregational Church.** In early 1859, Maynard (or Assabet as it was then known) provided little accommodation to those who desired to comply with the law "Thou shall keep the Sabbath Day." The church was built during the winter of 1852 and dedicated on March 24, 1853.

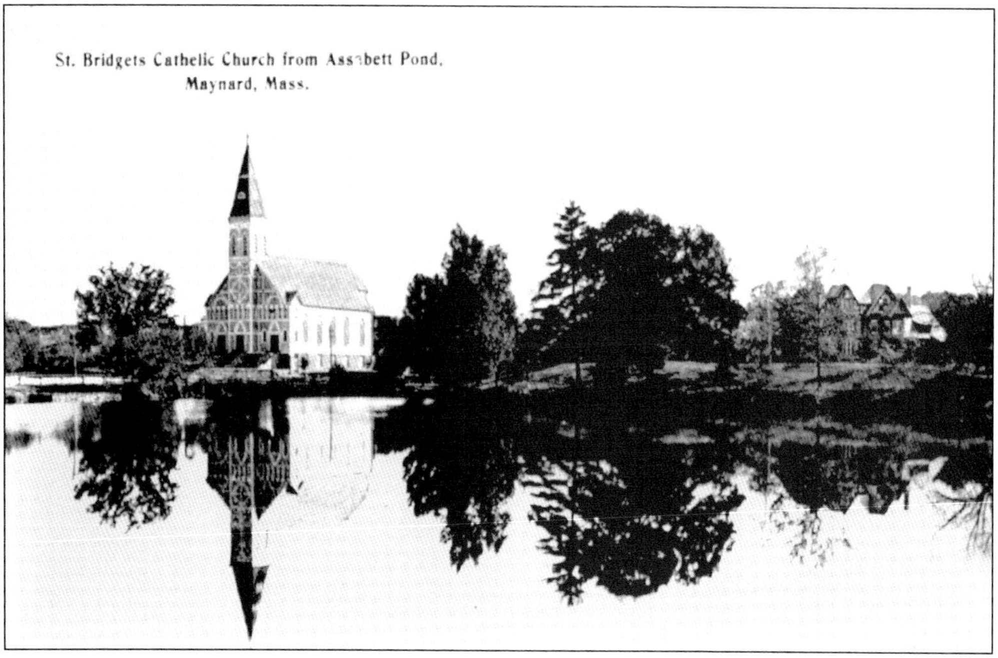


**St. Bridget's Parish by the Pond.** On January 1, 1894, St. Bridget's Parish was reestablished with John A. Crowe as pastor. A good portion of the pond was filled in for parking and the building of a parochial school.

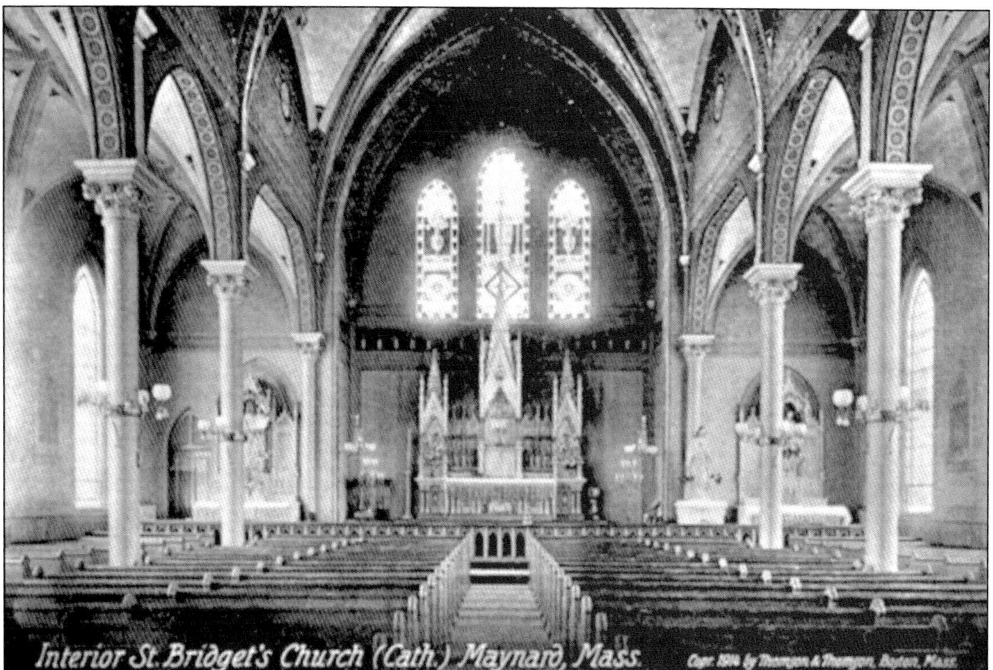


**Inside St. Bridget's Church.** This interior view of St. Bridget's Church shows the windows behind the altar that were destroyed during the 1938 hurricane.

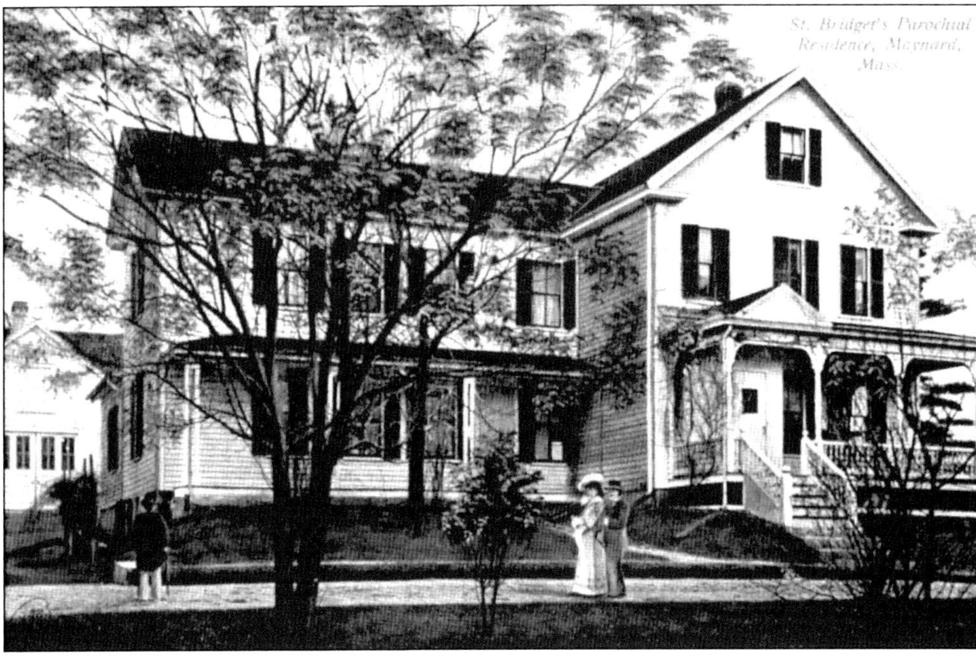


**ALFRED T. HAYNES HOUSE.** This house was purchased and converted into a parsonage. Later it was raffled off for $1.00 a chance when the new rectory was built and moved to Great Road.

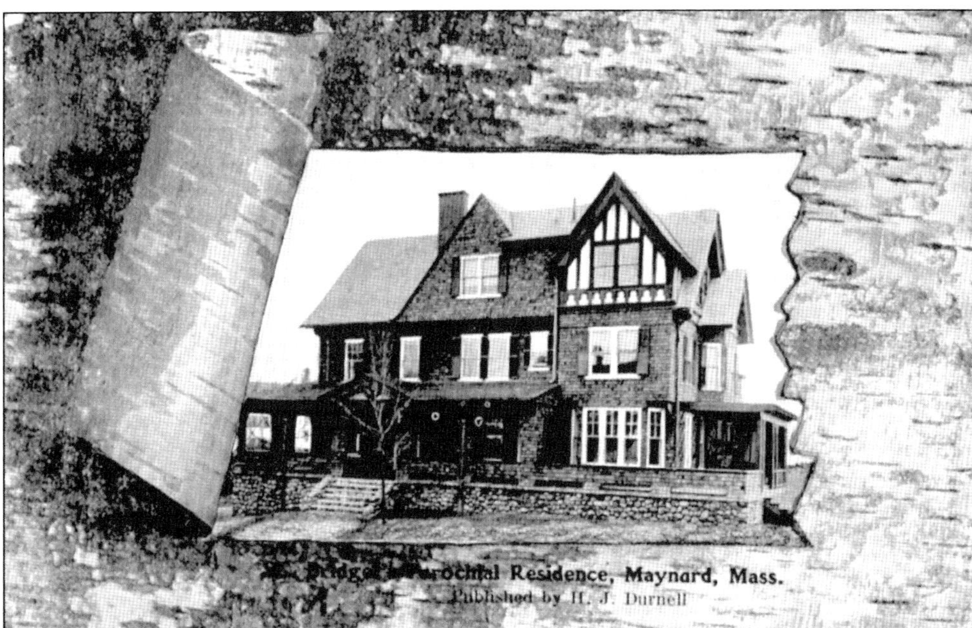


**ST. BRIDGET'S PAROCHIAL RESIDENCE.** This residence is located on Percival Street and was built in 1905.

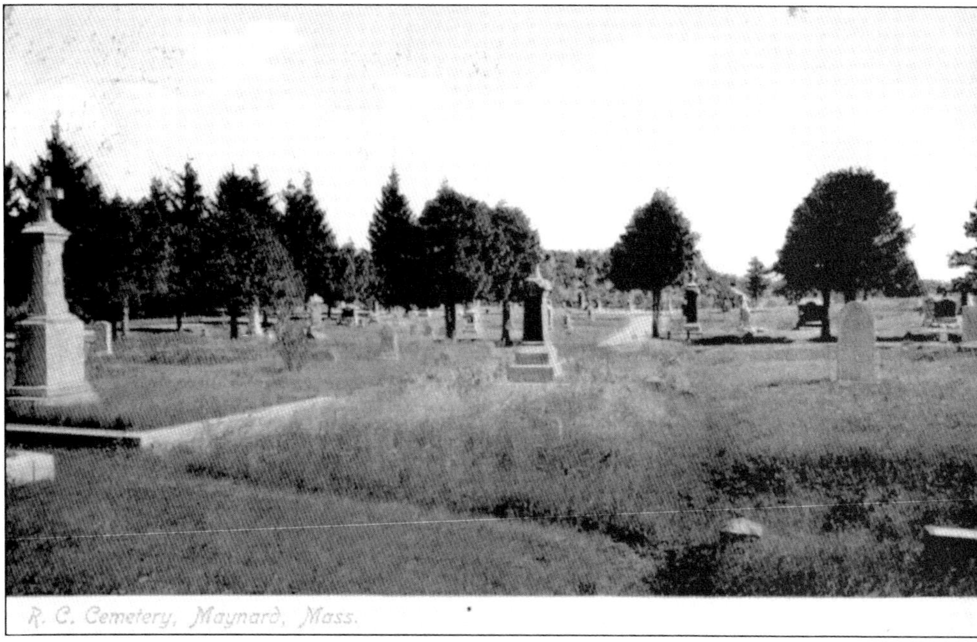


**ROMAN CATHOLIC CEMETERY ON GREAT ROAD.** A Civil War veteran, James Heffernan was the first one interred into this cemetery shortly after it was opened.

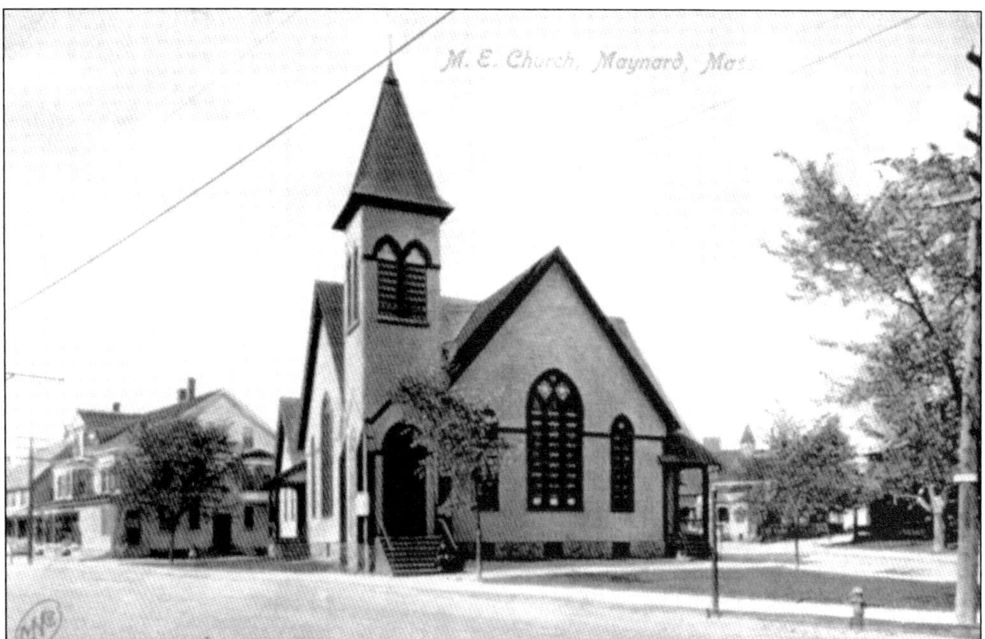


**MAYNARD METHODIST CHURCH.** Methodist services were carried on at Union Hall until the present Maynard Methodist Church was built and dedicated in 1895. Union Hall, in the background, is presently used as a multifamily home.

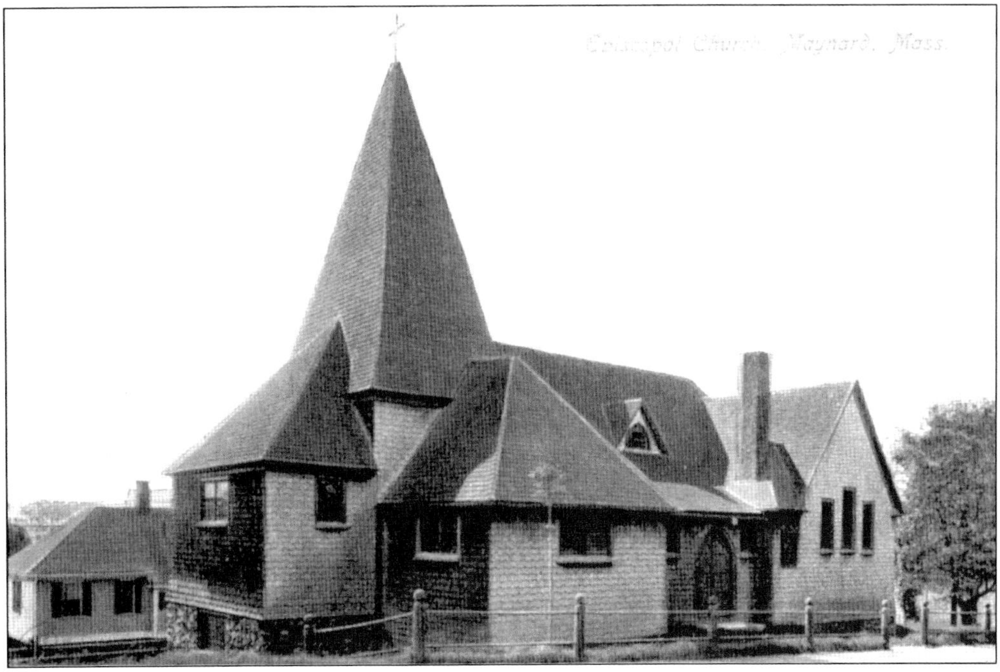


**EPISCOPAL CHURCH.** Episcopal services began in May 1899. The cornerstone of the present church was laid August 10, 1895, with the first service taking place the following Christmas.

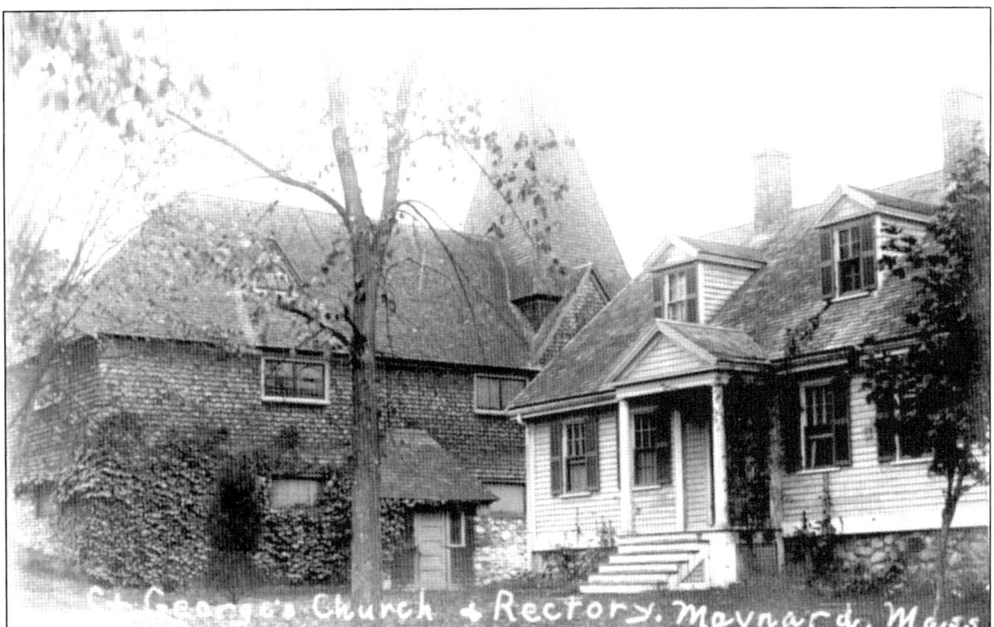


**ST. GEORGE'S CHURCH AND RECTORY.** St. George's Episcopal parsonage is located on 25 Florida Road and is next to the church. (Courtesy of MHS.)

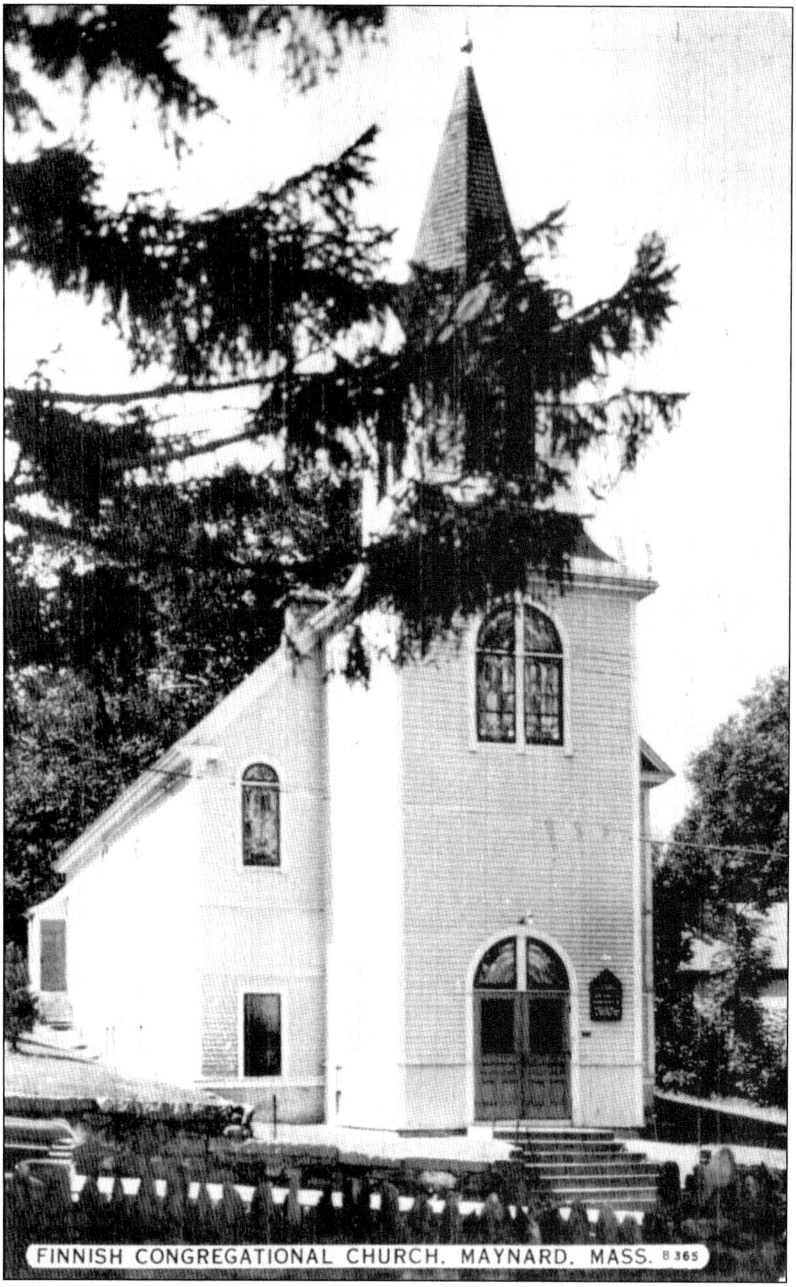


**FINNISH CONGREGATIONAL CHURCH.** This church was established as a pastorate in 1903, the cornerstone of the church building was laid at the corner of Walnut and Thompson Streets on May 23, 1913, and on December 19, the church dedication took place. H. C. Templeton, the mill superintendent, was asked if he would give the mill's famous and historic "curfew bell" to the church, and he did so. The curfew bell, as it was known, signaled to the mill employees each night that it was 9:00 and that they were to be at home and in bed. Amory Maynard, their employer, cautioned them that if they were found on the streets after the bell was sounded, the employees would lose their job in his company for failing to abide by its rules. This bell, cast in England in 1856, now is in the belfry of the Finnish Congregational Church.

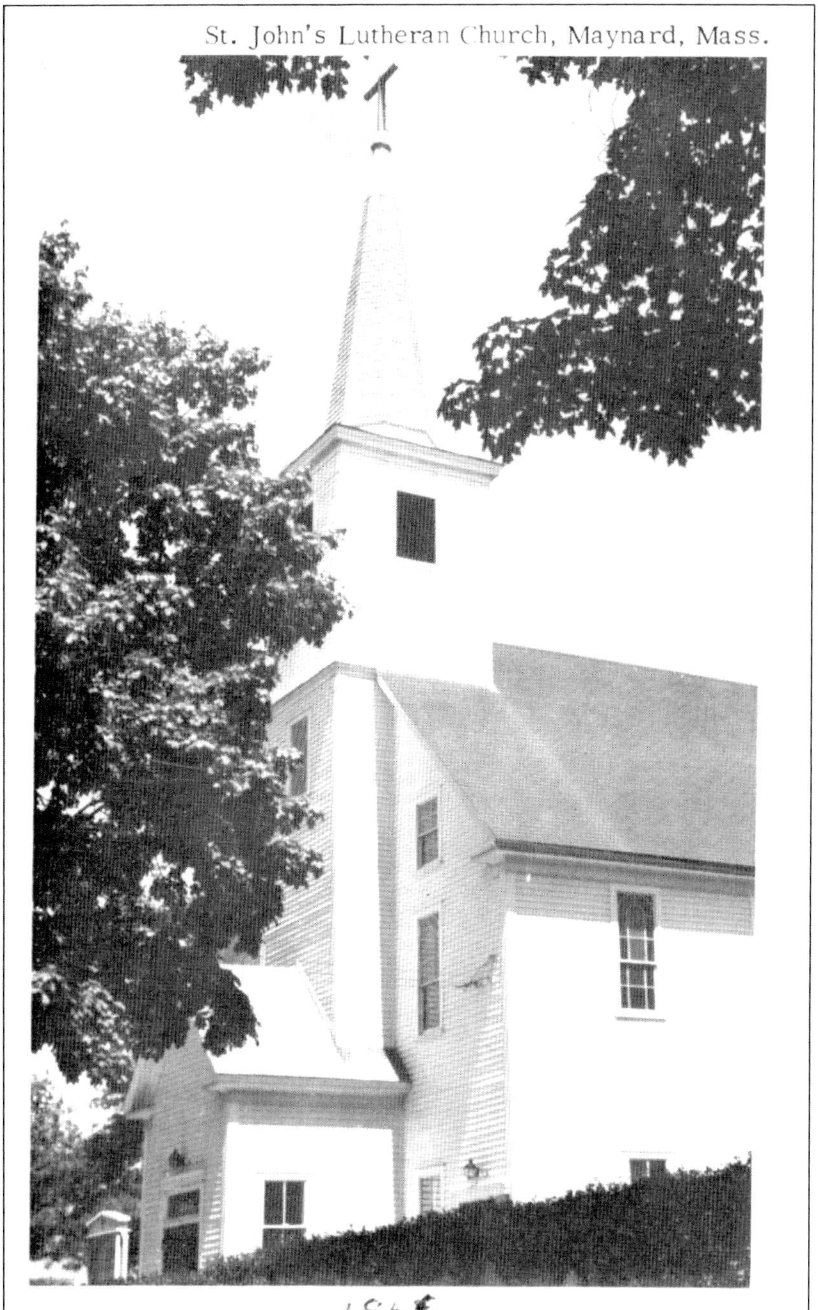


**ST. JOHN'S LUTHERAN CHURCH.** The first families of this church are reported to have settled on River Street. Topi Saisa, John H. Simons, John Hendrickson (Wirtala), Kansaoja, Henry Launola, and Weckstrom were among the first. Many of the later ones settled on farms throughout the entire Acton, Stow, Maynard, and Sudbury area. By 1894, they were numerous enough so that the Evangelical Lutheran Church was founded, and the church building was erected on Glendale Street in 1907–1908 and dedicated in June 1908. In 1967, the church moved to a new building over the town line in Sudbury, at the junction of Great Road and Waltham Street.

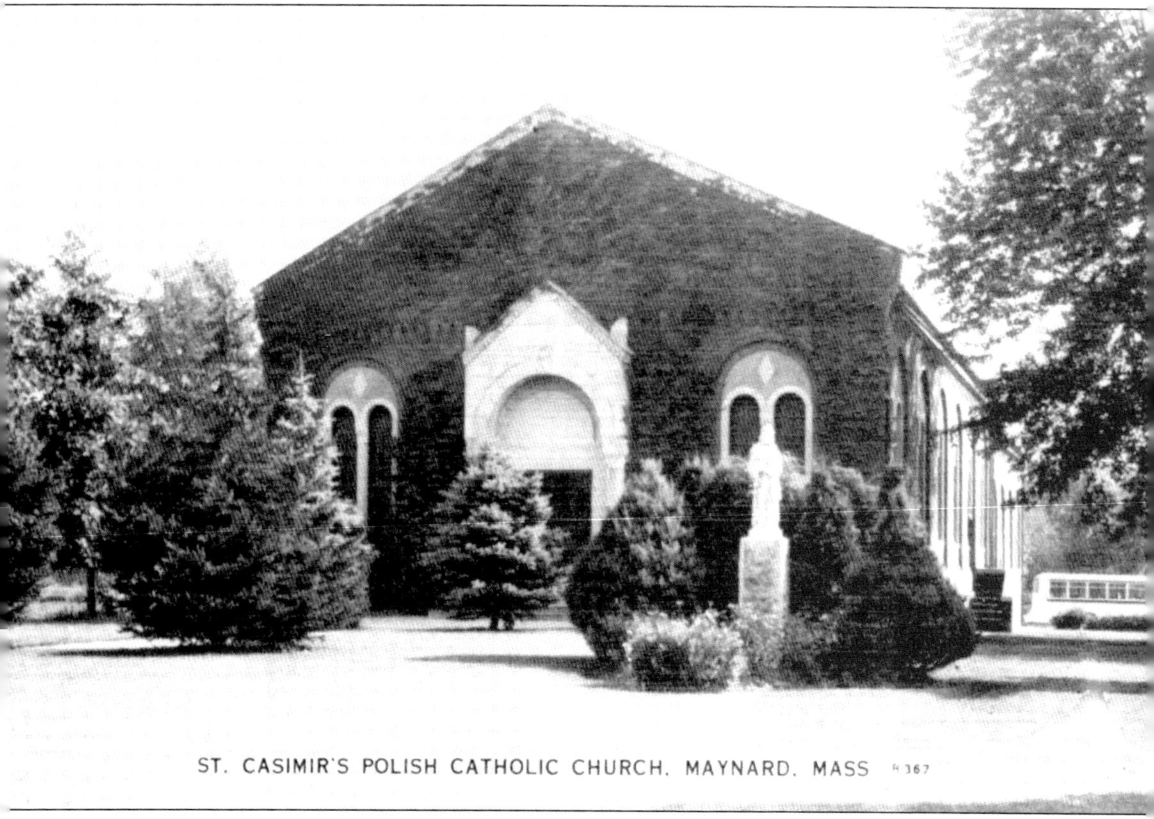


**ST. CASMIR'S ROMAN CATHOLIC CHURCH.** In 1926, St. Casmir's parish purchased the old streetcar company's power station and land. The building was remodeled into the present church. A Lovell bus can be seen in the back of the church. The Lovell Bus Company operated from 1925 until 1954 out of the old trolley barn that was located next door to the church.

## *Nine*

# EDUCATION

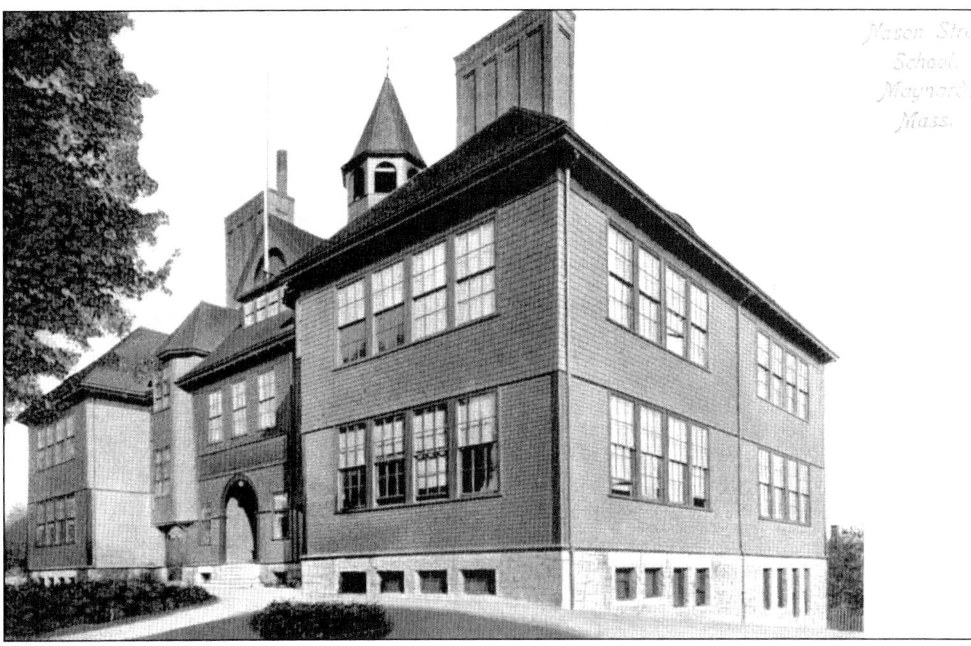


**THE SECOND NASON STREET SCHOOL.** On September 10, 1892, the new 12-room schoolhouse on Nason Street, costing $20,927, was opened, and it was dedicated on October 5. A September 12, 1916, fire caused $200 damage to the assembly hall on the top floor. On the night of September 20, 1916, the building was destroyed by fire.

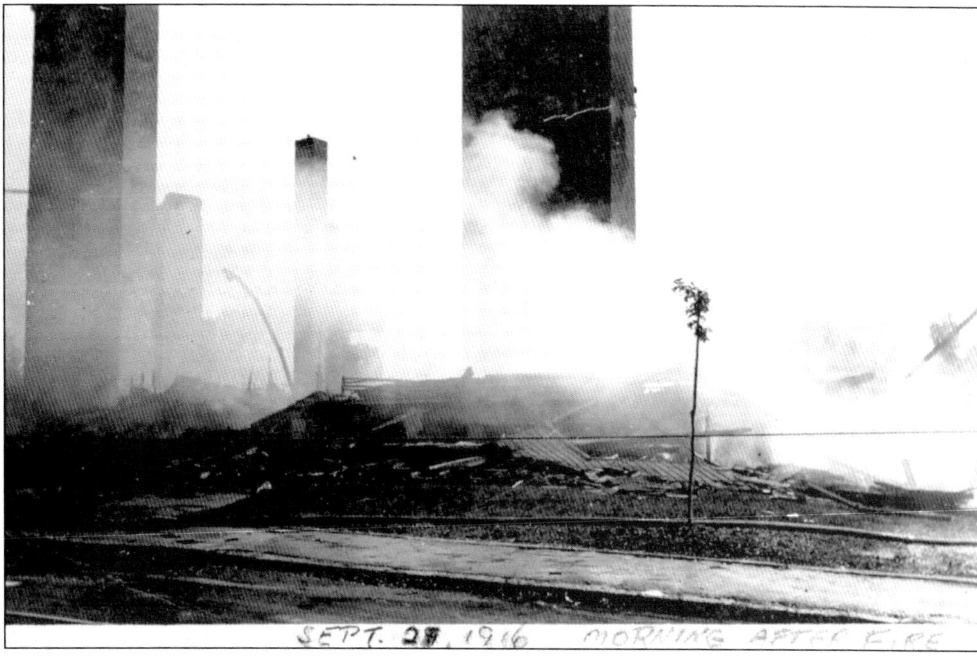


**Nason Street High School.** There is not much remaining of the school, which burnt to the ground on September 20, 1916. Roosevelt School was then built on the school's foundation. (Courtesy of MHS.)

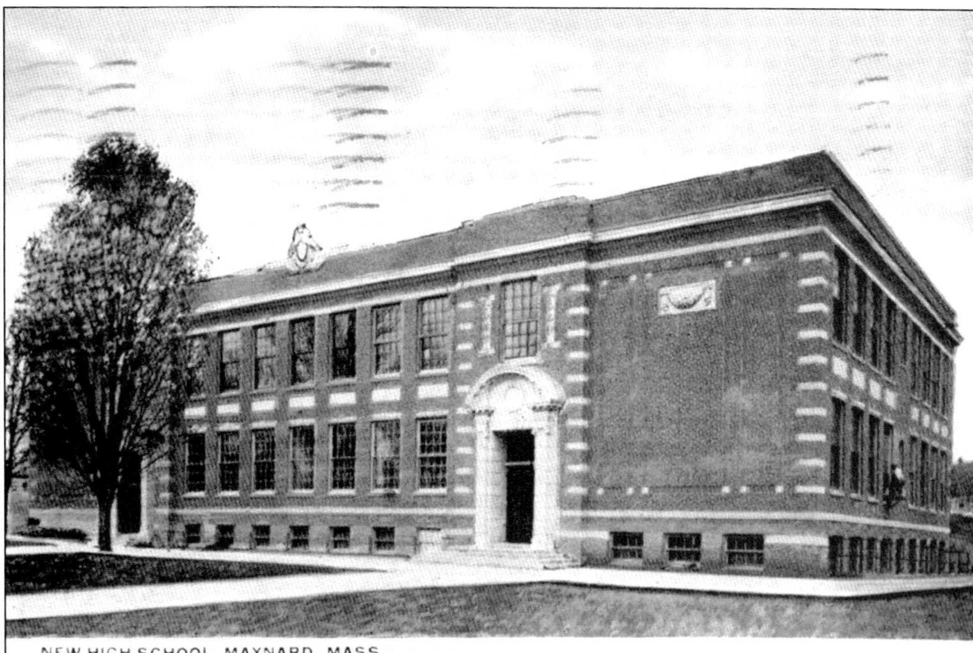


**Maynard High School.** On January 13, 1915, the town meeting voted to purchase land on Summer Street and to build a high school. The building, costing $61,600, was completed and occupied on October 2, 1916. On March 14, 1932, it was voted to name this the Maynard High School. In 1964, this school was renamed the Fowler School.

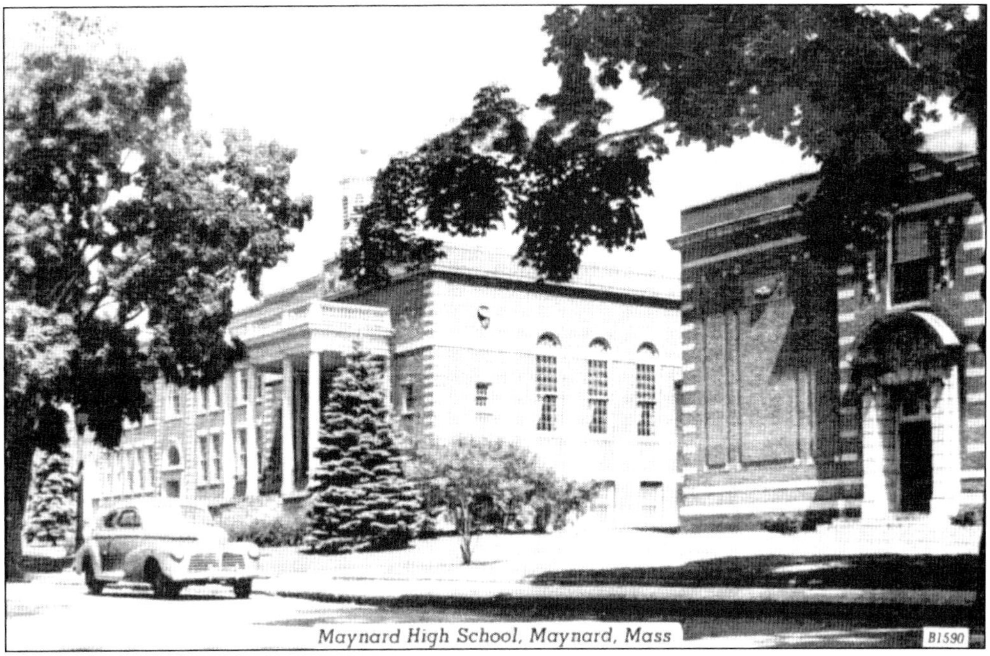


**GEORGE WASHINGTON AUDITORIUM AND GYMNASIUM.** This addition was opened in 1926. The gymnasium was found too small for regular indoor major meets, and a member of the building committee is said to have remarked, "half of the citizens wanted a gymnasium and the other half did not; so the town built half a gymnasium."

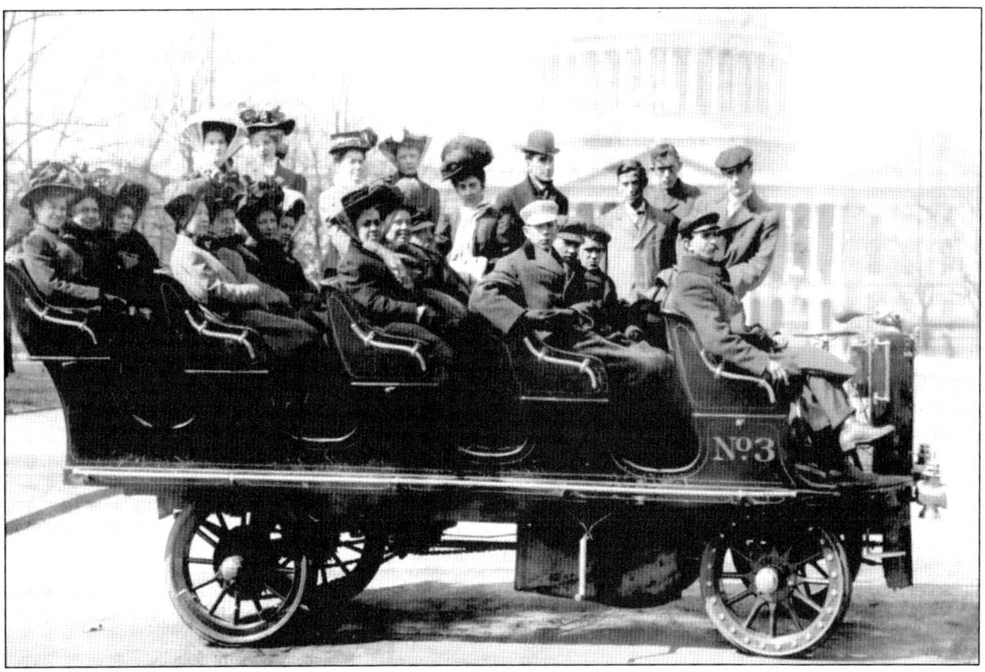


**WASHINGTON FIELD TRIP.** The Maynard High School class of 1909 poses in a tourist vehicle in Washington, D.C. The class was touring around Washington to visit its historic sites. (Courtesy of MHS.)

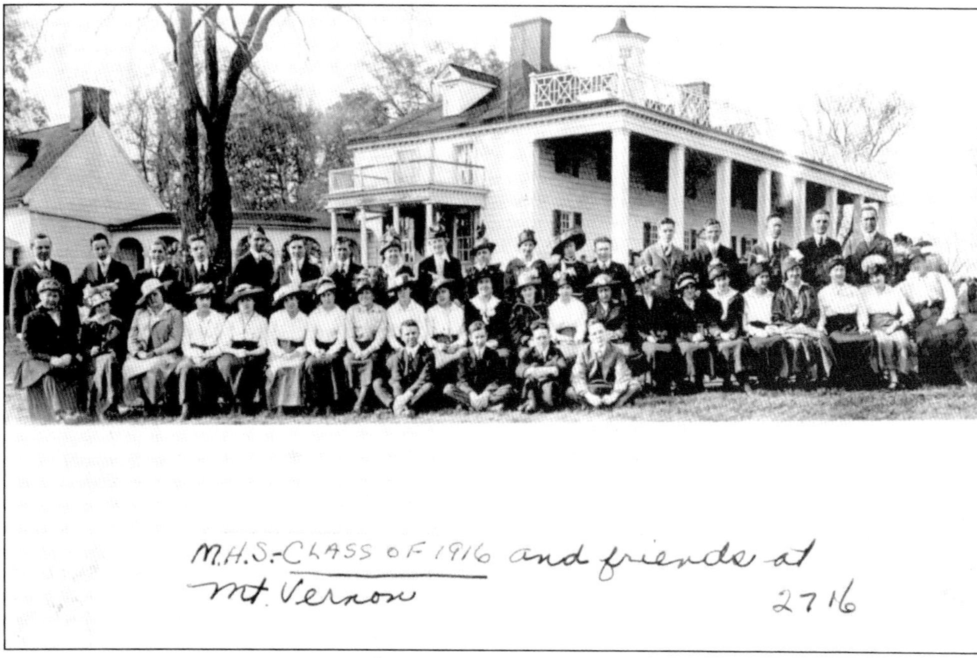


**MOUNT VERNON FIELD TRIP.** The Maynard High School class of 1916 lines up for a class picture in front of Mount Vernon during their class trip to the Washington, D.C. area. (Courtesy of MHS.)

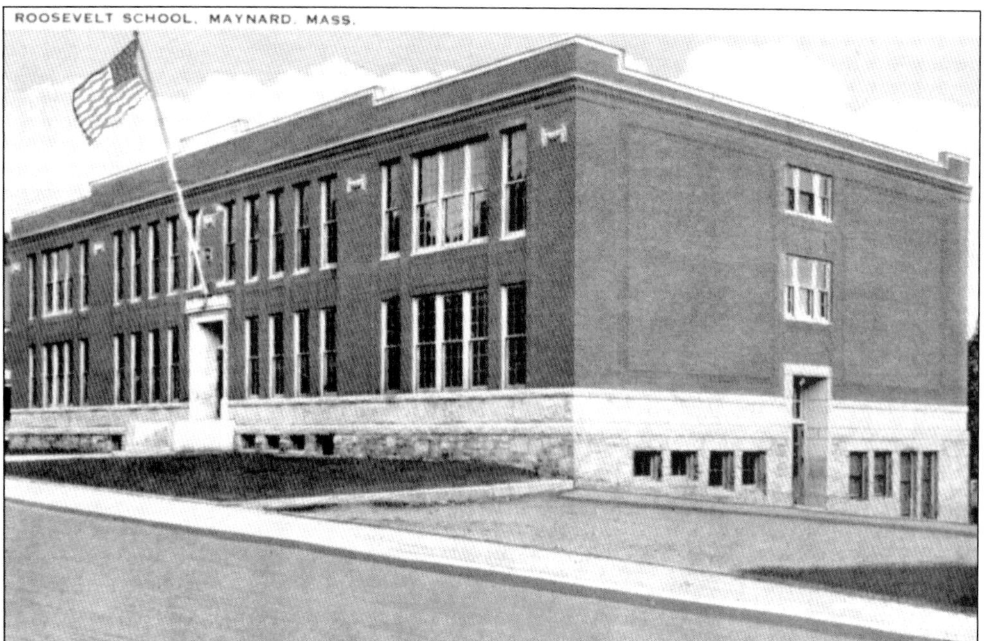


**THE THIRD NASON STREET SCHOOL.** On October 4, 1916, the town voted to build a two-story, 14-room grade school building on the Nason Street site. The new school was opened May 4, 1918, ready for classes. The fall classes started five weeks late that year due to an influenza epidemic. It was built at a cost of $70,000.

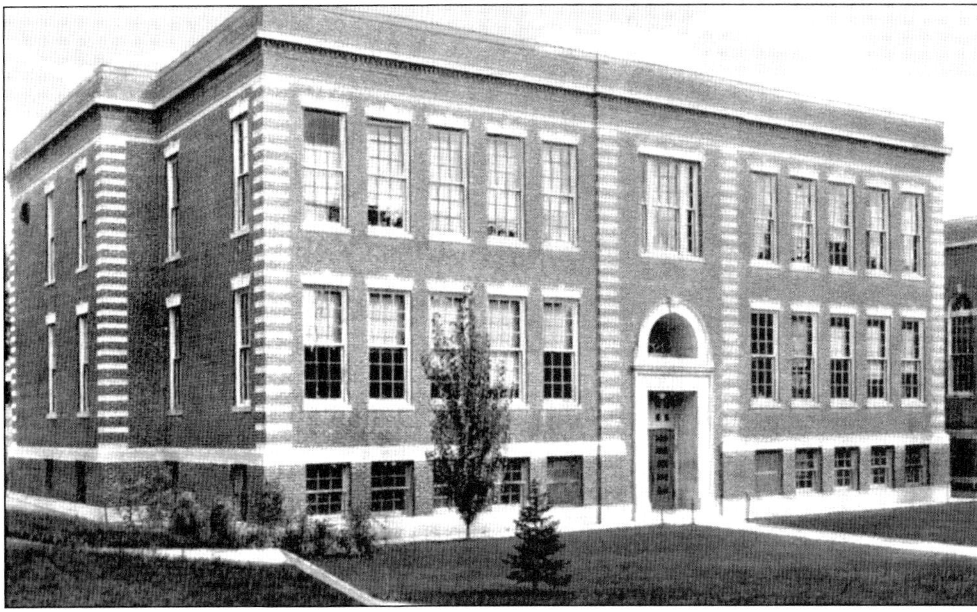

**Emerson Junior High School.** On March 9, 1925, a vote was passed to erect an eight-room school building on Summer Street. The junior high school was opened for classes on January 19, 1926. On March 14, 1932, a vote to name this school the Emerson Junior High School passed. In 1964, this school was renamed the Guyer W. Fowler Elementary School.

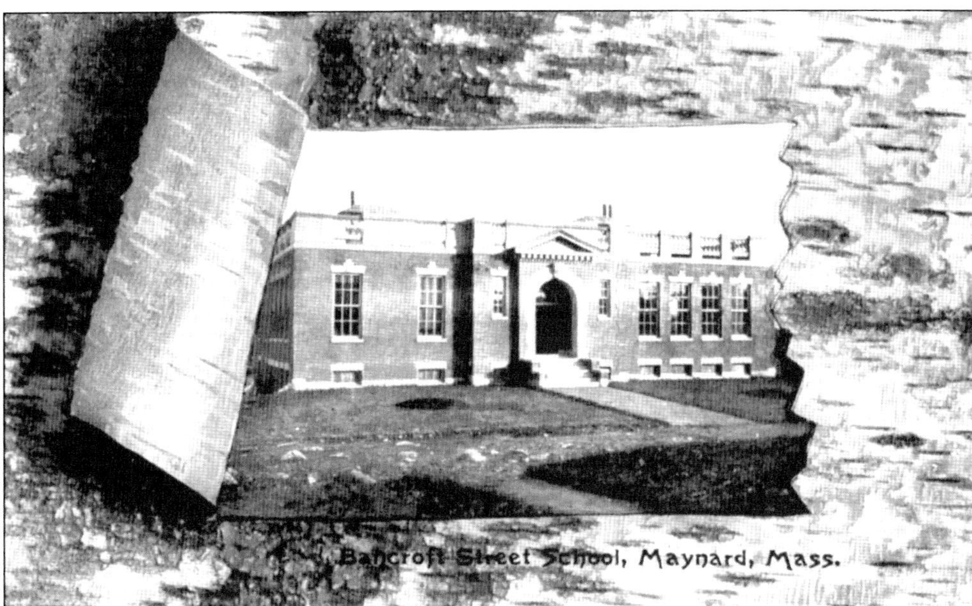


**Bancroft Street School.** This school was built in 1906 on Bancroft Street. In 1909, it was voted to add another story at a cost of $12,000.

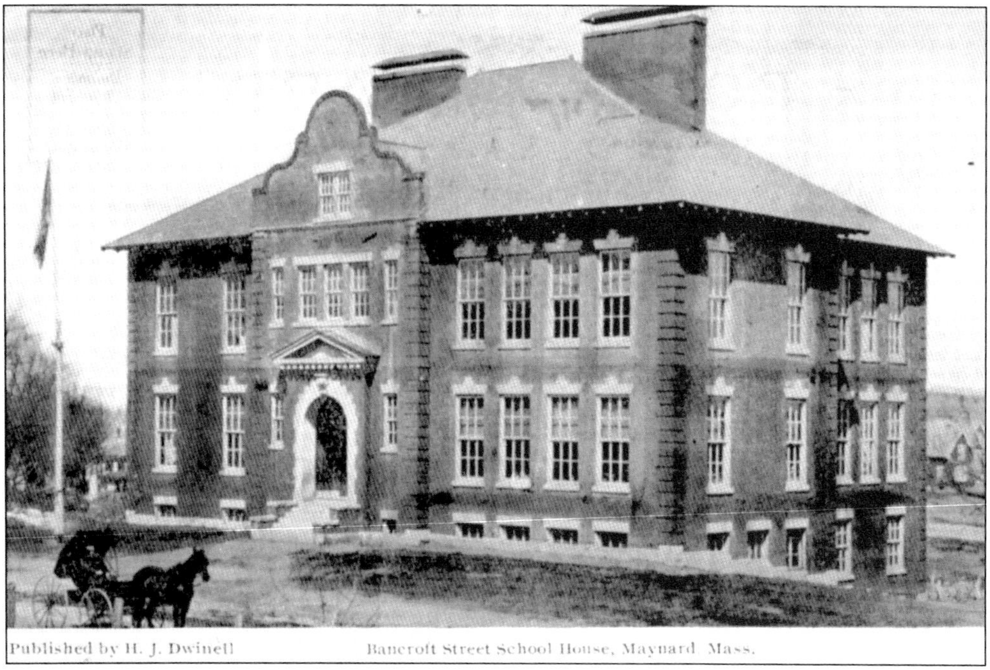


**BANCROFT STREET SCHOOL.** On May 16, 1905, it was voted to purchase 18 lots of land on Parker Street for $1,800 and to build on it a four-room brick school building. In September 1906, this school, known as the Bancroft Street School, was completed at a cost of $20,831. In 1910, another story to the building was added at a cost of $12,000. On March 14, 1932, the school was renamed Calvin Coolidge School.

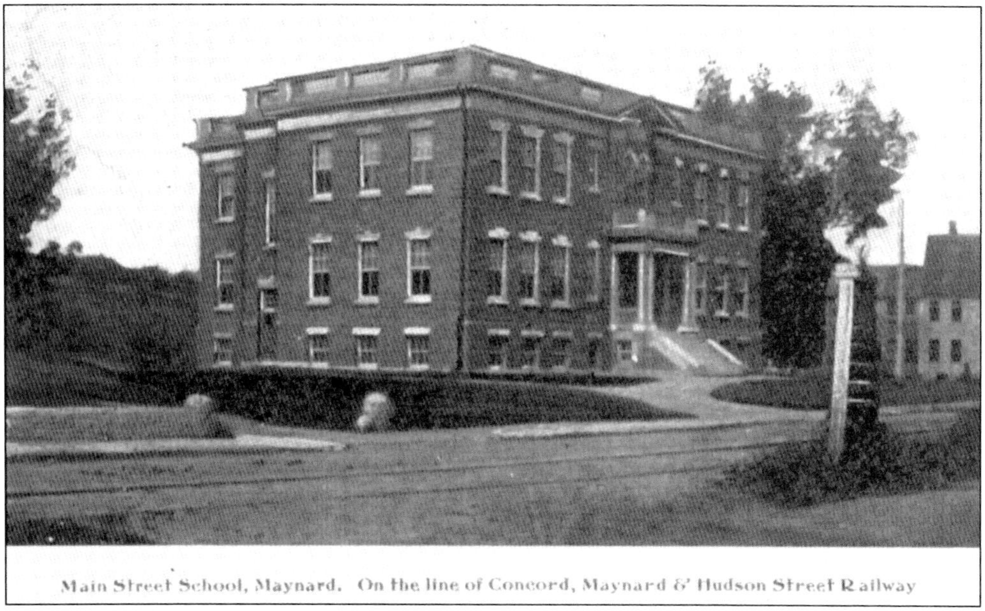


**THE SECOND MAIN STREET SCHOOL.** On April 7, 1902, it was decided to build a new brick school building of six rooms on the Main Street school site. The new school was the first town-owned building to be built of brick. The new building, which cost $25,000, was dedicated on April 19, 1903.

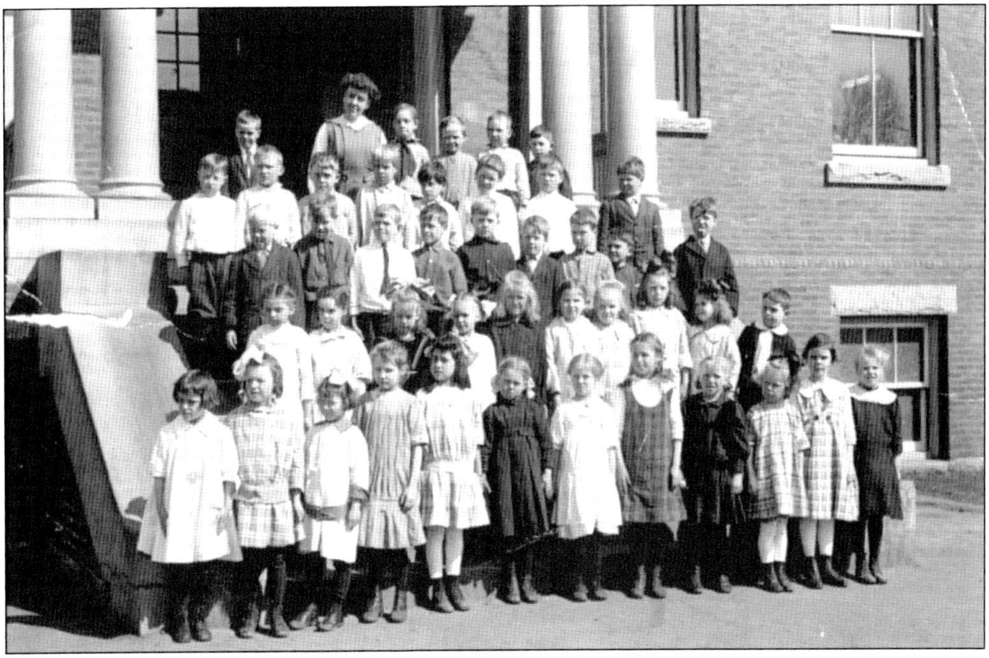

**WILSON SCHOOL PUPILS.** Students of the Woodrow Wilson School on Main Street line up on the front stairs to take a class picture. The picture was taken in the 1930s. (Courtesy of MHS.)

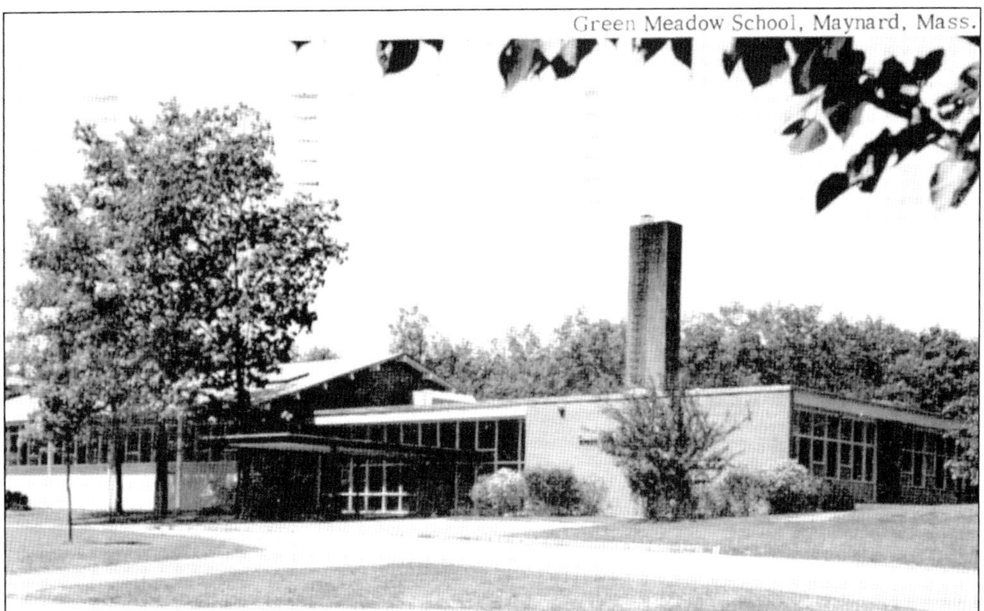


**GREEN MEADOW SCHOOL.** At a special town meeting held in the Peoples Theatre on April 26, 1954, it was voted to build an elementary school on the portion of the land that was originally annexed to the John A. Crowe Park. This school was built at a cost of $382,000 and was opened September 5, 1956. The school children suggested the name Green Meadow School.

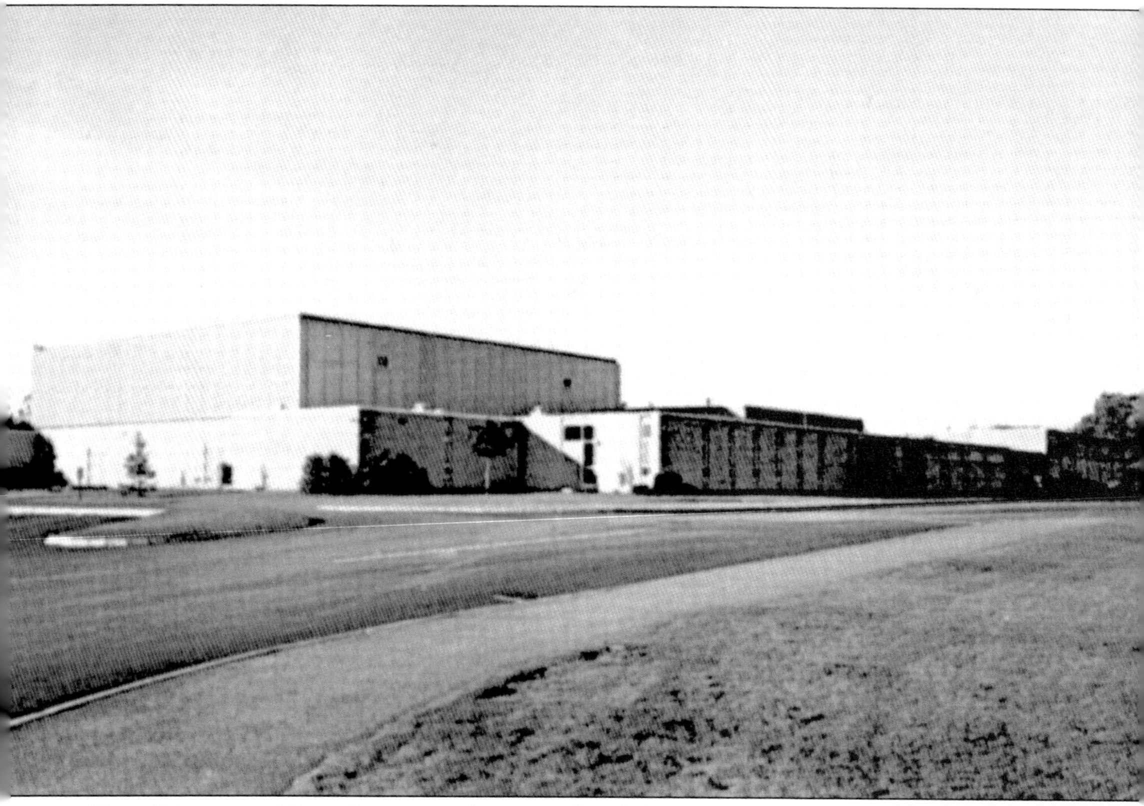

**NEW MAYNARD HIGH SCHOOL.** The town decided to construct a high school building on town-owned land off Great Road at a cost of $1,694,000. A motion to name this school the John F. Kennedy High School was defeated at town meeting; however, the gymnasium at the school was named the John F. Kennedy Memorial Gymnasium. The school opened for classes in September 1964.

*Ten*

# ORGANIZATIONS, SOCIETIES, AND POTPOURRI

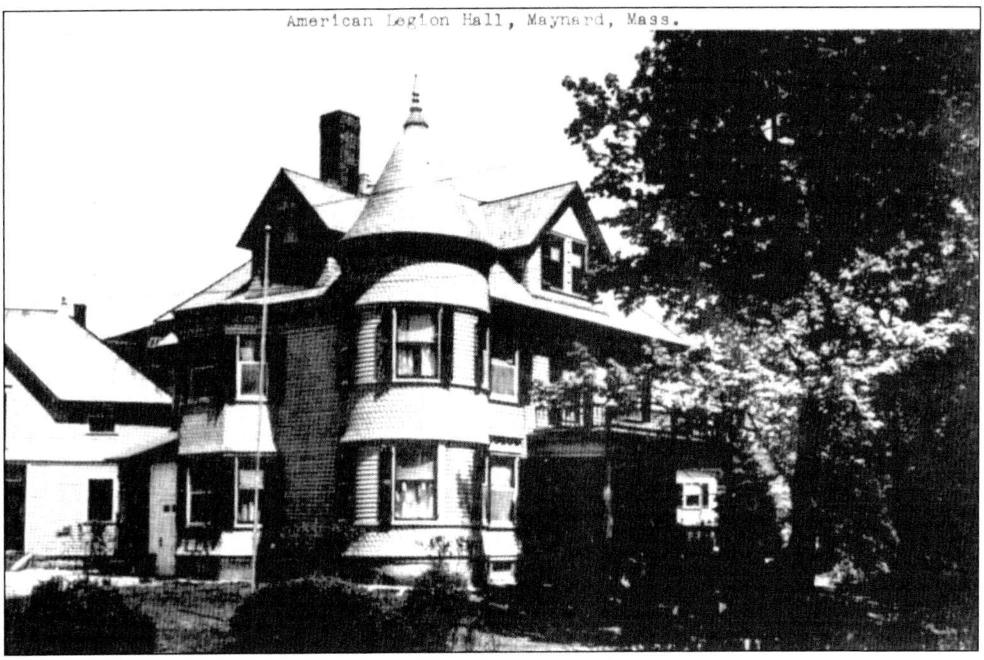


**AMERICAN LEGION.** On April 16, 1946, the Legion post purchased the former Abel G. Haynes residence on Summer Street to use as their headquarters. The American Legion post No. 235 was formed October 22, 1919.

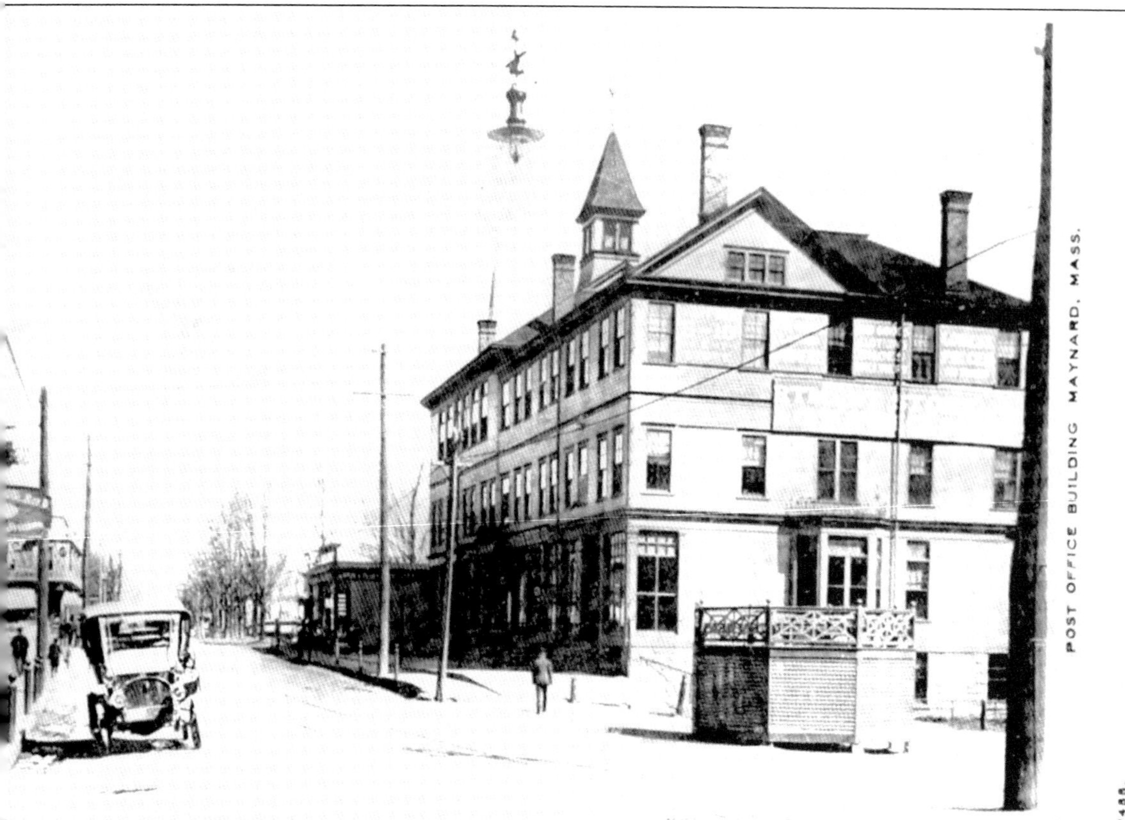


**TOWN BANDSTAND.** A bandstand was donated by Abel G. Haynes in 1904. It stood at the corner of Main and Walnut Streets until 1915. According to the local newspapers, thousands used to gather to hear concerts given by the three bands in town.

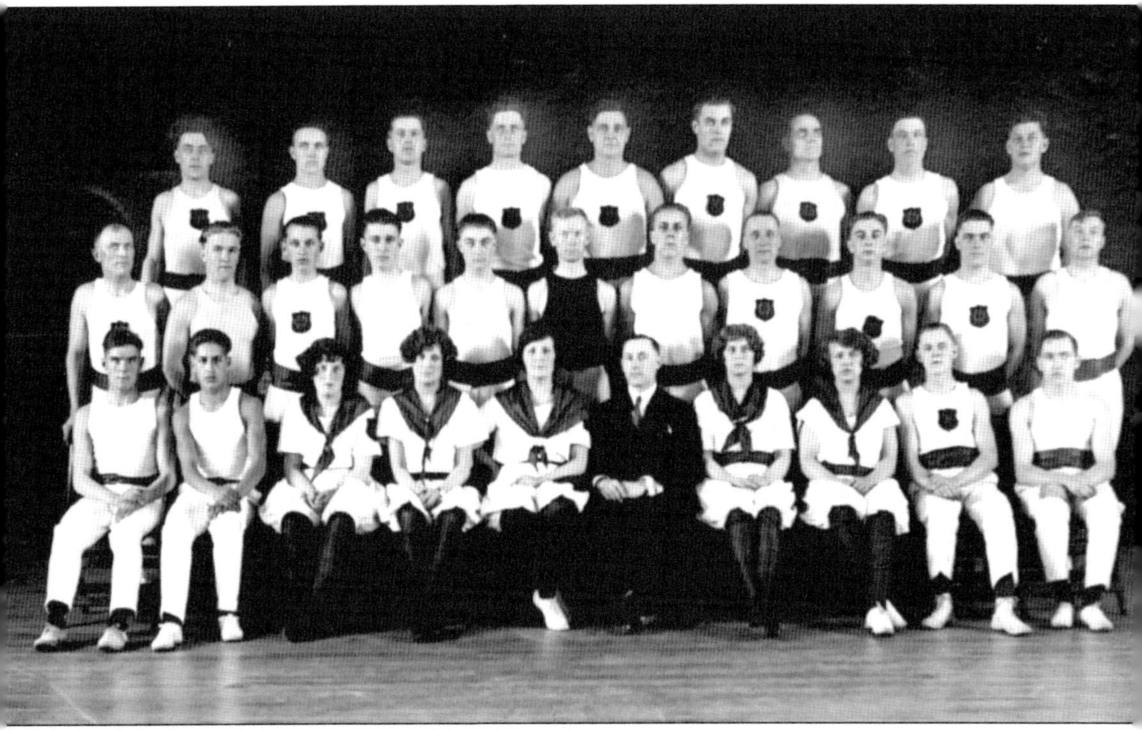

**GYMNASTIC TEAM.** The Finnish Workers' Federation was an off-shoot of the Finnish Workingmen's Socialist Society around 1920. The split was created by the emergence of the Soviet Union on the international scene, the federation people being sure that a socialist utopia was at hand. In many cases, the issue was taken so seriously there were divorces, or the husband would frequent one hall and the wife the other. A hall was built in 1922 (Waltham Street Hall), which was destroyed by fire in 1932, forcing the federation to move to the Russian Powder Mill Road Hall.

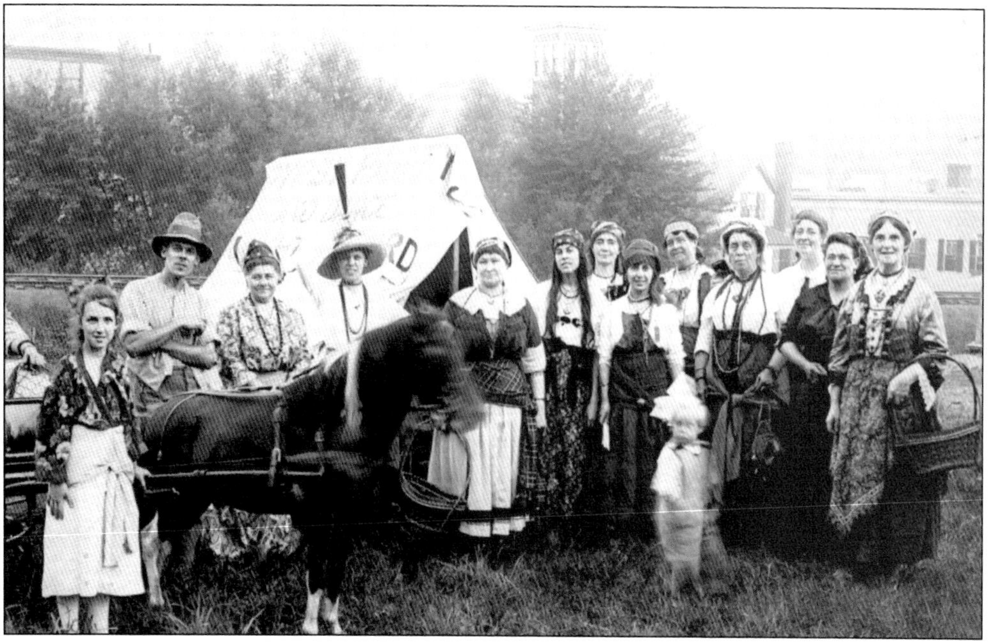

**GRANGE PARTY.** This picture shows a 1904 gathering of the Grange at a field off Summer Street at the present location of Century-21 Classic Properties.

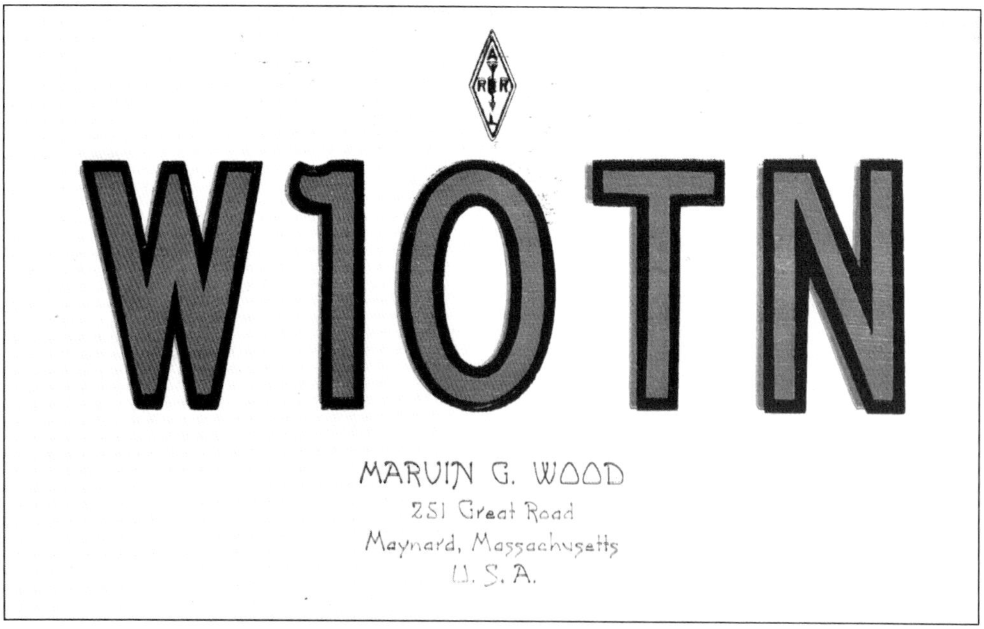


**HAM CARD.** When ham radio members contacted one another, they would send a confirmation card. Here is a 1959 card sent by ham radio enthusiast Marvin Wood of Maynard.

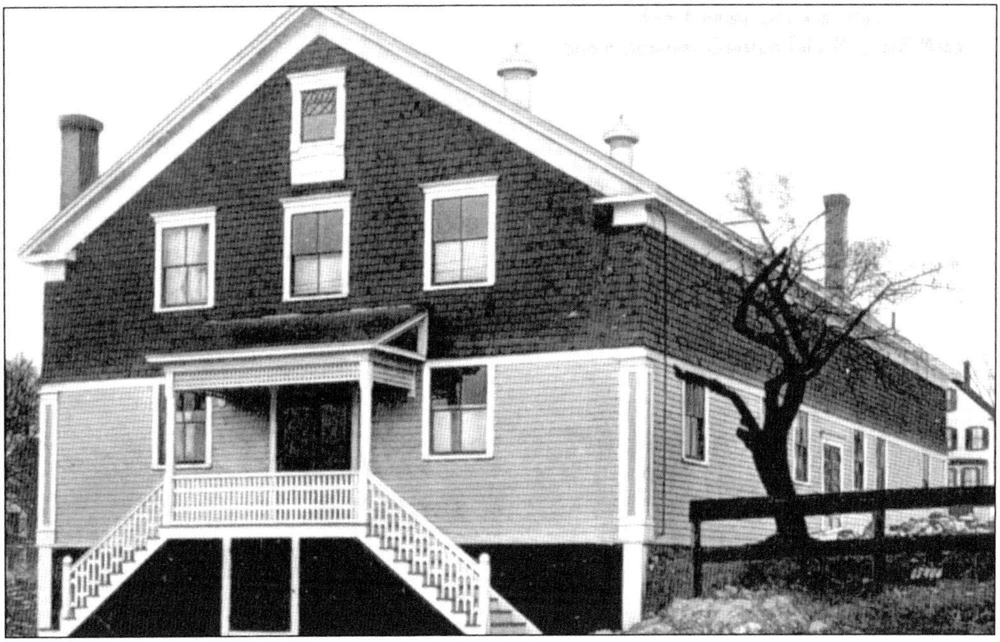

**PARKER STREET HALL AND IMATRA BAND.** In 1903, the Finnish Workingmen's Socialist Society was organized. It carried on socialist education, sports, dramas, gymnastics, wrestling, acrobatics, dances, and program evenings. It bought the Vose's Pond area and set up the pavilion and track and fixed up the pond for swimming. The Imatra Band (below) became part of this society, and the Tarmo Athletic Club was organized, which participated in all sports. Parker Street Hall was built by the society in 1909 and enlarged in 1916. The hall was sold in 1969. The United Cooperative Society was initiated by this group. With the passing of years, the Finnish Workingmen's Socialist Society as a viable group is now just a memory. The facility was sold to the Boys' Club in 1969.

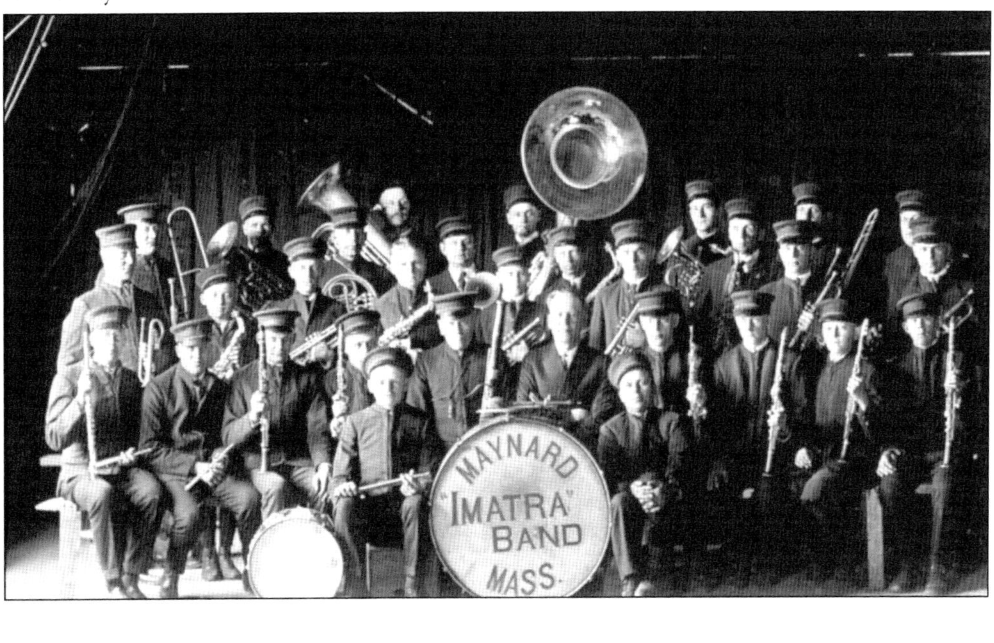

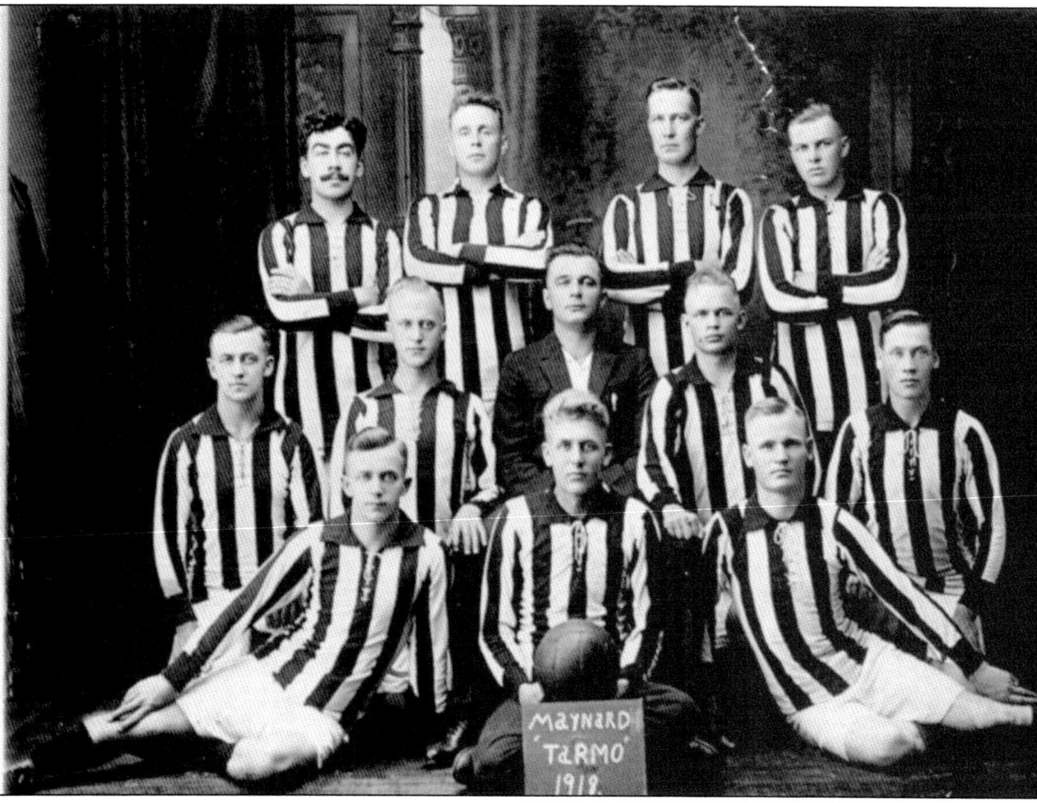


**GYMNASTIC TEAM.** The Alku Temperance Society was founded in 1895 and moved March 23, 1900, from Harriman Court to the Whitney Building on Acton Street. On July 29, 1910, the society moved to its new building on the corner of Harriman Court and Main Street, where it remained until the organization disbanded in the early 1960s. Activities of the society included program evenings, dramas, chorus, the National Band, and the Kanto Athletic Club. (Courtesy of MHS.)

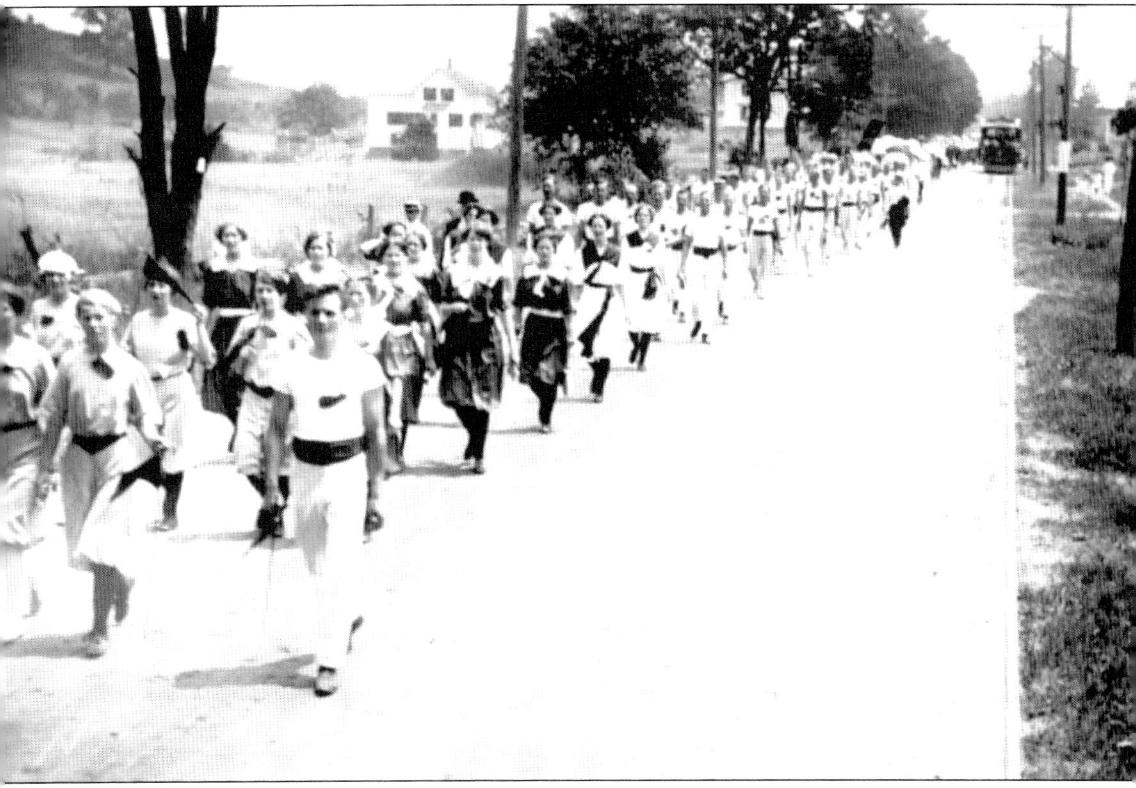

**WALKING TO SUMMER PLACE.** The Alku Temperance Society is walking on Power Mill Road toward their summer place at West Concord. Notice the trolley tracks on the right. In the distance is a trolley car on its way to Concord.

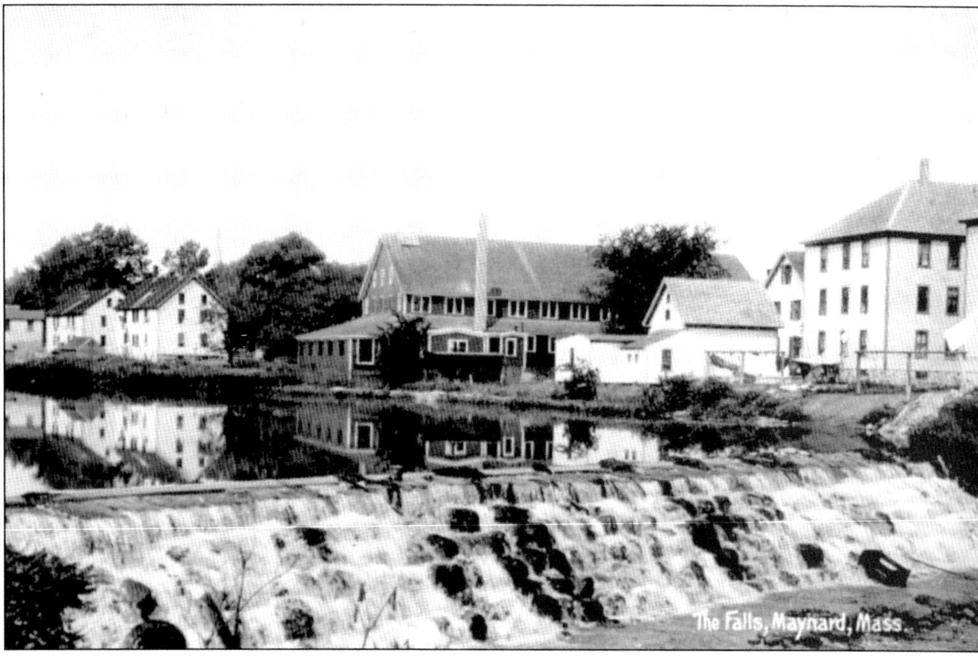


**Paper Mill Dam.** This is the way the paper mill dam looked in the early 20th century. The large building in the center is the Music Hall, or "Rink."

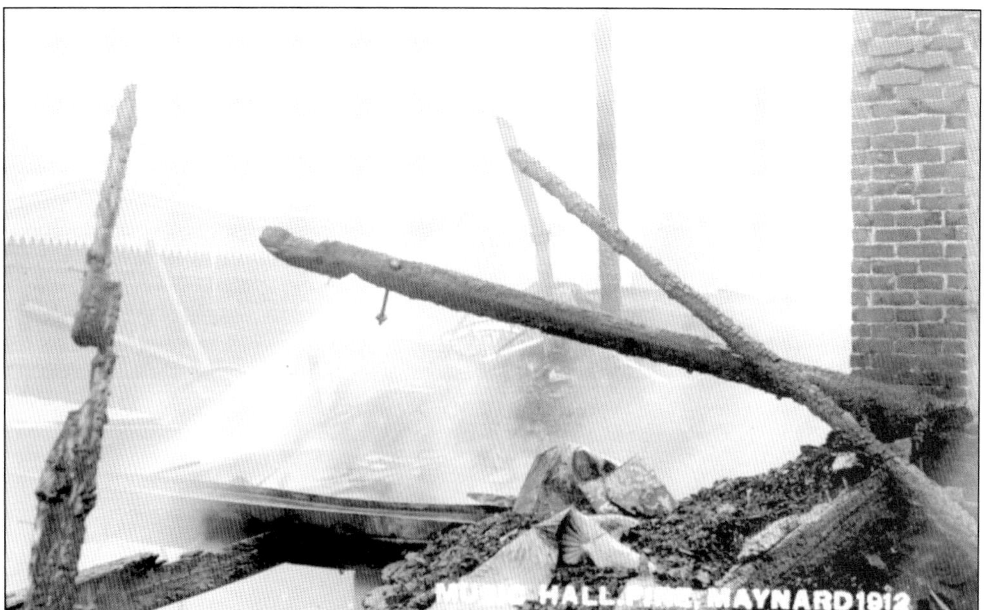


**Music Hall Fire in 1912.** The Music Hall, better known as the Rink, was erected in 1884 by Lorenzo Maynard on Main Street. It was originally built as a roller-skating rink, and the first operators of the rink were Frank and Arthur Locke. The manager of the skating floor was Edward Nutting. (Courtesy of MHS.)

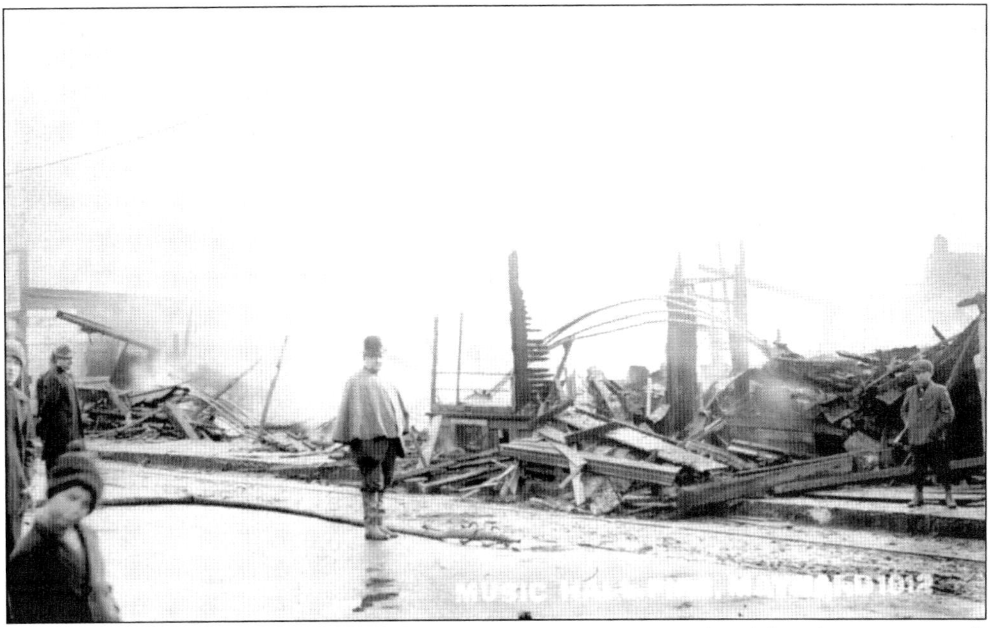

**RINK, 1912.** In this hall, many events of importance to the people of that day were staged. Many exciting roller polo games were played by the Maynard team, which was one of the best in New England. The basketball furor followed this, and Maynard became a hotbed for the sport with a team that took on most of the fastest teams in New England and some from upper New York State. (Courtesy of MHS.)

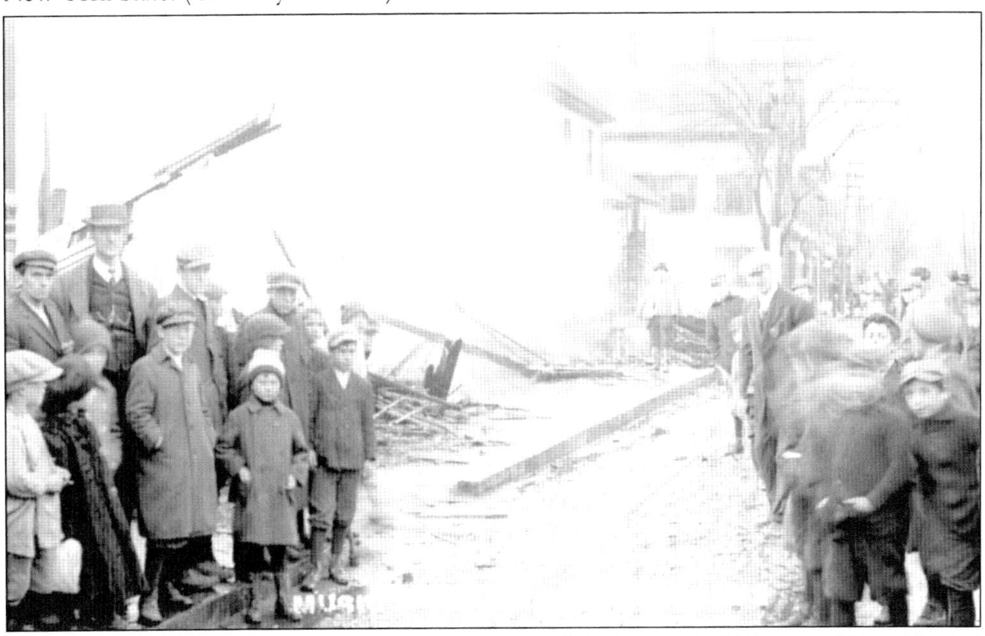

**DANCE HALL, 1912.** The great Merchant's Week exhibition was held here in 1901. Admiral William T. Sampson and Lt. Gov. John L. Bates honored the town with their presence. The building was later converted into a theater and general amusement hall. Many famous stock companies appeared on its stage. It was here that the original Maynard Dramatic Club performed during the early 20th century. (Courtesy of MHS.)

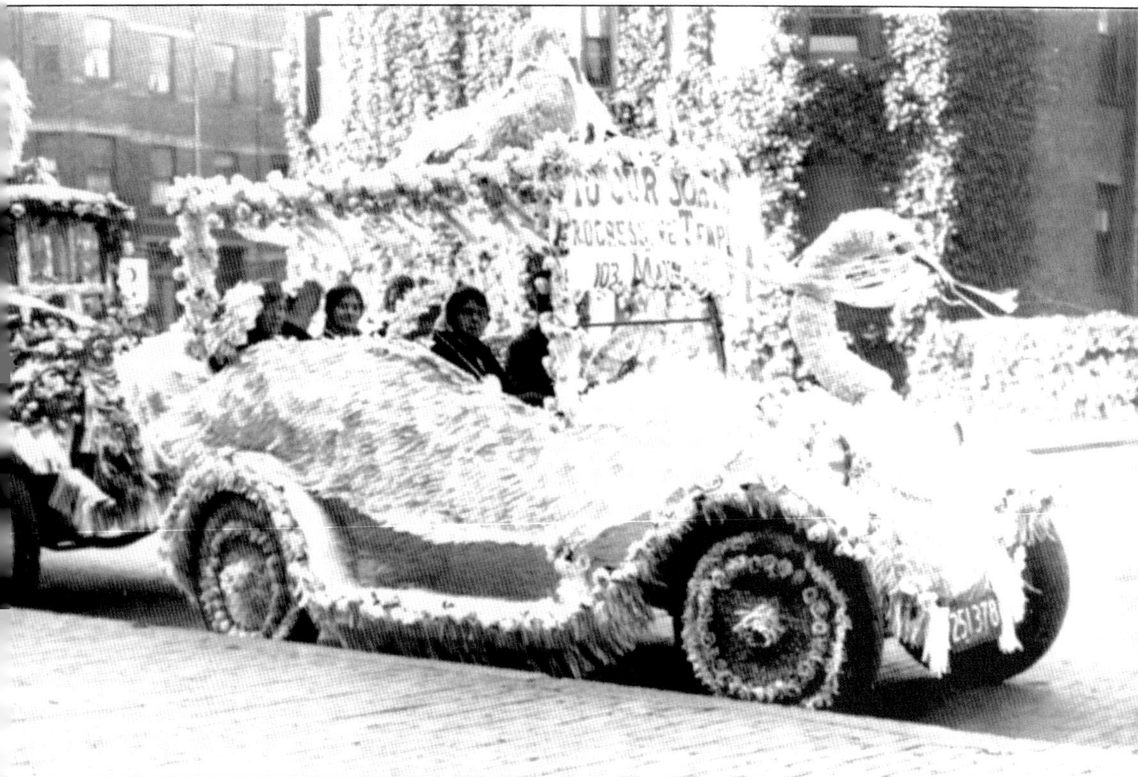

**KNIGHTS OF PYTHIAS FLOAT.** The Progressive Lodge of the Knights of Pythias was instituted July 25, 1898, to promote the principles of friendship, charity, and benevolence. Meetings were held at Masonic, Music and Riverside Cooperative Halls. At a meeting on July 15, 1921, a Temple of Pythian Sisters was instituted. The organization petered out during the 1940s, due possibly to the war.

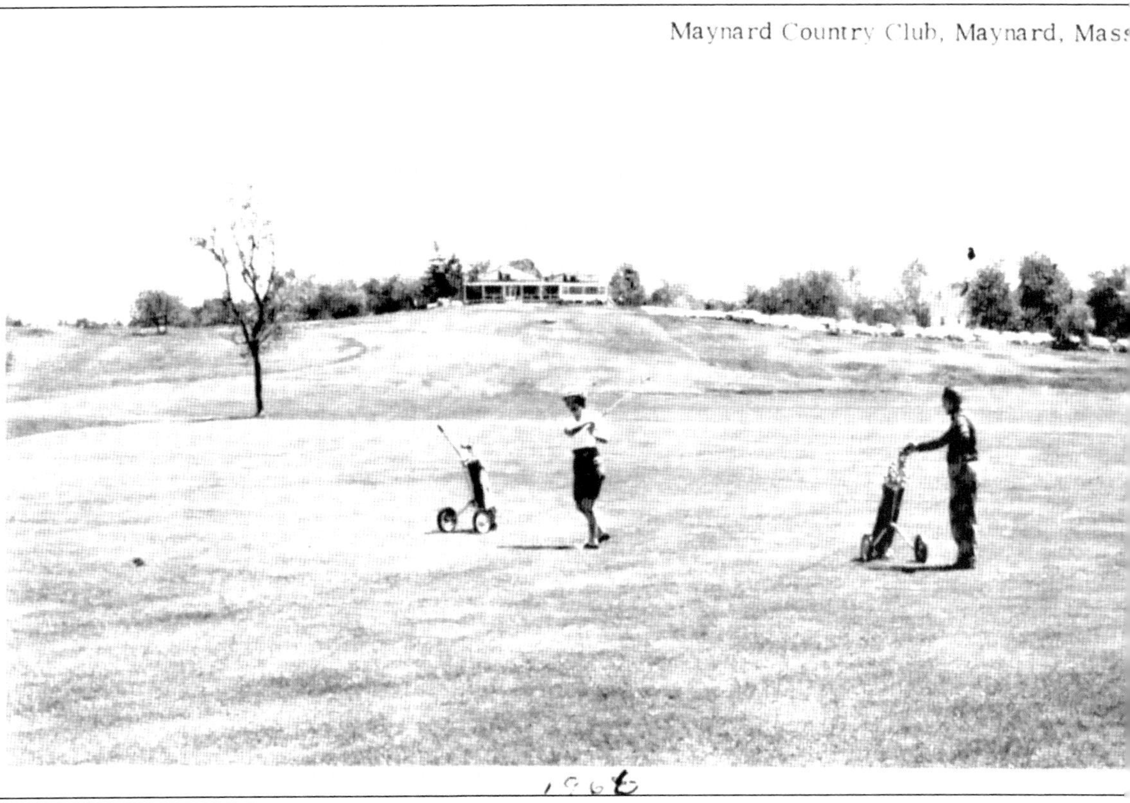


**MAYNARD COUNTRY CLUB.** The club was organized in 1921. The Calvin Whitney farm, comprising 68 acres of land, which was large enough to accommodate a nine-hole course, was purchased and the club started with 150 charter members. The present clubhouse was erected the following year, and several additions have been made to the original building. (Courtesy of MHS.)

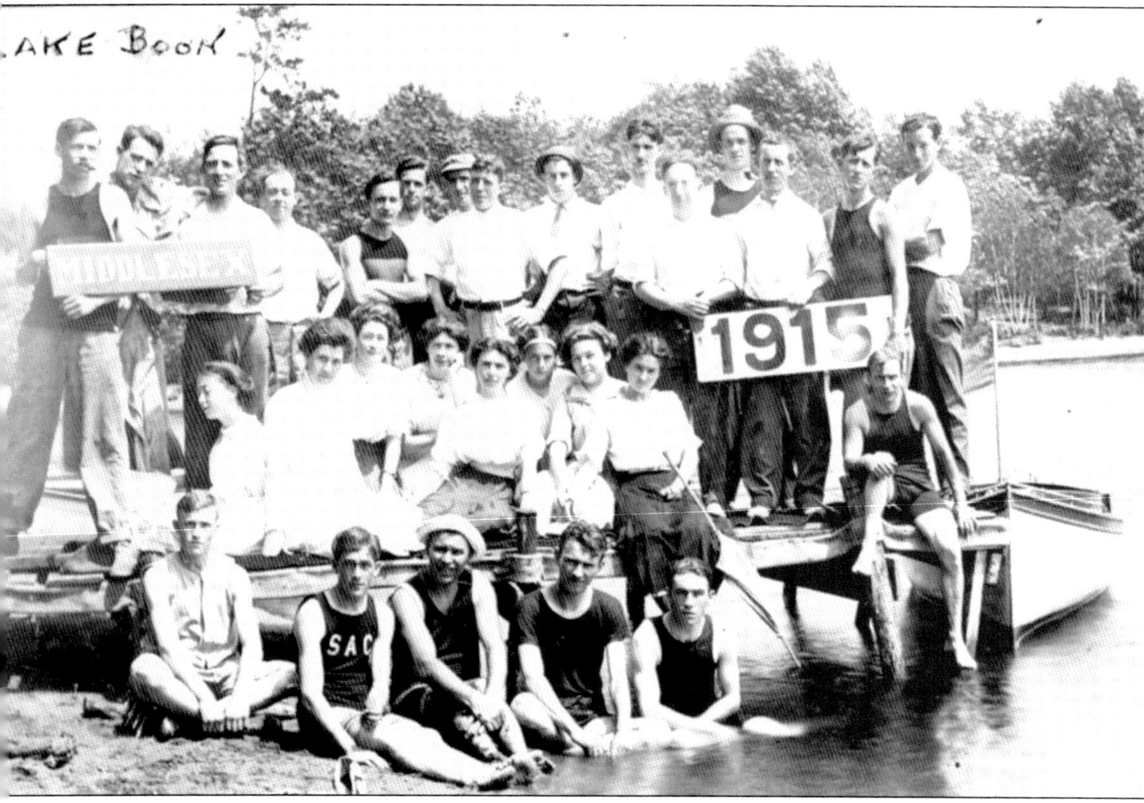


**THE MIDDLESEX CLUB.** This club was organized in 1910 by a group of Maynard young men who rented a cottage at Lake Boon. It disbanded in 1918 because almost the entire membership was in the armed forces of World War I. (Courtesy of MHS.)

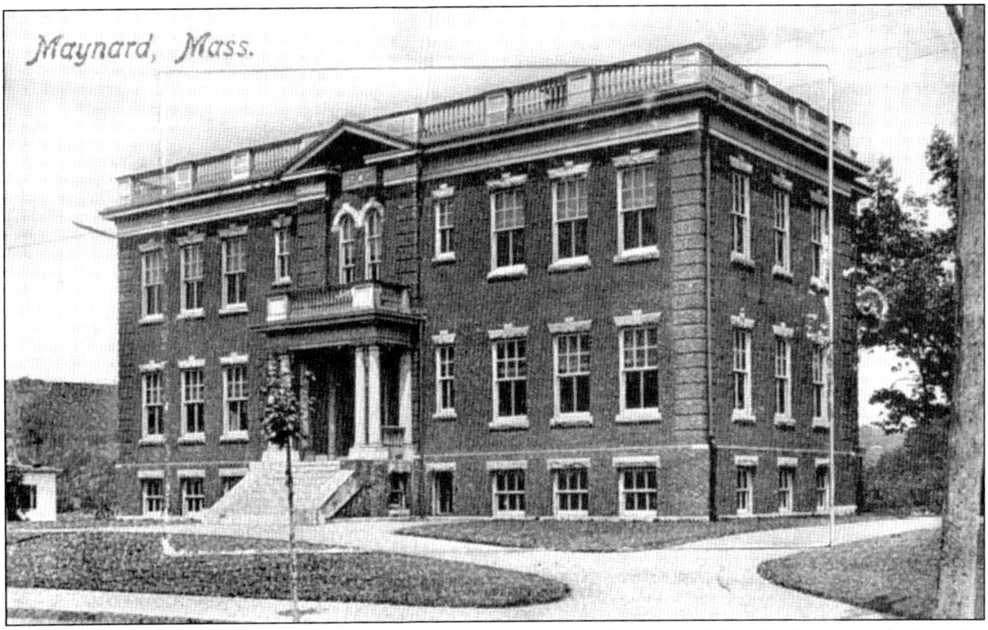


**SOUVENIR CARD.** In 1905, a Germany company created a special kind of postcard. On the address side it was identified as "Souvenir Mail Card" and was thicker and heavier than most postcards of the time. On the picture side was a local scene; here it showed one of the schools of Maynard. What made it unique was that a little flap opened on the picture to uncover a strip of 12 pictures of local sights. (See below).

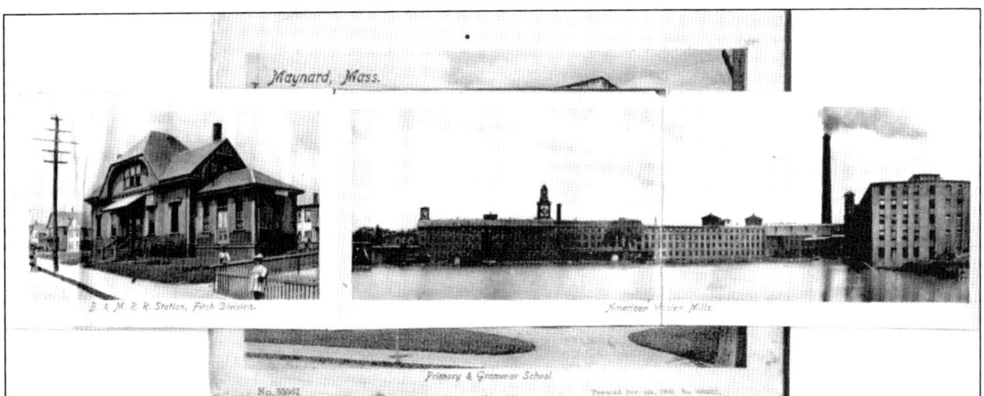


**HIDDEN PICTURES.** When the flap on this specially manufactured postcard was lifted, it unveiled a strip of smaller souvenir photographs of Maynard. Even though it was heavier and thicker than most postcards of the time, it still costs only 1¢ to mail.

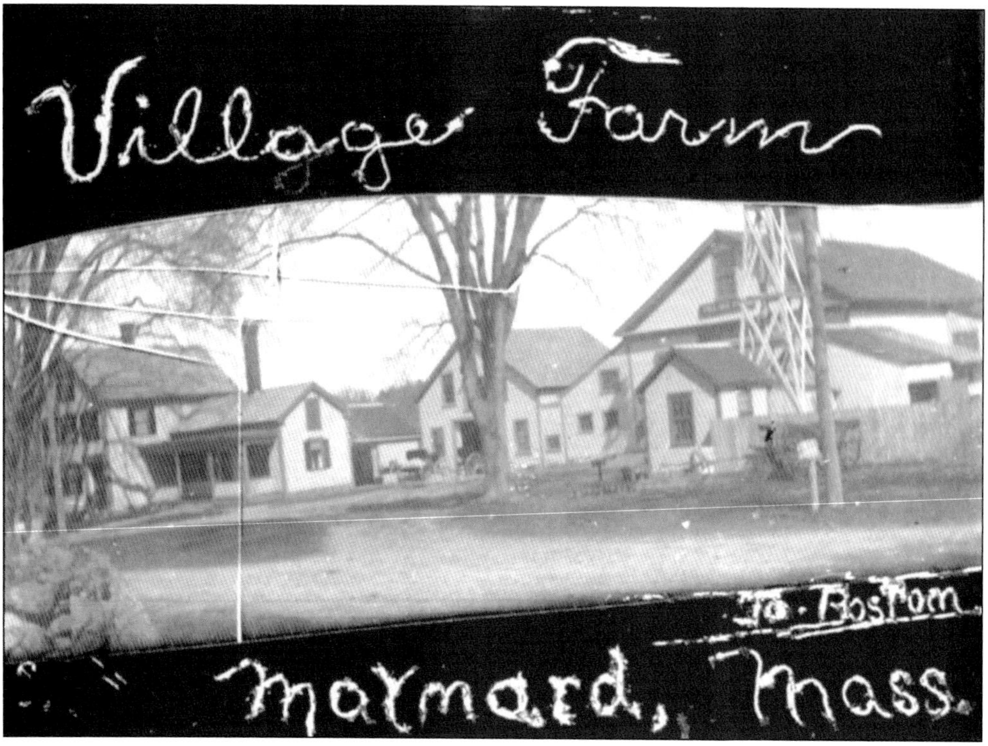


**WHERE WE LIVED.** Maynard was first a farming community with typical farm homes. As Maynard became an industrial community, the style of the homes changed into simple village Colonials, as shown in the picture below. (Courtesy of Paul Polewacyk.)

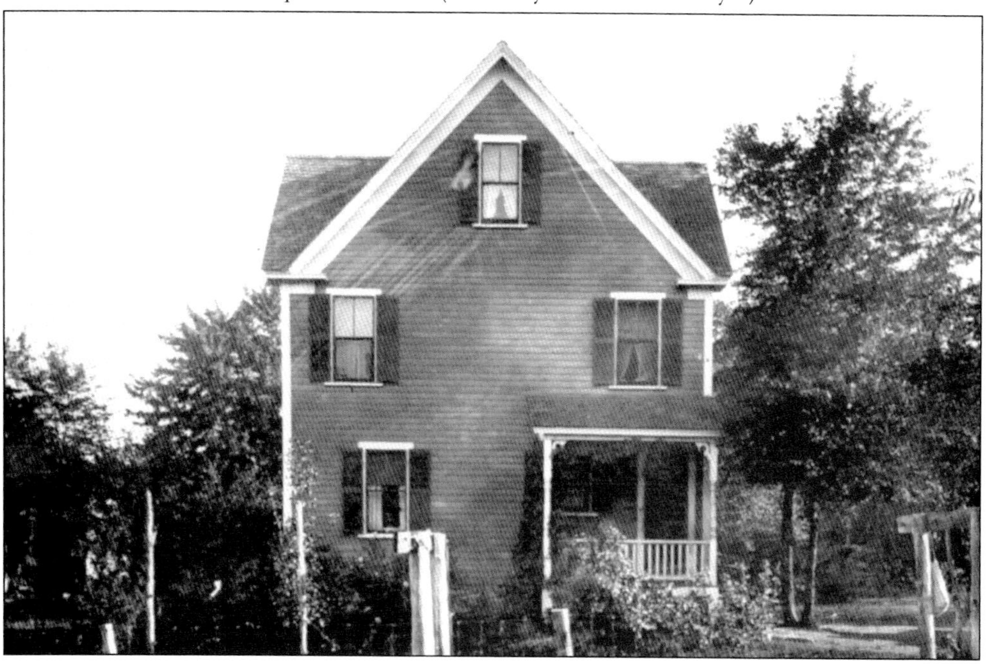

**TYPICAL MILL-WORKER'S HOUSE.** This is a typical village Colonial built for or by mill workers, this one on Butler Avenue. (Courtesy of MHS.)

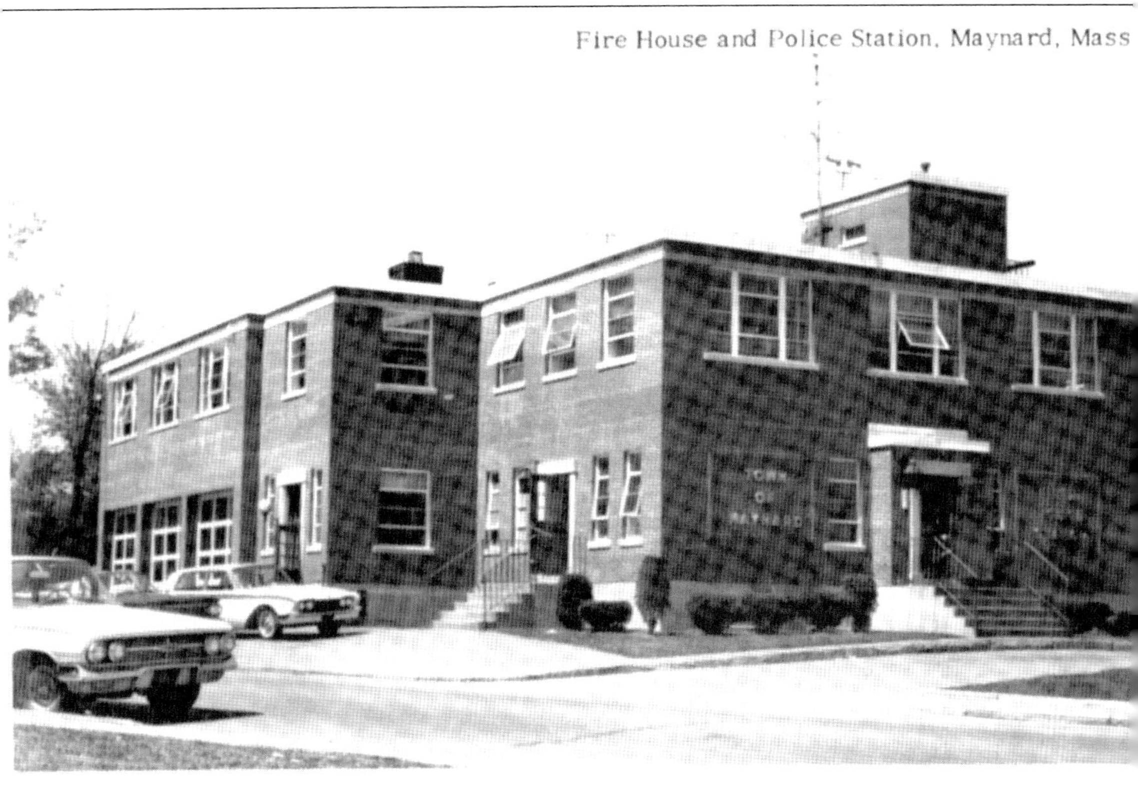


**MAYNARD FIREHOUSE AND POLICE STATION.** The police department received its first cruiser in 1938. The year 1946 saw the installation of the first two-way radio for the cruiser, and in 1950, the one and only traffic light in town was installed at Paper Mill Corner. Parking meters were installed in 1951. On October 4, 1955, the department moved into the new combination police and fire station shown above.

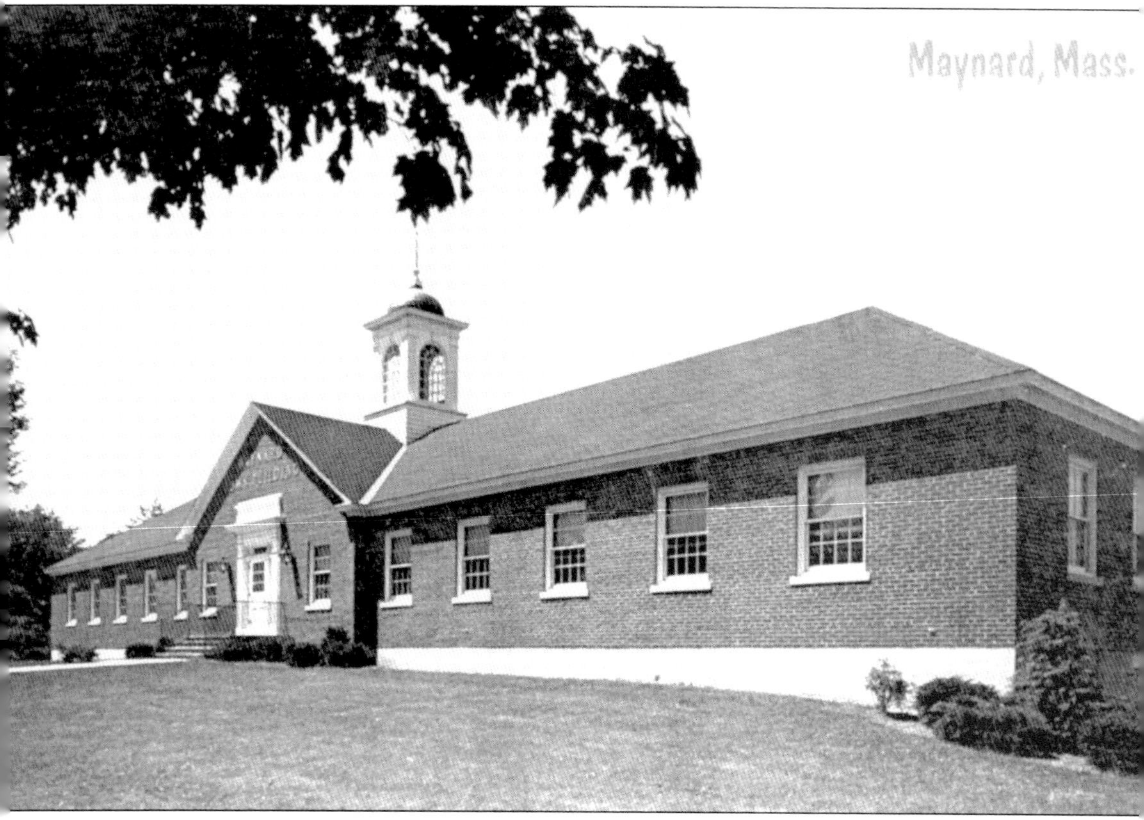


**MAYNARD TOWN BUILDING AND LIBRARY.** On March 7, 1960, it was voted to establish a town municipal building committee to formulate plans for a new municipal building. The committee appointed consisted of Jean T. Caisey, Richard T. White, R. Frank Punch, John H. MacDonald, and Stanley M. Kulik. On October 10, 1960, at a special town meeting, the committee recommended and it was voted to appropriate the sum of $329,999 to construct a combined town office and public library building on town-owned land on Main Street, known as the Wilson School property.